Why Grow Old?

To Josie,

Dr Finger

Why Grow Old?

The Antiaging, Feel Good, Look Good Bible

E. Ronald Finger, M.D., F.A.C.S.

Jones Street Publishing House
Savannah, Georgia
2009

Published in the United States of America by
Jones Street Publishing House
5356 Reynolds Street, Suite 505
Savannah, Georgia 31405

ISBN: 978-0-615-21720-8

Manufactured in the United States of America

First edition

INTRODUCTION

Good health is beautiful. Healthy people are more positive, vibrant, and more self-confident. Good health is attainable for the vast majority of people, and it's a part of science that has intrigued and interested me since childhood. Fortunately my background allowed me to pursue this great interest with vigor. My goal in writing this book is to explain the nature of the aging process to the nonscientist in a way that is easily read and understood and, I would hope, also interesting to read about. I will also discuss ways to slow and in many cases reverse the aging process.

Why include plastic surgery in this book? Our appearance also affects our health, mostly through self-esteem. We cannot separate our psychological feelings from our physical health. They are infinitely interrelated. An example would be aches and pains that often occur with anxiety or depression—referred to as psychosomatic disorders.

I have been involved in medicine since I was fourteen years of age. My father was a general surgeon in a small town in South Carolina from the end of the Second World War until he was about eighty-nine years old. As a young man, his practice expanded and eventually required the establishment of a thirty-five-bed hospital called the Finger Clinic Hospital. Much of my childhood was spent helping my father with his work in that hospital, and at age fourteen I began assisting him in surgery. Those days had a very positive impact on my goals in life and gave me invaluable experience. Beginning in my teenage years, I set my sights on a career in medicine with plastic surgery as my specialty. All my siblings were artists, and my mother was an artist and musician. She, in particular, encouraged me toward my goals.

I graduated from college at Emory University in Atlanta, Georgia, in 1960. From there my education took me to the Medical College of South Carolina in Charleston, where I graduated in 1964. Next on the agenda was a one-year internship at Grady Memorial Hospital in Atlanta followed by a four-year residency in general surgery at Tampa General Hospital in Florida, finishing in 1969. I then entered the United States Air Force as a general surgeon.

One year later in 1970 I began my plastic and reconstructive surgery residency program in the United States Air Force at Lackland Air Force Base in San Antonio, Texas. My residency occurred during the Vietnam War, which gave me experience with all types of war injuries, but oddly enough, with cosmetic surgery as well. The wives of our POWs and soldiers returning home wanted to look their best for their husbands upon their return, and in some cases their requests required cosmetic surgery. Some of the POWs had been in captivity for as long as eight years. My superiors in the military endorsed these procedures. As a result, I developed a deep appreciation for the efforts of our military forces as well as valuable experience in both reconstructive and aesthetic surgery. It also gave me a true grasp of the close relationship between the body and mind.

After my residency I owed the United States Air Force one additional year of service for my plastic surgery training. I spent that year as chief of plastic surgery at Travis Air Force Base at Fairfield, California, near San Francisco. Following these four years in the Air Force and just weeks after getting married, I moved to Savannah, Georgia, in 1973 to begin my private practice. I opened the first outpatient plastic surgery center in Georgia and South Carolina, and I continue my private practice there with two associates.

I am fortunate to have a large cosmetic surgery practice with facial rejuvenation being a major part. I noticed early in my practice that old-looking, environmentally damaged skin detracts from even the best facelift or eyelid lift. From this observation, my interest in skin care and health began early in my practice. Many fine topical products for the skin were available by prescription from physicians, though at the time none met my requirements and were available directly to the public. Ultimately (and with the assistance of several very fine biochemists), I created a line of skin products that is as effective as, and often more effective than those available by prescription. The name of this product line is the New Youth Skin Treatment System. In addition to plastic surgery and age management, creating and perfecting my skin product line has been both my passion and my mission. Simply put, our products are more effective than most others available because they promote skin repair on a cellular and microscopic level as a synergistic system. A healthy body, including the skin, involves the total synergistic approach.

This book is derived from my experience and observations as well as literature research regarding plastic surgery, the aging process and our aging skin, and the interventions available to address the causes and consequences of aging, including cancer and at least fifty other inflammation-based diseases as well as aging itself. My goal is to make scientific information available to the nonmedical, non-science-oriented public and to make the reader more of an expert on the many aspects of aging and age control.

Many people believe that health and appearance are totally influenced by genetic makeup, heritage, and destiny. In most cases nothing could be further from the truth. True health lies in our quest for knowledge and our discipline and determination to implement what we have learned. The fact that you are reading this book is proof that you are interested in the subject of slowing and reversing the ravages of age. The payoff for all this hard work will be feeling good and energetic and being and looking healthy. You can look much younger than your true age and actually be metabolically younger than your chronological age.

After decades of practice, it is clear to me that many people who seek plastic surgery are unaware of their options and the various advantages and disadvantages of the procedures and choices available to them. If you are dissatisfied with a physical aspect of your body, it is essential that you learn as much as possible about the different ways these problems can be corrected. If you are thinking about cosmetic surgery, this important information will help you communicate intelligently with your plastic surgeon.

It is the doctor's responsibility to tailor plastic surgery procedures to their patients' needs and desires. All patients are different in shape, size, and goals; and surgeons consulted for cosmetic surgery procedures must always carefully consider these variations. However, patients must become educated, so they can help surgeons with these important decisions. In short, your plastic surgeon may be the expert, but it is your face or body. Your knowledge and input are important, and you must make sure you are on the same wavelength as your surgeon. If your knowledge and opinions seem unimportant to your plastic surgeon, then I suggest that you run for the nearest door, or at least get a second opinion.

Through the years I have seen immense changes in patients' self-esteem and lives following well-conceived, well-performed plastic surgery. The plastic surgery–related information in Book VI is designed to help educate you to make informed decisions and get the best possible results if you have decided that cosmetic surgery might be right for you. So read on and get ready to look and feel better than ever.

I

Causes of Aging

1 Our Universal Wish

What do we all want? Or maybe I should ask, What should we all want? Because many of us don't appreciate good health until it is lost, the answer is good health and the ability to be active until our final days. To look and feel youthful would not be far down the list (and not far removed psychologically). To dissect what we mean by "youthful" a bit further, the general categories are how we feel and how we look. We would want to feel energetic, alert, sharp-minded, physically toned, strong, and well. Let's include happy in that list, too. Next we want to look good. This means not being overweight and, as mentioned, being physically well toned and young for our age. These are lofty goals to some people, small to others, but attainable by virtually all. Some people will achieve more than others, but everything in life is relative. We could wish for eternal youth or life, but that's not going to happen. However, looking young for our age and feeling vibrant and good is well within our reach.

One indisputable fact is that good health looks good. Healthy people are generally beautiful people—at least in appearance. I will add that healthy skin is beautiful skin. It all fits together. Have you ever seen children with bad skin? Probably not, as their skin has not had time to react to the various environmental hazards around us.

A positive attitude and determination are important factors in achieving our goals for health and, for that matter, any endeavor. I remember a comment that my mother (a very positive person) made when she was about eighty-four years old and, for the most part, bed-ridden from a stroke. Her comment to me was, "Ronnie, when am I going to feel old?" That comment has lingered with me for years. She kept a positive mental attitude under the worst of circumstances, though such an attitude becomes much easier when we are healthy.

Often an unhealthy state is also accompanied by some degree (or lots) of depression. In addition, we cannot completely separate the functions of the brain from those of the body. A depressed person looks and feels bad and may even have psychosomatic symptoms of pain, chronic fatigue, etc. I remember through the years of my practice performing plastic surgery on jailed criminals who had deep-seated insecurities about physical defects. More often than not, plastic surgery was a positive, life-altering experience for them. Many said that they were teased as children and lacked self-confidence and so felt angry and inferior. They responded by over-reacting, as many people with inferiority feelings do.

Another interesting case was a thirty-five-year-old high school teacher who had never had a date or even been asked to dance. She was unattractive and was severely insecure because of her appearance. She came to me in tears and basically asked me to do what I thought necessary to make her presentable. Her physical problems were very large lips (much larger than today's fad), a very large nose, flat cheekbones and a large face in the lower cheek and jaw area. She also had large hoods over her upper eyelids. The procedures I performed were removal of the buccal fat pad (a fat pad within the lower cheek) through an incision inside the mouth, surgical thinning of the lips, an upper eyelid lift and a "nose job" (rhinoplasty). I also inserted an implant over her cheekbones (the zygoma) through a lower eyelid incision. She was actually quite pretty after the procedures and also very appreciative. She began dating, and her self-esteem became immensely elevated. Later she told me that she was stopped at a traffic light and a gentleman in another car looked at her, looked ahead at the road, and then looked back at her. She asked me if I understood. I shook my head and she said, "He gave me a second look." That little incident affected her deeply. And I must say that it affected me deeply also and still does. This example represents one of my great pleasures of being a plastic surgeon.

So overall health is what this book is all about. In it I offer a combination of specific information about age management through nutrition, exercise, and lifestyle, as well as a consumer's guide to plastic surgery. After all, looking good goes a long way toward making us feel good. It also enhances the self-esteem that inspires us to take better care of ourselves. I will address specific questions regarding plastic surgery, including who should have it and how to decide if it is best for you. What should you avoid and what can you expect, both before surgery and during your recovery? What are the limitations of plastic surgery, and how do you choose between various techniques with the same goal—for example, sub-muscular (behind the pectoralis muscles) versus pre-muscular breast implants, a tummy tuck versus liposuction or lipodissolve for flattening the stomach, open or closed nose repairs, to mention a few?

A word about goals—I have found that achieving our goals can be most satisfying for both ourselves and others. I feel fortunate to have found an occupation and life that I love. In my late sixties, I have no intention of retiring until I can no longer perform to my satisfaction (or that of my patients). My dad practiced medicine until age eighty-nine, so I expect to be in my mid-eighties before retirement. If you are not lucky enough to have chosen an occupation you love, I suggest that you work on a hobby and/or goals of great interest to you.

The author Victor E. Frankl expresses the importance of goals in an extreme sense in his most wonderful book *Man's Search for Meaning* (1985). He survived concentration camps during World War II by having an important project or goal—in his case, the completion of his recent life's work, a thesis on new theories in psychiatry. Though he was much more frail than many other prisoners, he survived while most of the others perished. This goal gave him the determination to live. It may not have meant anything to anyone else, but it did to him, and it was a goal he intended to reach. Why not choose your health as one of your goals and/or hobbies? Health can be anyone's goal and project and it's an endless, interesting frontier. A healthy mind and body are a most valued gift. You wouldn't buy a Ferrari or another fine car and run it on poor fuel and oil, would you? You should take care of your health with the same enthusiasm as you do some of your prized possessions. I suggest finding a hobby or topic that greatly interests you and delving into it with enthusiasm. Such a project can invigorate you. It offers the excitement of reading and researching your hobby to whatever extent that intrigues you, followed by the practical satisfaction of applying what you have learned. It doesn't really matter what your goals or hobbies are as long as they interest you. Hobbies vary from gardening and traveling to sports and crafts. Read about them, investigate them, and become good at them.

For me, another activity of interest is creating skin products to repair and possibly reverse the damage caused by time and abuse, leaving results that you can see and feel. Despite the abundance of products available today, creating them is a new frontier because many of the most effective ingredients have not yet been fully utilized for skin repair or are not available in the proper combinations.

Your body and mind are one. Your body is your temple, so treat it with respect. What better reward is there than being happy, healthy, and interested in your own health project? And don't forget the satisfaction you derive from a positive self-esteem due to an attractive self-image and others commenting favorably on your appearance. Once about ten years ago I was at an airport waiting for my flight when a gentleman approached me and asked, "How do you do it?" I naturally asked, "Do what?" He said, "Stay in such good shape." I gave the obvious answer of eating well and exercising, but the point of the story is that it meant so much to me that a total stranger noticed.

There was a time not so far in the past when the kinds of health and aesthetic surgery available today were not available to most people regardless of their wealth or positions in life. Like great health, plastic surgery can be of great emotional and physical value, and a plastic surgeon can fulfill this part of the picture. A patient's knowledgeable input is too often a missing ingredient, however. To live long and look your best, you must also create a healthy lifestyle. Otherwise, you will be like people who come in for liposuction once a year because they continue to gain weight year after year.

Lack of attention to health and appearance is a habit, and behavior is difficult to change. However, habits definitely can be changed. During my third year as a medical student, I worked at the M. D. Anderson Tumor and Cancer Institute in Houston. Too often, I had the unpleasant task of doing physical examinations on patients with suspected cancer that in fact turned out to be invasive lung cancer. It shouldn't surprise anyone that virtually every patient given that diagnosis removed the cigarettes from his or her pocket and stopped smoking immediately. Unfortunately, it sometimes takes a lot of incentive to end a bad habit, but any habit can be changed.

2 Why We Grow Old

To understand the process of aging and how we can slow it down, we must start with the basics. What causes us to grow old, and what exactly happens on a cellular level? With this knowledge we can more easily understand how to avoid the aging processes as much as possible. Living long and healthy lives usually translates into looking our best.

We are the sum of our complex body parts and our numerous complex chemical reactions. Consider the numerous parts as trees in the forest that is the body, with the trees representing the 100 trillion cells constituting the body. We must then look to the trees (our cells) to understand our past and present and how they affect our future regarding our age, age control, and overall health.

Our physiological age does not necessarily correlate with our chronological age, and most often we are responsible for much of this disparity. Good health is a gift. Physically, we are all made up of the same elements, and we are all the product of oxidation as are all living things on earth, including plants. However, plants require carbon dioxide for metabolism and breathe out oxygen. If we fail to fertilize and water a plant, it would certainly not thrive, and its lifespan would be shortened. We are similar in that sense, and we must care for our bodies thoughtfully from nutrition to physical activity. Chronological age cannot be altered. However, to remain younger physically and mentally, commitment to treating our bodies with respect is as important as our date of birth. Some of us have been blessed with stronger, healthier bodies than others. But we all have known gifted people who have aged poorly, died young, or had a miserable quality of life during middle and later years on account of, perhaps, stroke, heart disease, or cancer. On the other hand, we have also seen great athletes and even Olympians born with physical handicaps. The question boils down to how much effort you are willing to put into your body's proper maintenance to respect it as your temple. Regarding health and the body, my father once said to me, "You are not going to be given another one." As a former race-car driver, I was an "adrenalin junkie" and had to learn some of what he meant the hard way. But as far as exercising regularly and eating a nutritionally sound diet, I took, and still take, his advice to heart.

There are many factors that influence age control. Some require common sense. Others require more study and effort, which, incidentally, is good exercise for your brain. What could be more interesting and offer a larger reward than being healthy? Regarding what we control in our environment and nutrients, we are much like the computer cliché, "garbage in, garbage out." Our efforts toward health will serve us well. Many people, however, have no plan, and many more succumb to gluttony and the couch-potato lifestyle. This book will give you the ingredients for a plan, but most of all, an understanding of the how and why such a plan can succeed.

The following sections describe some specifics that increase physiological age and diseases of the aged:

Bad Habits: Smoking, Unhealthy Diet, and Excess Caffeine

To begin with, we do not know all the answers to the questions of aging and anti-aging. We do know that proper nutrition and good health habits can dramatically decrease the risk of stroke, heart disease, certain cancers, and much more, including keeping us from looking older than we are. Many bad habits are the starting points for numerous diseases.

Smoking

Smoking most definitely causes heart disease, blood vessel disease, lung and bladder cancer, cancer of the throat and tongue, emphysema, bronchitis, and many other diseases. Since Johnny Carson was known to be a heavy smoker, it is hardly surprising that his death resulted from emphysema and heart disease. Passive (second-hand) smoke can be one of the causes of these same diseases; reports show that pets of smokers have an increased incidence of these diseases and die at younger ages than pets in nonsmoking households. Only in very unusual circumstances will I perform a facelift on smokers because they typically have small artery disease that increases the risk of flap necrosis (a medical term for something like gangrene). In fact, I refrain from doing any kind of flap surgeries (tummy tucks, breast uplifts, and reductions) on smokers, because the body cannot supply enough blood to the flap for healthy recovery or flap survival. I have recently found that nicotine-chewing gums cause the same problems with these kinds of surgeries. Each cigarette smoked metabolizes 25 to 30 mg. of vitamin C, meaning that this necessary vitamin and antioxidant would not be available to the individual for other necessary metabolic needs such as maintaining good health and recovery from disease.

A primary problem with cigarette smoking is the resulting increase in free radical formation. The Centers for Disease Control (CDC) estimates that more than 440,000 deaths each year and one out of five deaths overall are from tobacco and that another 50,000 die each year from problems related to second-hand smoke. Living with or working alongside smokers can be deadly. Some diseases occur almost exclusively among smokers such as Buerger's disease, which is a blood-vessel disease primarily of the toes and feet. These parts lose their blood supply because of constriction of small vessels (a process called vasoconstriction) and may ultimately develop into gangrene, leading to amputation. I have seen patients with Buerger's disease asking for "just one more cigarette," presumably for pain relief, knowing that smoking is the cause of their disease and will only make it worse. I have also seen a cancer patient with a surgically removed larynx and a permanent tracheotomy actually smoke through the hole in his neck. Unbelievable, but true. Along with cancer of the tongue, cancer of the larynx is almost unheard of among nonsmokers or those who do not chew tobacco or smoke cigars.

Another story I remember quite vividly occurred when I was a resident in general surgery. In order to breathe without his lungs filling with fluid, a gentleman in the intensive-care unit always sat and leaned forward with his elbows resting on his thighs, even when attempting to sleep. I was amazed to see the dents in his thighs caused by his elbows from this constant behavior. Formerly an excellent athlete, he began smoking heavily later in life, causing the emphysema and heart disease that eventually led to his death. This was indeed a sad ending for someone who at one time enjoyed robust health.

According to a report from the CDC issued in 2000, an estimated 10 million people have died from smoking-related diseases (mostly heart disease, lung cancer, emphysema, and other respiratory diseases) in the United States since the release of the first Surgeon General's report on smoking in 1964. Staggering, isn't it? Ten million! Tobacco lobbyists are powerful, and so are the adverse effects of smoking.

Improper nutrition

Improper nutrition is another bad health habit. We have all seen overweight people filling their plates with simple carbohydrates and saturated fats, definitely an unhealthy thing to do. We might also witness anorexics with saggy skin, making them look old before their time. These examples are the opposite of what we are trying to achieve. Overall, the answer to staying young is certainly balance and moderation. That approach along with fundamental knowledge about healthful living will do much for promoting good health, and we now know that healthy people feel better and look better and younger as well.

This book will not help those who have no self-discipline. It will, however, educate and assist those who want help and are serious about improving their health and appearance. I hope some readers will be inspired to live a healthier lifestyle. To do this, they must first have realistic goals. Second, they must develop the knowledge and persistence to pursue these goals. Readers must, however, develop a plan in order to achieve these goals. As part of an overall plan to maintain a healthy life-style, I suggest taking the time and striving to acquire at least moderate knowledge on the subject of nutrition. The references in the back of this book provide additional suggested reading material and sources on this very important subject.

Caffeine

Caffeine certainly gives us a boost and gets us going in the morning or after a large meal. It does so by releasing norepinephrine, a brain stimulant. That is the good side of caffeine. Excess caffeine, however, can cause hypertension and "the shakes." If you don't believe caffeine gives you the shakes, try to do delicate work with your hands after a couple of cups of coffee and you might be surprised at the results. Furthermore, in many people caffeine also causes gastrointestinal problems such as stomach ulcers or spastic colon, a kind of colitis with diarrhea, pain, and/or cramps. People who suffer from esophageal reflux (heartburn) should ingest no caffeine. Caffeine increases acid production in the stomach, and in individuals with reflux this acid backs up into the esophagus. The lining of the esophagus cannot tolerate acid, so this process can result in strictures, ulceration, and sometimes cancer.

Fibrocystic disease of the breast, very common in American women, can be reduced and even eliminated by discontinuing all sources of caffeine, including soft drinks, tea, and chocolate. Among men, caffeine can cause chronic or acute prostatitis (inflammation of the prostate gland), an unpleasant but common condition.

So the question we should ask is this: Should we drink any coffee? Like most things in life, moderation is the key, but we should know the various medical issues related to its consumption. Get both sides of the story and then judge if and how caffeine may affect you. I have seen numerous heavy coffee drinkers suffer from stomach ulcers or prostatitis without realizing the correlation between their problems and caffeine. To do my job as a plastic surgeon I must be totally caffeine-free. This means not only no coffee, but I must also avoid black and green tea, many soft drinks, and many over-the-counter medications, such as Excedrin, that contain caffeine. On the positive side, coffee contains many anti-oxidants and it does increase alertness. Knowledge of potential problems and moderation are the keys.

Free Radicals and Antioxidants

Free radical formation is one cause of aging on a molecular level that we certainly cannot overlook. We must also be aware of the important protective effect of antioxidants. University of Nebraska professor Denham Harman, M.D., Ph.D., first discovered free radicals in the 1950s. Think of human beings and all other animals as products of oxidation, which means that we burn oxygen to live. Now think of each of us as 100 trillion microscopic cells all using oxygen to produce heat, which is converted into chemical reactions, motion, thought processes, and much, much more. That is the good news about oxidation: the part that makes life possible. However, while burning a match produces the desired flame and heat, it also results in smoke and ashes, which is the negative side of oxidation. Obvious common effects of oxidation that we see every day are rust, faded paint, fish getting that fishy smell, any type of corrosion, and the subject of this book, people aging. Of course, our oxygen-burning furnaces—our cells—do not produce smoke and ashes, but they do produce undesirable by-products such as free radicals. (See Figure 2-1.)

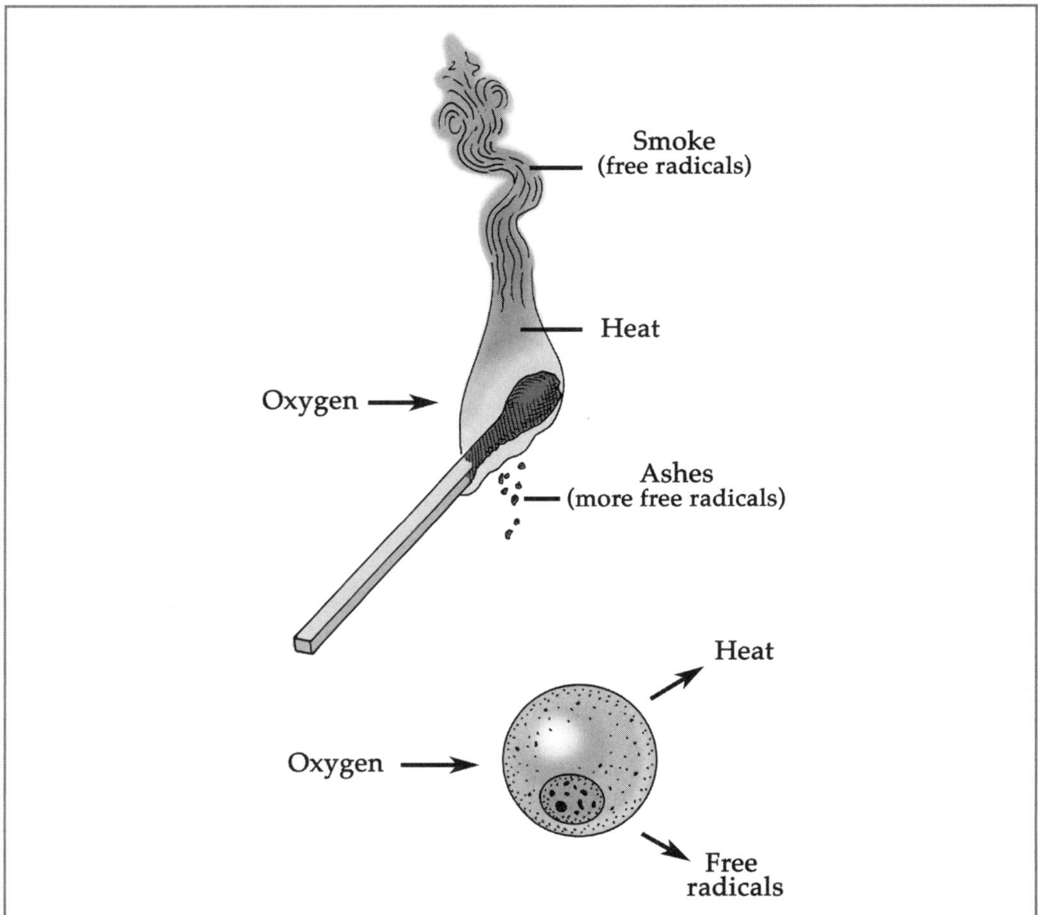

FIGURE 2-1. The burning match is an example of heat produced by the burning of oxygen, called oxidation. With the match, we have smoke and ashes as the byproduct. The toxic debris from cellular oxidation is the free radical.

A free radical is a molecule that lacks an electron (a negative electrical charge). Actually, it has one electron, but electrons must exist in pairs. Free radicals, therefore, try to steal electrons from various parts of our cells such as the cell membrane, the mitochondria (energy-generating sites within the cytoplasm of the cell), and DNA. The electrons create damage by robbing these structures of their electrons. This damage is continuous and cumulative and ultimately results in cellular malfunction. In addition, when free radicals steal a charge, they cause an additional problem: the creation of a toxic chemical that the body must deal with. So free radicals are bad and, as you will see, are directly linked to our life-style and habits.

Free radicals—products of burning oxygen (O2)—come from several sources:

External sources:

- Sun exposure
- Smoking
- Pollutants
- Poor diet

Internal sources:

- A by-product of mitochondria burning O2 for energy
- Other metabolic reactions using O2
- Glycation—a free-radical-producing "factory"

Antioxidants, some of which our body produces, are molecules that satisfy free radicals' quest for an additional electron by providing the extra charge, thus rendering the free radical harmless. There are many different types of free radicals, but fortunately there are also many different kinds of antioxidants available to neutralize them by giving them the missing electron. For an analogy of a molecule missing an electron, think of Wild Bill Hickock missing one of his two guns. He would have no problem stealing or taking another, but he wouldn't have to if someone else gave him the gun. The someone else would be like an anti-oxidant offering an extra electron to a free radical. Everyone goes away happy. No electron or gun is stolen. (See Figure 2-2.)

Antioxidants represent one form of anti-aging therapy. Free radicals hit each cell for that extra electron about 10,000 times a day, ultimately damaging different parts of the cell. It is estimated that each puff of a cigarette sends billions of free radicals into our system, resulting in the acceleration of aging, cancer, and other diseases. In fact, scientists are discovering that free radical damage contributes to virtually every known disease, as well as to the degeneration that accompanies aging.

FIGURE 2-2. Wild Bill Hickock's guns were in pairs and he is missing a gun in the illustration, as a free radical lacks an electron. Both have the need to steal another. The analogy is the antioxidants offer electrons to satisfy the free radicals, avoiding damage, just as the gun is offered to Bill Hickock.

As we well know, DNA (deoxyribonucleic acid) contains the genetic instructions for the function of all living cells. It is the blueprint for our chemical, hormonal, and genetic makeup as well as our aging pattern. DNA damage due to free radicals is like changing a blueprint for a house everyday before the house is finished. Remember that the human being is a continuous "work in progress"—we never stop replacing cells and repairing damage of some sort, so our "building" is never complete. DNA contains the instructions that the cells need to perform all of their many needed tasks. Ongoing DNA damage ultimately results in micro-mutations (changes in the DNA) when the cell replicates itself, as all cells do hundreds of times, depending on the cell. (Actually, adult specialty cells such as nerve and muscle cells rarely replicate, whereas others like skin and gut-lining cells replicate almost every twenty-four hours.) DNA mutations lead to chronic disease, premature aging and ultimately in some cases cancer. No cancer occurs without mutations in or inherited damage to DNA. When free radicals change DNA, cell replication creates a new cell that is not an exact copy. Thus, we actually become mutants of our original selves. A part of any age-control plan, therefore, is to decrease free radical levels by increasing antioxidants in our diet and supplements to neutralize them. The good news is that we can do this.

Because of the complexity of the body's defense system, we know that prolonged life requires a well-coordinated approach incorporating various nutrients for assimilation and utilization throughout our body. This approach includes numerous antioxidants, anti-glycation agents, anti-inflammatory agents, a proper diet, and more, all of which we will explain a little later in this book. Of the hundreds of different antioxidants, some of the important ones are vitamins C and E, beta-carotene, lecithin, alpha lipoic acid, superoxide dismutase (SOD), glutathione, selenium, melatonin, astaxanthin, and coenzyme Q10 (CoQ10).

Any discussion about antioxidants would be incomplete without mentioning Oxygen Radical Absorbance Capacity, or ORAC, which is a test-tube analysis of the amount of antioxidant power of various foods and nutrients. Each food is given a value; the higher the value, the higher the ORAC (or antioxidant power). Research by Drs. Ronald Prior and Guahau Cao indicates that we need roughly 3,000 to 5,000 ORAC units a day. Surprisingly, most people living in the United States take in under 1,400 units a day by consuming about three vegetables or fruits daily, which leaves us woefully deficient in ORAC. This deficiency is believed to be one of the foundations of degenerative diseases and poor aging quality. To learn the powerhouse antioxidant foods, conduct an Internet search for ORAC. The immense resulting list of antioxidants includes fruits and vegetables at the top. We should look for foods with bright and varied colors, as these usually contain ORAC-enhancing carotenoids, lycopenes, lutein, and flavonoids.

High on the ORAC list are dried fruits because they are so much more concentrated. Spinach is also high on the list. These and other foods will be discussed in the section of the book on nutrition, but at this point it is enough to know that we can now monitor the antioxidant capacity of any food. Just knowing the above should make us want to increase our intake of vegetables and fruit to a total of eight to ten helpings a day, even in small quantities per serving. According to Jean Carper's *Your Miracle Brain* (2000), our brain produces more free radicals than any other organ because it uses so much more oxygen and because it is the fattest organ in the body. But don't assume antioxidants are the complete story. Many different nutrient functions are necessary for healthy metabolism.

In a Nutshell

1. Make life inhospitable to free radicals to reduce their damage to cells and DNA.
2. Eat plenty of fresh vegetables, especially green and brightly colored ones, to furnish antioxidants. In other words, eat the rainbow.
3. Eat a combination of eight to ten fruits and vegetables a day.
4. Take nutritional supplements, which we will discuss later. If free radicals want electrons, give them plenty. This is war!

Glycation

A seldom-mentioned result of metabolism, which I believe will become more publicized in the future to both medical and lay people, is a process called glycosylation, more commonly called glycation. This process results in an abnormal bond between sugar and protein molecules and between protein molecules themselves. In short, glycation is bad. It is increased by simple carbohydrate intake and by eating rapidly cooked meat, especially overcooking meats. This abnormal bond results in a sticky molecule that is difficult to break. These micro-substances are appropriately and prophetically named Advanced Glycation End Products, or AGEs. AGEs attach themselves to large proteins such as collagen and elastin (elastic) fibers, hemoglobin, enzymes, and even immunoglobulins (blood proteins necessary for proper immune response).

> Metabolism consists of anabolism, or building up, and catabolism, tearing down.

Glycation is a catabolic process, and when these AGEs attach themselves to the above-listed proteins, the proteins stop working properly. The actions of AGEs plus proteins impact enzymes involved in every chemical reaction in the body, and glycated enzymes simply do not do their jobs well.

> AGEs (advanced glycation end products) attach to proteins such as:
>
> Collagen
> Elastin fibers
> Immunoproteins
> Hemoglobin
> Enzyme proteins

Glycated proteins do not function properly. Think of our elastin fibers as micro-bungee cords that stretch and the AGEs as a sticky substance like honey or tar being applied to the bungee cord. Eventually the bungee cord becomes saturated and will not contract to its original length after stretching. The cord becomes permanently stretched. Similarly, research indicates that AGEs attaching to our elastin and collagen fibers contribute to the loss of elasticity, causing our skin to sag with age because the elastin fibers simply cannot contract back to their original size and shape.

AGEs also contribute to hardening of the arteries, also called arteriosclerosis or atherosclerosis (formation of dangerous plaques of calcium and fat in arteries). Ultimately, all arteries are affected, leading to heart disease, hypertension, strokes, kidney disease, diseases of the retina, and other arterial diseases. We have arteries everywhere from our toes to and including our brain. In addition, glycation is a virtual free-radical production machine itself, so it is a significant factor in aging as we have already seen.

AGEs also attach themselves to immunoglobulins. This attachment reduces the effectiveness of the immune system, leading to, among other things, a decreased ability to respond to inflammatory disorders as we age. Such disorders include virtually all diseases from Alzheimer's to heart disease, skin disorders, stomach ulcers, and other diseases too numerous to count.

It is fair to say that AGEs adversely affect the entire body, as outlined in the box below.

Since AGEs result from sugar attaching to protein, the need to dramatically reduce the simple carbohydrates in our diet (for example, sugar, honey, white potatoes, white bread, and pasta) begins to make sense. Simple carbohydrates such as sugar cause many additional problems that will be discussed later in the book. At this point it is sufficient to note that diabetics suffer accelerated small vessel disease, resulting in a dramatic increase in strokes, heart disease, kidney disease, blindness, macular degeneration, and more. It is well known that sugar and other simple carbohydrates contribute these same health hazards to individuals other than diabetics and usually occur in people who consume large amounts of simple carbohydrates. These folks are on a high-speed aging trip.

AGEs affect:

All blood vessels in all organs and tissues
Hardening of blood vessels, causing heart disease, stroke, and other diseases.
Sagging of the skin and subcutaneous tissues
The immune system
All chemical reactions in the body

Do any products delay or inhibit glycation? Studies show that there definitely are and an effective one is carnosine, which is available in most health food stores as a supplement and well worth taking in my opinion. Also vitamins C and E, flavonoids (found in fruits, vegetables, and whole grains), and alpha lipoic acid help reduce glycation. From a chemical standpoint, AGEs have been shown to deplete our bodies of the antioxidants glutathione and vitamin C. Lipoic acid reduces this

Glycation produces AGEs:

Sugar + Protein = AGEs =

Loss of elasticity
Sagging skin and other tissues
Impairment of the immune response system
Damage to all organ systems, leading to:
Heart disease
Hypertension (high blood pressure)
Strokes
Kidney disease
Cataracts
. . . and many other disorders

depletion. This is another example of how the body works like a symphony orchestra: each instrument must work in harmony with all the others. Another inhibitor of glycation is kombucha, a fermented tea from Russia. However, I doubt if any of these products will offer much help for sugar addicts. As time moves ahead, more anti-glycation substances will be discovered and studied in humans. Some of these will be discussed later under Supplements on page 53.

In a Nutshell

1. Simple carbohydrates increase AGEs and are Bad! Bad! Bad!
2. Over-cooking or rapidly cooking meats increases AGEs and that is Bad!
3. AGEs (the products of glycation) attach to elastin, collagen, hemoglobin, enzymes, and immunoglobulins, causing:
   Sagging of the skin
   Hardening of the arteries—with reduced blood supply everywhere, including your brain
   High blood pressure
   Deficient immune response
   Chronic inflammatory diseases
   High-speed aging
   Cataracts

Simple Carbohydrates

We can maintain good health and good looks by limiting our intake of simple carbohydrates. Foods, such as the aforementioned sugar, bread, pasta, white potatoes, and white rice, absorb rapidly into the blood system without having to be broken down. Simple carbohydrates differ from complex carbohydrates, which are broken down and absorbed into the blood stream more slowly. Eating many simple carbohydrates causes health problems. For instance, adult-type diabetics have blood sugar that is too high and insulin levels varying from normal to excessive, depending on the quantity of simple carbohydrates they ingest. Slower absorption from eating complex carbohydrates causes no spike in blood sugar and no corresponding spike in blood insulin. In conclusion, high simple carbohydrate intake causes a spike in blood sugar, causing a corresponding high spike in insulin output to reduce the high blood sugar level, leading in turn to hypoglycemia, which causes craving for more sugar (simple carbohydrates). (See Figure 2-3.)

The vicious cycle begins when we eat more sugar, resulting in increased insulin secretion. As the cycle continues, the body develops insulin resistance, a situation where insulin blood levels remain elevated. When insulin levels stay high, our sugar craving continues, and we develop the same diseases as diabetics, or we may even become diabetic.

Therein lies the crux of the problem: chronically elevated insulin levels. Unfortunately, when we consume excess simple carbohydrates causing a spike in excess blood sugar and increased insulin secretion, the metabolic result is much like that in the diabetic for a period of time, albeit not always as severe. We get the increase in small-vessel disease, heart disease, stroke, and so on due to AGEs, free

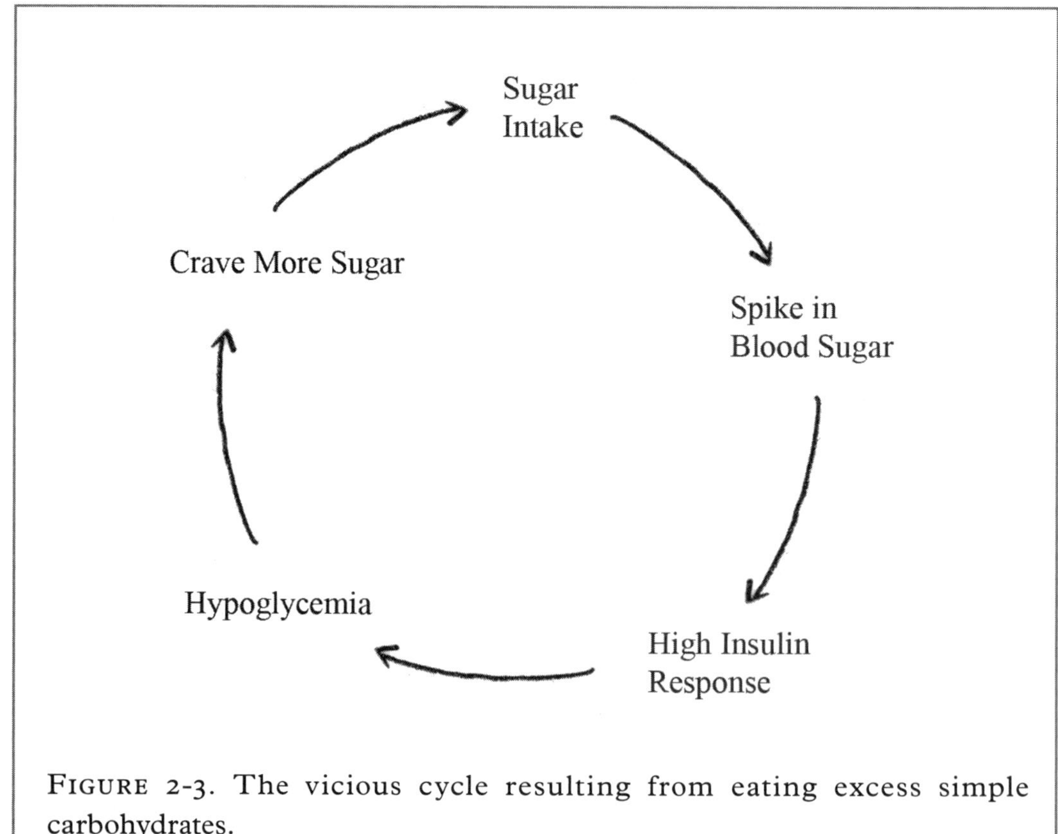

Figure 2-3. The vicious cycle resulting from eating excess simple carbohydrates.

radicals, inflammation, and DNA damage. In that sense, sugar and other simple carbohydrates are truly toxins.

In a Nutshell

1. Eat lots of leafy and brightly colored vegetables and fruit to increase your complex carbohydrate intake. As it has been said, "eat the rainbow" for those marvelous nutrients.
2. Limit your simple carbohydrate intake, such as sugar, white potato, bread (especially white), pasta, and white rice.
3. Two-thirds of your plate should contain complex carbohydrates, especially fruits and vegetables, and the remaining third should contain lean protein. Because this cannot be emphasized enough, carbohydrates will be discussed in more depth in Chapter 3.

Ultraviolet Light

Our bodies receive ultraviolet (UV) light mostly from sunlight. UV light comes in various wavelengths. The most damaging type is called UVB, which refers to its wavelength (between 280 and 320 nm., making it one of the shorter wavelengths). Fortunately, the ozone layer absorbs a portion of this wavelength and almost entirely absorbs a still shorter wavelength, UV-C. Depletion of the ozone layer results in our exposure to more UVB light. In principle, UV-C would also increase, but ozone absorbs it so efficiently that a very large depletion of the ozone layer would be necessary for significant amounts of UV-C to reach the earth's surface. Our DNA and other large biological molecules absorb UVB and UV-C, causing photochemical reactions.

Most skin cancers are due to exposure to UVB. UVA radiation has a wavelength longer than 320 nm. Ozone does not absorb these longer wavelengths, but are not usually considered as harmful to humans as UVB. However, UVA does cause immunosuppression of the skin, which could be an important factor in skin diseases as well as development of skin cancer. We must have some exposure to sunshine in order to create vitamin D, so as with many other factors that promote good health, moderation is the key. Vitamin D supplements will be discussed in Chapter 4.

The major concerns regarding UV damage are visible aging and various forms of skin cancer. Free radicals produced by UV exposure cause DNA damage leading to mutations, and remember that DNA forms our genetic blueprint. According to the American Cancer Society in 2006, more than a million Americans were diagnosed with one of two types of skin cancer, namely, basal cell and squamous cell cancers. In 2006 the American Cancer Society also reported that 62,190 people would develop melanoma, and an estimated 7,910 would die from this malignant cancer. Studies show that all of these skin cancers occur because of excessive exposure to sunlight. Fitzpatrick's classification of skin types related to susceptibility of cancer appears on page 93.

The following are nutrients that help reduce UV damage:

1. Vitamin A: Many studies show that vitamin A prevents and reverses cancerous changes in cells in some parts of the body, including the skin. One study showed that taking 25,000 international units (IU) of vitamin A per day for five years reduced the risk of developing skin cancer by thirty-two percent. However, taking large amounts of beta-carotene, a precursor to vitamin A, did not provide the same benefit as taking vitamin A because the extent of conversion of beta-carotene to vitamin A was limited.
2. Lycopene: Lycopene may be a good defense against the harmful effects of UV radiation on the skin. The best food sources of lycopene are any red fruits and vegetables, tomatoes being the single richest source.
3. Lutein: Certain antioxidants prevent skin damage induced by UV light by protecting against the body's own reactive oxidation in the skin from the UV exposure. Lutein can be effective in this way. The best sources of lutein are dark green, leafy vegetables such as spinach, kale, and collard greens.
4. Astaxanthin: This is a powerful carotenoid pigment from red marine algae. It is the pigment that gives the pink color to salmon, lobsters, shrimp and pink flamingo. It protects against free radical damage from excess exposure to UV light, and is one of the most powerful antioxidants known, many times stronger than vitamin C and beta-carotine. Astaxanthin is also an effective anti-inflammatory and booster of the immune system. The usual dose is four milligrams per day.
5. Other nutrients that help reduce UV damage are green tea, vitamin E, and EPA (eicosapentanoic acid) fatty acids (i.e., Omega-3 fatty acids), the latter of which I will discuss in detail in Chapter 3, page 33.

In a Nutshell

Too much sunlight is downright dangerous, and a tanning bed is no better. If you love the outdoors or must work outdoors in the sun, use a good sun block, a hat, and preferably long sleeves, though even then you may still get excess exposure to harmful UV rays. Ultraviolet light can rip through your cells and destroy their membranes, causing a leak of cellular contents. This sounds bad because it is. This leakage creates the redness, inflammation, and itching we experience as sunburn. The cells die in massive numbers, and as we have observed in ourselves and others, they peel off in layers. This damage to the skin's protective properties often results in the aforementioned skin cancers, the most malignant being melanoma, which too often leads to death. A diet in vegetables and fruits will provide the nutrients to help protect you. Of course, limiting your exposure to the UV rays is the most important factor in avoiding the results of UV damage.

Inflammation

The definition of inflammation according to one medical dictionary is "a localized protective reaction of tissue to irritation, injury, or infection characterized by pain, redness, swelling and sometimes loss of function." It is also a reaction to the ravages of age and the environment, so although we certainly need inflammation to protect us from our surroundings, we can have too much of a good thing. The good part is we can control inflammation in most cases.

Inflammatory response presents the proverbial double-edged sword. We need inflammation for defensive purposes, but it can also go awry, causing great destruction. When we think of inflammation, we visualize a red, swollen, infected wound. A reddened joint resulting from an injury or arthritis and sinusitis are other examples of inflammation. In its role of healing an injury or infection, inflammation dilates surrounding capillaries and brings in the various building blocks required to repair the injury. Also, various phagocytes (white blood cells and mast cells that ingest and destroy bacteria, viruses, and debris) enter the wound area. These mast cells and white cells are formidable warriors that kill and ingest invading pathogens such as bacteria and viruses.

How does the body know when to send these warriors to the front line for duty? Our immune system rapidly transports news of any injury to various parts of the body via chemical messengers secreted by white blood cells. Interesting reading, but certainly not required to be committed to memory, is the long list of chemicals released from the specialty cells that stimulate the inflammatory response. The following are the body's chemical responses that cause inflammation:

1. Prostaglandins, a group of compounds derived from unsaturated fatty acids that produce many inflammatory effects in the body.
2. Histamine, a chemical found in every body tissue, which causes the unpleasant minor effects in allergic reactions.
3. Cytokines, a class of inflammatory hormones that includes:
   - Leukotrienes
   - Tumor necrosis factor (TNF)
   - Interleukins of various types.
4. Our antibody system.

Aspirin is the granddaddy of all prostaglandin-inhibiting agents. We have used it for decades to treat the pain and inflammation of arthritis as well as for headaches and virtually any other type of pain. We also now use aspirin to ward off heart disease, and evidence indicates that it may even help reduce the incidence of colon polyps and cancer. Its anticoagulant and anti-prostaglandin (anti-inflammation) activity are the basis for aspirin's analgesic effects. Other anti-prostaglandin relievers of pain and inflammation are ibuprofen, Aleve, and Celebrex.

The newly developed COX-2 inhibitors Celebrex, Vioxx, and Bextra are also anti-prostaglandins, but they are more specialized. They supposedly do not reduce one's blood clotting ability and are much easier on the gastrointestinal tract. They have recently received bad press because of an alleged increase in heart attacks, in spite of their effectiveness at treating arthritis symptoms. Additional studies have shown a reduction in other inflammatory disorders, the risk of memory loss with aging, and breast cancer. Sometimes junk science (which I define as faulty science presented to advance an underlying agenda) interferes with objectivity when treating diseases. These issues make medicine more difficult to assess, but also make science an interesting and continuous frontier. Had aspirin been subjected to the type of scrutiny imposed today on newly discovered pharmaceuticals, I have no doubt that it would not have been approved and made available over the counter to the public. It causes gastric ulcers in many people and reduces the blood clotting ability in everyone. Every medication, even every food and all vaccines, including the polio vaccine, pose some type of risk that we must balance with the known therapeutic benefits.

Another COX-2 anti-prostaglandin, Vioxx, as of this publication, has been pulled from the market. This drug effectively relieved pain in some patients, but had been prescribed for long-term therapy instead of suggested treatment for acute pain.

In the box below are some of the diseases that involve inflammation which are listed according to the organ affected.

1. Brain—Alzheimer's disease, Parkinson's disease, ALS (Lou Gehrig's disease), stroke, multiple sclerosis, cancer, encephalitis
2. Heart and arteries—heart attacks, strokes, angina, blindness, hypertension, small vessel disease of the kidneys, arms, and legs
3. Lungs—bronchitis, bronchiectasis, any chronic lung disease, cancer
4. Stomach and intestines—esophagitis, gastritis, stomach and duodenal ulcers, spastic colon, Crohn's disease, ulcerative colitis, diverticulitis, cancer
5. Kidneys—stones, infection, hypertension, nephritis
6. Joints—rheumatoid and osteoarthritis, tendonitis, gout, tennis elbow, carpal tunnel syndrome
7. Skin—wrinkles, age spots, basal cell and squamous cell cancer, melanoma, actinic keratoses (sun spots), rashes, eczema, acne
8. Systemic—lupus erythematosis, rheumatoid arthritis, scleroderma, other autoimmune diseases

Inflammation is linked to aging and chronic diseases. Inflammation was a very little publicized factor in the aging process until it became mainstream in a February 23, 2004 issue of *Time* magazine, the cover article of which was entitled, "The Fires Within," by Christine Gorman, Alice Park, and Kristina Dell. Inflammation is certainly a part and result of the process of aging and a cause of many unwanted aspects of aging. Whether it is an independent cause of aging is not yet clear, though I have suspected so for many years.

Inflammation is certainly involved in heart disease, kidney disease, small vessel disease (atherosclerosis), arthritis, stomach and intestinal problems, Alzheimer's disease, allergies, lung diseases, and the many other chronic disease entities listed above. Few organ systems, if any, get a reprieve from the assault of inflammation. Inflammation is also an important component of disorders of the skin, including wrinkles and even cancer. This condition often results from the harmful effects of a poor diet and the production of free radicals, which is interrelated with excessive UV exposure as well as damage from such habits as smoking, contributing to illnesses and premature aging.

A healing wound is a positive result of inflammation, but cancer has many similar characteristics to a healing wound. However, in the case of cancer the inflammatory process doesn't stop, and it becomes more aggressive. Acute inflammation offers good protection against invaders such as infective bacteria or viruses, but chronic inflammation wreaks havoc. A logical question would be: What turns inflammation off so that it doesn't become malignant? I don't have all the answers, and neither does anyone else. Pertinent, however, is that all of the mentioned bad habits do cause inflammation.

Let's concentrate on reducing inflammation as a goal toward age control, which is a great start. We know that certain foods induce generalized inflammation, while others have an anti-inflammatory effect. The unsaturated fats, Omega-6 fatty acids, for example, increases the inflammatory response while Omega-3 fatty acids, also unsaturated, are anti-inflammatory. Excess simple carbohydrates and elevated insulin are inflammatory (remember the relationship?). Add high intake of saturated and trans-fats to the list of inflammation producers. Also, our fat cells secrete inflammatory cytokines, so it's no wonder that people with more fat cells usually have more inflammatory diseases and have shorter life spans. Glycation end products (AGEs) and free radicals are very inflammatory, so we have another reason to reduce them as we discussed in this chapter (and will again in Chapter 3). As with other aspects of the aging problem, it all boils down to how committed we are to taking care of ourselves.

As a plastic surgeon my interest has always been directed toward skin health and beauty (as well as skin cancers and reconstructive surgery). When focusing on skin disorders, inflammation was a priority when formulating the New Youth Skin Treatment System of skin products (see Chapter 8), of which I have a financial interest. Accordingly, several ingredients in various skin products in this system and others are effective in reducing inflammation of the skin.

In a Nutshell

1. Chronic inflammation causes diseases and the deterioration of advanced aging people.
2. Important causes of inflammation are elevated blood sugar, elevated blood insulin, an imbalance of Omega fatty acids (excess Omega-6 and insufficient Omega-3), and excess saturated and trans-fat intake.
3. Inflammation can be thwarted by commonsense nutrition and other good health habits.

Dietary Abuse

A proper diet is absolutely necessary in our goal toward health and beauty. This is where age-defiance begins. As adults, we should know what to eat (and more important, what not to eat) and be dedicated to our goals. Unfortunately, children don't have much choice. It's no surprise, therefore, to see children eating like their parents—and looking like them as well. So we have an obligation to other people in addition to ourselves. For now, let's just leave it at this: dietary abuse is certainly a bad habit. The subject of diet is discussed in more depth in Chapter 4.

It is appropriate to touch upon the relationship between excess calories, especially those due to excess sugar and other simple carbohydrates, to the formation of free radicals, glycation, inflammation, and other factors that accelerate aging. A study in rodents revealed that a caloric reduction of 40% reduced the animals' weight by about 40% and also increased their longevity by 40%. This study demonstrated that caloric restriction slows the rate of aging in mice. These results suggest that we can draw the same conclusion with people, but we need human studies for a direct correlation. This study would be quite difficult because it would take decades, and it would be practically impossible to control another human's diet. Nevertheless, the study in rodents reflects the fact that increased caloric intake yields more free radicals and thus more cellular damage. However, caloric restriction does not mean anorexia as a way to reduce excessive caloric intake. We are, again, talking about moderation.

Glycation is enhanced by the excessive intake of sugars and certain foods that become sugars and are released rapidly into the bloodstream. These foods are sugar (of course) and other simple carbohydrates such as white potatoes, white bread, white rice, pasta (except for whole wheat or grain), and even some fruits and vegetables such as beets, raisins, and bananas. The fruits, however, also offer fiber (which slows their absorption) and nutrients. Fruit should not be eliminated from your diet, although you may want to reduce them if weight loss is your primary goal. All the damage from simple carbohydrates causes premature aging and inflammation, resulting in degenerative diseases and more premature aging, setting up a vicious cycle.

As discussed, the body responds to excess intake of simple carbohydrates by creating excess insulin. A spike in blood sugar, therefore, also causes an abnormal spike in blood insulin, and the spike in blood insulin makes the blood sugar level drop like a falling stone. A low blood sugar level is called hypoglycemia, which causes a craving for more sugar. Thus, the vicious cycle is sustained.

Additional in-depth scientific sources on aging and anti-aging directed toward the general public are listed in the references section at the back of this book.

Stress, Proper Breathing, the Importance of a Good Attitude, and Laughter

As a plastic surgeon, I have seen how looking good also reflects what is inside a person and vice versa. Healthy people look better, especially when combined with happiness, less stress, and a positive attitude.

On a more abstract plane in our quest toward our health goals, let us consider stress. Stress is definitely another cause of premature aging. It can be job-related, or it can result from a significant loss, like a death, a job, divorce, or a number of issues such as problems with loved ones or inherent personalities, such as in the Type A individual (the hard-driving, impatient, success oriented, easily-angered man or woman). External forces such as our legal and political systems and the economy can induce stress, if you allow it.

Stress too often results in hypertension, heart disease, stomach ulcers, spastic colon, stroke, insomnia, and many more afflictions, and it is even thought to be an important cause of cancer. Stress can cause many psychosomatic problems such as low back or neck pain, which are often the result of muscle spasm. It can interfere with our breathing properly. Hostility and anger are also high on the stress list and are detrimental to our health. As would be expected, the Type A personality is more prone to all the above. Associated emotions induce rapid aging by increasing our cortisol and adrenalin levels, which put our metabolism into overdrive. Such people are, therefore, in a perpetual flight-and-fight mode, and it's reasonable to expect this chronic state to cause health problems.

A physician-friend told me an interesting story of the power of stress. A patient was admitted to the hospital with uncontrolled diabetes. His blood sugar simply could not be kept under control. Three days later it became stable. Why? His son had been declared missing-in-action in a war for several days until he was reported to be alive and well on the third day of the patient's hospitalization. This situation was an example of extreme stress, but we too often seem to have similar reactions to everyday occurrences. We can't, however, change the little things like too much traffic. How many times have you seen traffic causing road rage? In this situation, it's best to just sit back and enjoy listening to your favorite radio station. Or obtain and listen to books on CD or CDs about self-help or any other topic that interests you. Breathe deeply and do nothing but relax. Try to think of how insignificant the problem is in relation to the big picture that is your life. The only thing you accomplish by losing your patience is shortening your life span. It doesn't solve problems.

People approach stress relief in many different ways. For instance, once a friend of mine owed me a large sum of money. He seemed to vanish and could not be found. Three years later I got a call from him a few days before Christmas. He said he was sending me a check for the total amount. His most interesting remark was that he was paying me back for himself, for stress relief. This man went well beyond the usual to achieve personal stress relief, but to my mind he also had great character and honor.

One method of stress relief is proper breathing, which is almost the essence of meditation. Some people spend their entire lives concentrating on how to breathe. That sounds odd to someone who lives the typical stressful life and has no time to breathe. Here is a test for you. Take your deepest breath. Did your stomach go in or out? If it went out, you may have done it perfectly. If it went in, then you took only about half of your deepest breath. Also, your shoulders should not elevate. They have nothing to do with expansion of the lungs.

Here we must discuss some anatomy. During inhalation certain muscles elevate the ribs and lift the chest which creates negative pressure within the rib cage. This negative pressure expands the lungs and in turn causes air to flow into your lungs from your mouth and nose. However, equally important for breathing is your diaphragm, the muscle that separates your lungs from your abdominal cavity. The diaphragm is shaped like a large upside-down salad bowl. When it contracts, it moves downward, and this pulls the lungs down creating even more negative pressure. The biggest breath requires your abdomen to protrude from the diaphragm contracting followed by your chest expanding. This is the maximum in breathing.

When I was angry as a child (and young adult), my mother would say, "Count to ten and take a deep breath." She was correct. Shallow breathing is typical of someone under stress. Muscles tighten and the chest can't expand. Also, our interest in keeping our abdomens tight and our stomach flat keeps us from breathing deeply. If your abdominal contents are large (containing fat and stuffed, dilated intestines), breathing is considerably more difficult. Shallow breathing itself causes more stress and muscle tension, leading to yet another vicious cycle. Breathe deeply and savor it.

Everyone knows the importance of oxygen. You may not know, however, that we retain carbon dioxide (CO2) when we breathe shallowly. Our blood's CO2 levels elevate, and this level upsets our body's acid-base balance causing our blood to become more acidic. Every chemical reaction in our body responds adversely to that state of CO2 retention, which in turn causes a lower (more acidic) pH. A reverse example is hyperventilation. With this disorder you blow off too much CO2 and the pH (the measure of acidity versus alkalinity) goes up, indicating a more alkaline state (the opposite of an acidic state). This state removes calcium from the bloodstream, causing muscles to go into a spasm, called tetany. Hence, first aid manuals suggest that hyperventilating people breathe into a bag. By doing so, the individual re-breathes some of his or her own CO2 and maintains a pH balance compatible with normal metabolism. Life would not exist without oxygen, and our existence is better with proper breathing.

Several techniques can get you started in deep breathing:

1. Start each breath with the abdomen expanding, that is, going out. The chest then expands with the rib cage.
2. Do this slowly, but comfortably.
3. Take twice as long breathing out as breathing in.
4. Do this conscientiously several times a day, especially at night.
5. Think of the air coming into your nose, and then imagine it traveling everywhere in your body, even to the tips of the toes and fingers.
6. Focus only on your breathing.

We must emphasize a positive attitude as well. Remember to consider the glass half full instead of half empty. Be happy. There are always things to appreciate. Anger and hostility are extremely stressful. After all, who wants to be around a sour person with frown lines and an angry, stressed face? Such emotions are difficult to change once they become habits. They can be changed, however, and it is worth striving toward such change through meditation, yoga, Pilates, and/or other types of exercise.

Let's also talk about laughter. Laughter is also good therapy. Every issue of *Reader*'s *Digest* includes a section called "Laughter, the Best Medicine." There is an old saying that we get the face that we deserve. People who have been ill-tempered or even sad for long periods of time have lines that reflect those feelings the same way that happy people have happy lines. A good example was Johnny Carson, who almost always had those happy lines. Happy faces simply look younger. Testing this assertion is as simple as looking into a mirror and frowning and then smiling.

This chapter, along with its subchapters, has presented an overview of some of the reasons why we grow old and particularly, why some people grow older and look older (or younger) than their chronological age. There are many more aspects of aging and anti-aging yet to be reviewed.

In a Nutshell

Self-abuse (poor diet, smoking, excessive UV exposure, and stress) leads to . . .
Free radicals, glycation, inflammation, which lead to . . .
  DNA damage and mutation that leads to . . .
    Premature aging and many diseases, including cancer, which can lead to . . .
      Premature death.

Feeling and looking bad can fit anywhere in the above scenario.

What can we do about it? Knowing the information in this chapter is a great start. I will discuss in more detail diet and nutrients and what to do in later chapters. Don't forget to reduce free radicals by engaging in good health habits, about which we will have more to say.

II

Nutrition and Supplements

3 Nutrition for a Long, Youthful Life

The importance of good nutrition is nothing new. Around 400 B.C., Hippocrates said, "Let food be your medicine and let medicine be your food." In past centuries death was caused by war, battles, infections, plagues, or starvation, while today it is usually related to poor nutrition.

A brief and very interesting discussion of human history may help us understand our genetic needs regarding our diet. The early Homo sapiens, our ancient human ancestors, originated in Africa about 150,000 years ago. This seems like eons ago until we realize that the dinosaurs ruled the earth for about 165 million years. Evidence indicates that the most ancient humans inhabited the earth four to five million years ago, while other mammals began life about 60 million years ago. DNA testing and fossil research indicates that our metabolic, hormonal, and digestive systems developed over many millions of years. With this long history we can understand how we adapted to recent changes in our diets (since the agricultural revolution about 10,000 years ago), very slowly, probably in terms of tens to hundreds of thousands of years. Over 100,000 years ago our Homo sapiens ancestors migrated to coastal areas and developed tools that helped them catch fish and shellfish that live on a base diet of algae and are very high in Omega-3 fats. As will be discussed later in this chapter, Omega-3 fats (fatty acids) were important in the development of the human brain and our increased intelligence. With the consumption of Omega-3 fats from fish and shellfish sources, intelligence made a giant leap forward. They remain necessary for maintenance of intelligence and proper mental function.

Ten thousand years ago at the beginning of the agricultural revolution, we began using grains as our staple food—hence, carbohydrates became substitutes for vegetables, berries, and lean meats. Today these grains, along with meats from farmed animals (that are also fed high carbohydrate diets) and now processed vegetables, are responsible for many of our degenerative diseases. Most grains convert rapidly into simple carbohydrates when our bodies process them. Cereals and breads were our first exposure to high-density carbohydrates, and we know these stimulate rapid elevations in blood sugar and thus blood insulin levels. We certainly cannot live without insulin, but in excess amounts this hormone is dangerous. Excessively elevated insulin levels are related to obesity and most of the degenerating diseases that continue to increase in American society. I emphasize that prior to this introduction of grains into our diets, lean meats and wild plants were staple foods for our hunter-gatherer-forager ancestors. Their diet consisted of wild animals, fish, mussels, snails, birds, bird eggs, reptiles, and shellfish as protein sources, plus roots, berries, shoots, seeds, nuts, and other plants and various leaves. This protein- and nutrient-dense diet often included mostly complex carbohydrates and often up to five times the protein of our American diet because protein from wild animals is of a much higher quality and more protein-dense than the protein from today's food-lot animals. Just like our ancestors, the animals themselves had to hunt for their food. They ran wild and were not fed fattening high-carbohydrate diets. (It is of interest that many of the amino acids that make up proteins are essential, but no simple carbohydrates are actually essential.) We have thus undergone a dramatic change in dietary habits over a relatively short period of time with regard to genetic adaptation relating to evolution of the primate.

These dietary changes caused humans to decrease in height of up to six inches after the agricultural revolution began. The average height of males during the Upper Paleolithic Era (10,000 years ago and beyond) was five feet ten inches to six feet tall, and the average women stood five feet six inches tall. This reduction due to diet is ironic considering the increased availability of food. Unbelievable, but true!

These nutritional problems only worsened with the invention of food processing, which yielded white flour, white bread, rice, pasta and, finally, sugar in virtually everything from meats to salad dressings to canned goods. People got shorter and fatter. They also became unhealthier, as is indicated by healthy teeth noted by archaeologists in Paleolithic man versus the rotten teeth predominating after the advent of grains as a primary part of our diet. This phenomenon occurred even before our modern-day sweet tooth. For example, examination of various ancient Egyptian mummies reveals obesity, degenerative diseases, bad teeth, and shortened life spans due to heart disease and stroke. The Egyptian diet at that time consisted mainly of grains, fruits, and some vegetables, with less than optimal protein intake. The ancient Egyptians also drank beer and made their staple food, grain, into numerous different recipes, often with honey. They thus consumed a high-carbohydrate, low-protein diet.

To add insult to injury, over the last twenty-five years until recently we have learned an "I hate fat" philosophy, influenced at that time by the Surgeon General, the American Diabetes Association, and the American Heart Association. This trend was remarkable, since the value of a low-carbohydrate diet was reported in a book by Dr. William Banting in the early 1800's. In spite of this and other evidence through the years, health officials strongly encouraged us to eat a low-fat, high-carbohydrate diet, resulting in Americans now being among the fattest, unhealthiest populations on earth. An excellent source of information regarding the benefits of a high-protein, balanced diet is *Protein Power* (1996) by Michael R. Eades, M.D., and Mary Dan Eades, M.D.

Of course, gluttony has not helped the matter any. How many times have I seen an obese person eat only a salad for lunch? Not surprisingly, the plate is often stacked with bacon chips, croutons, cheese and so much salad dressing that it looks soupy. We are not stuffing sausage when we eat. Our bodies are not warehouses for food. In fact, the only proven way to extend life is caloric restriction, which doesn't mean we have to starve ourselves. We just shouldn't stuff ourselves until we are miserable or even to where we feel uncomfortably full. We will adapt to less intake and our stomachs will shrink to accommodate, just as it stretches to accommodate gluttony. Also, we should eat more slowly so our brains get the message that our stomachs are getting full. I can often look at how much food one puts on a fork and predict whether or not that person will become obese.

Dietary supplements, exercise, and a healthful diet dramatically improve the quality of life in our later years and may even extend our lives—the latter is yet to be proven, though I feel confident that it will be. It's just a matter of time, as it takes generations for such studies to be completed. We do, however, know how to increase heart disease, cancer, and stroke (not that we would want to do this), and that is with obesity, high simple carbohydrate intake, smoking, and high saturated fats. We can reduce these diseases also, so it is logical that reducing these diseases would prolong life.

Dietary Fats

Is fat intake as evil as we have been led to believe? Let us review some history and then you decide. The first hormones developed by a living organism were fats called eicosanoids. Primarily from algae, these are long-chained, unsaturated fats (polyunsaturated fats). Because our ancestors for the past 100,000 years lived in great part on shellfish, which live on algae, and also on fish that eat both shellfish and algae, they consumed an abundance of these eicosanoids. Unfortunately eicosanoids have been severely lacking in our diets for many recent decades. In addition, since the Surgeon General suggested fat intake as the primary cause of obesity and ill health in 1988, numerous publications have suggested fat and cholesterol intake of any type to be a cause of heart disease, stroke, hypertension, diabetes, and other diseases. In the past, even the American Diabetes Association implicated fat as a villain in diabetes and recommended a low-fat, high-carbohydrate diet. As a result, many health-conscious people stopped eating nuts, shellfish, and virtually any type of fat. Evidence now indicates that such a diet is entirely the wrong approach. Fats are essential for health, as they make up 60%

of the brain and are the main ingredient in the insulation covering of nerves (the neurolemma sheath) throughout our bodies. They also maintain our trillions of cell membranes. A proper balance of fat intake is essential. Let's think about this again in more depth. Each cell membrane contains high concentrations of fats and cholesterol. What does the cell membrane do? First, it is not a simple, semipermeable membrane like a piece of filter paper. It is actually a functioning entity consisting of multiple specific pumps. When functioning properly, these pumps orchestrate the flow of nutrients into and out of each cell to maintain the appropriate environment for the cell to conduct its vital functions. Our survival requires the contents within each cell to be constant and significantly different from the environment outside the cell, such as our serum or the spaces between the cells. For instance, the cell membrane functions as a "sodium pump" which keeps sodium out of the cell and high concentrations of potassium inside the cell. Common sense indicates the health catastrophe resulting from eating no fat: the cell membranes no longer work properly—which is what has happened on our no-fat diets.

These cells are our trillion factories that perform our vital functions so when our cell membranes become functionally deficient with a depletion of fat and become more vulnerable to the ravages of free radicals, this damage leads to damage within the cells, to the mitochondria, to the DNA, and more. Mutations (changes in DNA) then occur, and we age faster and acquire more chronic diseases, including cancer. Also in simple terms, the cell contents also leak out.

With Cro-Magnon man's migration to the coastal areas and increased intake of seafood, the frontal lobe and cerebrum of the brain developed and modern intelligence began. This new diet of fish and shellfish, both high in long chain polyunsaturated fats, coincided with the emergence of modern intelligence. Hence, without certain fats abundant in fish and shellfish (the Omega-3 fats discussed later in this chapter), modern intelligence could not have occurred. So as it turns out, Grandmother's old adage of fish being brain food was true after all. This is only the tip of the iceberg and takes us into a discussion of specific fats.

Fats come in a variety of forms, ranging from healthy to unhealthy. Saturated fats are generally from animal sources. People on the same diets today that people were on in the early 1900s will consume more fats because of the way animals are raised. Free-range cattle and even chickens raised 100 years ago were much leaner than today's feedlot animals. The saturated fat content in cattle has gone from about 5% to 30% over that period of time. The U.S. Department of Agriculture's Feedlot Guidelines suggest feeding cattle 61% carbohydrate (which are starches), 25% fat, and 14% protein. These, unfortunately, are the same high-carb ratios that were recommended in USDA guidelines for people. With this decrease in protein intake and increase in saturated fats, it's no wonder that many Americans are fat and unhealthy. This high carbohydrate diet is even bad for our animals. It stimulates production of excess insulin, which is a major problem. Most interesting—fat does not stimulate production of insulin.

Fat Classification

Saturated fats—bad if taken in excess. Meat fats and fats from dairy products are never good for you.

Monosaturated fats—a healthful form of unsaturated fats, such as olive oil.

Unsaturated (polyunsaturated) fats—the other good fat.

Types of unsaturated fats:

- Omega-3—beneficial fats consisting of:
  - Eicosapentanoic acid (EPA)—for general health
  - Docosahexanoic acid (DHA)—for growth of brain and nerve cells
- Omega-6—considered bad if used in excess

Trans-fats—partially hydrogenated vegetable fats. Man-made, very unhealthful fats.

Saturated fats have more hydrogen bonds, which makes them thicker and stickier at room temperature, much like lard, butter, and animal fat, like that around the edge of a steak. These fats stick to the walls of our blood vessels, contributing to heart disease, currently the number one killer in our society. Saturated fats should therefore be kept to a minimum. I recommend reading the labels on all foods when possible, paying attention to these facts. Make it a habit.

Monosaturated fats (Omega-9 fats), which include olive oil and canola oil, are among the most healthful fats. Try to include these in your diet and also as your cooking oil. When you must eat bread, eat wheat bread, and dip it in a saucer of extra virgin olive oil. It retards absorption of the carbohydrate, it's delicious, and it's good for you.

Trans-fats (also called trans-fatty acids or partially hydrogenated fats) are made from vegetable oils processed so that they become more solid, as in most margarines. Trans-fats are man-made and not natural to the body. They are the most dangerous fats, even worse than saturated fats, and are responsible for not only heart disease but certain cancers as well. Unfortunately, they are also the most popular fats in America. It's difficult to find processed foods without these hydrogenated or partially hydrogenated trans-fatty acids, and they now account for more of our fat consumption than does beef. In fact, if you pick up any package of cookies, crackers, or cereals, you will probably find partially hydrogenated corn, soy, coconut, sesame, or some other vegetable oil. These oils are all trans-fats. Manufacturers prefer trans-fats because they are more stable than unsaturated fats and have longer shelf lives. Their problem shouldn't be our problem, however.

It takes effort to avoid trans-fats, but the reward is better health. Again, read the labels. One bit of evidence that food suppliers are listening to current evidence against trans-fats is that now some margarines, breads, and cookies contain no trans-fats. Another is the fairly recent federal requirement that trans-fat contents of packaged foods be disclosed on labels.

Unsaturated fats (polyunsaturated fats) are divided into Omega-6 and Omega-3 fatty acids. Omega-3 fats are considered healthful and Omega-6 fats thought to be bad. However, both are necessary, though we must have a proper balance of them to be healthy.

The Omega-3 fatty acids are considered essential because they cannot be synthesized by the human body. Dietary sources of Omega-3 fats include plants (especially flax seed, canola, walnuts, and avocado) and ocean fish (particularly salmon, sardines, mackerel), krill, and shellfish that dine on algae.

Sources of Omega-3:

- Fish, shellfish—Omega-3
- Plants (walnuts, flax seed, avocado, canola) > alpha linolenic acid > Omega-3
- Omega-3—consist of EPA and DHA

We can get our EPA and DHA from the above-listed plants because the high amount of alpha linolenic acid (ALA) they contain is converted into Omega-3 fats. Omega-3 fatty acids are divided into EPA (eicosapentanoic acid) and DHA (docosahexanoic acid). The function of EPA is for general health, and DHA more specifically enhances nerve cell and brain development and maintenance. Sixty percent of the brain is fat and the majority requires DHA, which is also necessary for the function of our nerve synapses, the connections between nerve cells. Just like an electric cord has insulation, each nerve fiber has an insulation covering made up mostly of DHA fats. Without DHA, we short out—that is, our nerve cells don't function normally. An example of the ultimate lack of DHA and EPA occurs in anorexic patients, who often eliminate all fats from their diets. In the later stages, anorexics cannot think logically, and they function instead on habit and momentum. In addition, they often develop neurological symptoms such as stinging and pain in the legs and arms, indicating destruction of the nerve insulation sheath, the neurolemma.

Interestingly, much work has been done on the relationship between Omega-3 fatty acids and depression, and results show that depression is often directly related to insufficient intake of Omega-3 from fish. Those who eat more fish have less depression and vice versa. This relationship exists when comparing certain countries to others and even when comparing various areas within the same country. EPA, or lack thereof, is the important component. This observation is not only academic. Since the low-fat craze began, depression has risen to an all-time high. Now that the public is more aware of the necessity of adequate Omega-3 intake, we hope to see less depression and chronic inflammatory diseases as well.

Adequate intake of Omega-3 fats can also reduce discomfort and inflammation from arthritis. Inflammation is also involved in Alzheimer's disease, Parkinson's disease, gastrointestinal diseases, and virtually every other disease. Truly, almost all inflammatory diseases are due in some part to excess Omega-6 fats and inadequate Omega-3 intake. In fact, the blood vessel disease known as arteriosclerosis, which involves blood vessel plaques and obstruction, has a strong inflammatory component. Therefore, a strong indicator of such disease is the C-reactive protein blood test, a generalized test for inflammation.

Important benefits from optimal Omega-3 intake are as follows:

Inflammation reduction
Pain reduction
Improvement of arthritis symptoms
Reduction of premature clotting of the blood
Dilation of small blood vessels
Enhanced immune function
Improved brain function
Psychological stability

Omega-6 does the opposite:

Stimulates inflammation
Increases pain (including joint pain)
Increases blood clotting
Constricts blood vessels
Reduces immune function
Reduces brain function
Promotes psychological instability (especially depression)

As we can see, Omega-6 fats cause inflammation and Omega-3 fats are anti-inflammatory. Consider the following diseases and conditions as significant results of inflammation:

Alzheimer's disease
Parkinson's disease
Ulcerative colitis
Crohn's disease
Heart disease
Stroke
Arteriosclerosis
Certain cancers
Bronchitis

Arthritis
Inflammatory skin disorders
Tendonitis
Depression
Rapid aging

Most of us have some symptoms of one of the above-mentioned disorders, whether it is a sore shoulder, knee, or hands; high cholesterol levels; or a rash of some sort. Hence, we should wonder how much of our problems is related to diet, particularly, in terms of an imbalance of Omega-3 and Omega-6 fats (and also the balance of insulin to glucagon to be discussed later under carbohydrates). Is your memory as good as it was in the past? If not, look to your Omega-3 intake for a possible answer. This brief review of the list of characteristics related to excess Omega-6 intake explains why we should make every attempt to manage Omega-6 intake and assure adequate Omega-3 intake. Who of us has not had one or more of these signs or symptoms mentioned?

Let me emphasize, however, that Omega-6 fatty acids are not entirely bad. In fact, we could not live without them. They contribute to our inflammatory process, and we need them for an adequate inflammation to fight various bacteria and viruses and to assist in repairing various wounds, including surgery. We are constantly subjected to physical insults requiring our defensive inflammatory process.

The most common source of Omega-6 fats are meats, liver, egg yolks, and refined cooking oils from corn, safflower, cottonseed, peanuts, sesame seeds, and sunflower seeds.

The challenge is consuming the proper balance of Omega-6 to Omega-3 fatty acids in our diets. This is important! Experts have reported that the most healthful ratio of Omega-6 to Omega-3 intake is 1 to 1. In the present American diet the ratio is as high as 20:1, with the excess being Omega-6! (See also www.memanweb.com/article-15.htm and www.healingdaily.com/detoxification-diethealing-fats.htm.)

Because of the unfortunate low-fat craze, it is no surprise that western countries have seen a significant drop in Omega-3 fatty acid intake over the last century and especially the last 30 years. The opposite, however, can be said of Omega-6 intake from meats and egg yolks, which contain arachidonic acid. (Arachidonic acid is linked to the production of Omega-6 fatty acids and is also found in various vegetable oils from corn, safflower, sunflower, cottonseed, and sesame seeds).

Remember, both Omega-3 and 6 are essential fats, but we consume both excess Omega-6 and inadequate Omega-3 in our diets. The average intake of the EPA/DHA fatty acids in North America is about 130 milligrams. The recommended intake is 870 milligrams, and for heart disease patients the American Heart Association now recommends 1,000 milligrams per day. Now that we know a proper intake of fats is necessary for good health, we should make shellfish, algae, fish, the proper vegetable sources, and Omega-3 supplements an important part of our diet. The fish containing the most Omega-3 fats are salmon, tuna, mackerel, and sardines. Good vegetable sources of Omega-3 are avocados, walnuts, flax, and canola oil.

We must also keep in mind that many types of fish, particularly farmed fish, contain high levels of mercury, polychlorinated biphenyls (PCB), and other toxins. In addition, a list of fish to consider avoiding for environmental reasons includes Chilean sea bass, Atlantic cod, king crab (imported), monkfish, orange roughy, rockfish (Pacific snapper), farmed or Atlantic salmon, bluefin tuna, and Atlantic swordfish. Information regarding these and other commercial fish can be found on www.montereybayaquarium.org. These issues make your choices more complex, but are worth looking into. Because of the notoriety of the heavy metal problem in farmed fish, I would expect that more care will be made to minimize that problem in the near future.

If your doctor has you on anticoagulant therapy, discuss Omega-3 supplementation with him or her.

Very good sources of Omega-3 dietary supplements are from the following laboratories (among others):

Nordic Naturals: www.nordicnaturals.com
Sears Labs: www.searslabs.com
Omega Natural Health: www.Omegabrite.com
Coromega: www.coromega.com
Natural Factors—Dr. Michael Murray's Fish Oil: www.naturalfactors.com
Carlson Cod Liver Oil and Fish Oil: www.carlsonlabs.com
Country Life Fish Oils: www.country-life.com

These are some of the pharmaceutical sources with higher concentrations of Omega-3 than found in many health food stores and pharmacies, which often provide 60% Omega-3 at the most. I take Omega-3 supplements and recommend them to reduce symptoms and diseases of aging. You can also ask a knowledgeable health food store nutritionist for a good product.

Barry Sears, Ph.D. (author of the "Zone" books, including *The Omega Zone*) recommends that daily maintenance should begin with 2 to 2.5 grams of long-chain Omega-3 fatty acids, which would be two capsules or one teaspoon of pharmaceutical-grade fish oil each day, divided into morning and evening doses. The dose can be increased to two capsules or one teaspoon in the morning and in the evening. Too much too soon will result in diarrhea so you may have to work your way up to that dose.

Although many excellent products are available, most of my experience with Omega-3 supplementation is from the Sears Labs (DrSears.com), Dr. Michael Murray's Fish Oil, Nordic Naturals, and for those adverse to taking fish oil, Coromega. All have been satisfactory. Children will love the Coromega brand fish oil as it looks and tastes like pudding. It's almost impossible to influence children to take any other type of fish oil supplement.

Finally, we are back to the monounsaturated fats, also referred to as monosaturated fats, which are considered to be some of the most healthful of the unsaturated fats and should be a part of everyone's diet. They help lower LDL (the bad cholesterol) and elevate HDL (the good cholesterol). They also help reduce age-related memory loss. The best sources are virgin olive oil and canola oil. Extra virgin olive oil also contains squalene, a potent antioxidant. Because of the instability of unsaturated fats due to oxidation, antioxidants help preserve these fatty acids from oxidation once they are in the bloodstream. Other good sources of healthy unsaturated fatty acids are nuts (especially cashews, macadamia nuts, and almonds) and avocados.

For weight loss, remember that each gram of fat yields nine calories, whereas protein and carbohydrates yield four calories per gram, so while we absolutely require certain fats in our diet, moderation is the goal. You do not have to clean your plate, even though your mother and/or grandmother may have told you to. We are not warehouses for food. You may have to change your dietary habits, and sometimes this is difficult. For instance, two patients came to my office for total body lifts following stomach bypass surgery. Each had lost about a hundred pounds. Months later one had continued to lose more weight, and the other had started to gain again, approaching his pre-surgery weight. When I asked the first patient what happened, he said that the other patient had "learned how to cheat by eating small portions of the wrong foods all day." Maybe he was punishing himself, or attempting to get attention, but for emotional reasons he simply had to defeat every effort to help him with his dietary problems. It's difficult to change one's behavior. In cases like this where something much deeper is wrong, a psychiatrist may be the only answer.

Cholesterol

There is more to know about the issue of fats, including cholesterol, LDL, HDL, and arachidonic acid. Very high blood cholesterol levels have been proven time and again to cause harmful deposits in our coronary arteries (the arteries that feed the heart) and arteries to the brain, as well as everywhere else. So we should keep cholesterol levels within acceptable ranges: from 160 to 200 is usually considered acceptable, providing other parameters such as LDL and HDL are OK. But that's only the tip of another iceberg.

In my medical college years and even now in many medical circles, many have believed that we should get cholesterol as low as possible, meaning the lowest possible cholesterol level is the best. I have heard people bragging about cholesterol levels of 120 or less. A multitude of medications, such as Lipitor, Mevacor, and Zocor, are designed to lower blood cholesterol. Their value should not be minimized because they do work to lower cholesterol levels. However, it is our obligation to ourselves to understand what cholesterol is before we take such drugs in this attempt to get levels as low as possible.

First of all, cholesterol is not a fat. It is a solid alcohol wax substance insoluble in blood. Thus it makes a great source for obstruction of our arteries due to plaque formation. Cholesterol is not all bad, however. It is manufactured in every one of our trillions of cells and is necessary for the formation of many hormones, including our sex hormones (testosterone and estrogen) and cortisol, all of which are necessary for life. Cholesterol is a main component of bile, which is necessary for absorption of certain foods, especially fats, including the fat-soluble vitamins A, D, E, and K. Cholesterol is another substance necessary for normal growth of the entire nervous system, including the brain. It has many more functions, and because it is necessary for life itself, we don't really want our cholesterol levels extremely low.

Cholesterol is made in every cell but primarily within the liver, though about 20% is from our diet. When our diet is inadequate our cells make more. The amount of cholesterol within our cells is stable, and a feedback regulatory mechanism within the cell regulates how much is made. But there is no such feedback system within our circulatory system, so blood levels of cholesterol vary widely. On the typical American diet, however, cholesterol levels range from high to higher (in addition to our superfluous levels of simple carbohydrate intake). Fortunately, these high blood cholesterol levels can be controlled by diet in most cases; and as only 20% of our blood cholesterol comes from diet, its control surprisingly doesn't reduce dietary cholesterol or fat as much as one might expect.

To understand cholesterol we must also understand lipoproteins. The total blood cholesterol level is made up by the combination of LDL (low density lipoprotein), VLDL (very low density lipoprotein) and HDL (high density lipoprotein) levels. These lipoproteins carry insoluble cholesterol and also insoluble triglycerides.

> LDL wears the black hat. It is the bad cholesterol and levels should be kept low.
>
> VLDL is also bad.
>
> HDL is the white-hat lipoprotein and is good. Its levels should be kept as high possible.

LDL (bad) carries cholesterol to the cells to be transferred through the cell membrane by LDL receptors. LDL with cholesterol that is not used by the cells is either destroyed or deposited onto the arterial walls (not good).

VLDL carries mostly triglycerides with some cholesterol and usually is an indicator of carbohydrate intake.

HDL (good), the most dense lipoprotein, carries cholesterol back to the liver to be destroyed.

HDL is thus protective and counters high levels of LDL.

This paragraph is for those of you who want to know more of the technical details. Cells both manufacture and use cholesterol, and when the cells' need for cholesterol exceeds what they can manufacture, they send the messenger (the LDL receptor) to the cell membrane to capture LDL and its cholesterol from the blood stream. If the cell needs more cholesterol than it can manufacture, it will take more from the blood stream and the cholesterol blood levels will decrease—a good thing. If the cellular cholesterol production mechanism slows, more LDL receptors are made within the cell to snare more cholesterol. And that's what we want. So what do we do to achieve this? We go back to the basic—eat lean meats or fish (1/3 of your plate) and lots of small helpings of vegetables (2/3 of your plate). The supplement niacin also lowers cholesterol, raises HDL, and lowers LDL. Supplements will be discussed below.

Cholesterol is made up of:
- HDL—The Good
- LDL—The Bad
- VLDL—The Ugly (mostly triglycerides)

If you understand how these lipoproteins work, you will know their importance and how to keep them at healthful levels. You now understand cholesterol, both the good and bad as well as where it is made—that is, within every cell. Blood levels of cholesterol are governed a small degree by how much cholesterol we consume, but mostly by how much cholesterol our cells need to perform their functions.

Fat intake does not have to be low and our discussion above explains why. Very low total fat intake dieters are unhealthy, usually get fatter, and die younger.

Homocysteine

Most discussions about heart and blood disease focus on cholesterol. But there are other causes of heart disease. Cholesterol is far from the entire story.

Homocysteine is a toxic, nonessential amino acid present in everyone. Although Dr. Kilmer McCully first discussed the significance of homocysteine in the 1960s, not until 1994 did a study by Harvard's Dr. Meir Samfer endorse its importance. So what is its importance? Elevated blood homocysteine may kill you by accelerating vascular disease. We still have much to learn about elevated homocysteine, but we do know that it's bad. High blood levels of homocysteine are related to vascular and other diseases, but there are nutrients that can change it into methionine, an essential amino acid.

High homocysteine levels = vascular disease

When one's homocysteine level is elevated, nutritional intervention can reduce homocysteine levels to normal in 95% of cases. This process is called methylation because a combination of atoms (a methyl group) attaches to homocysteine. (The above supplements work by giving a methyl group to the homocysteine creating the essential amino acid methionine. For folic acid to make this transformation, vitamin B12 is required. Vitamin B6 detoxifies homocysteine by another pathway, but is equally important. However, B6 can be destroyed by food processing, by use of birth-control tablets or patches, and by cigarette smoking). TMG (betaine), folic acid, and vitamins B12 and B6 can all be purchased at any health food store. Sometimes all four nutrients can be bought in a single capsule or tablet.

> The knights in white armor that lower homocysteine are:
>
> Folic acid with vitamin B12
> Trimethylglycine (TMG, betaine)
> Vitamin B6
>
> All three can be bought over the counter.

As a matter of interest, the methylation process is involved in many other biological functions such as processing fats, maintaining DNA integrity, maintaining neurological function, and virtually every metabolic process in the body. Therefore we should make every effort to take supplements with TMG, folic acid, and vitamins B6 and B12. Recent studies show a 60% decrease in vascular disease among those who take these supplement combinations.

> Homocysteine (+) methyl group = methionine (an essential amino acid)

Carbohydrates

In the introduction to *The Schwarzbein Principle* (1999), by the endocrinologist Diana Schwarzbein, M.D., and Nancy Deville, they describe the American Diabetes Association's diet as a high-carbohydrate, low-fat, low-protein program.

Seeing that her patients not only got worse but also became obese on that plan, she began measuring their blood sugar levels before and after meals—up to seven times a day in some patients. After these exhaustive experiments, the conclusion was obvious—the high-carbohydrate, low-fat, low-protein diet made her patients' diabetes worse and made them fat.

Since there are only three classes of nutrients in food, consider carbohydrates as anything other than protein or fat. Carbohydrates' purpose is to serve as fuel for our bodies. Starches are complex carbohydrates, but some such as white bread, white rice, pasta, and potatoes act as simple carbohydrates because they are absorbed rapidly. (Generally, those complex carbohydrates with more fiber, such as whole grain bread, brown rice, whole wheat pasta, and vegetables are absorbed more slowly.) Simple carbohydrates consist of one or two molecules and complex carbohydrates have three or more molecules. All carbohydrates are broken down by digestion before absorption into the blood system. One can easily see that simple sugars with fewer molecules are broken down and absorbed faster, which is not good because a spike in insulin follows soon afterward. Sugars stimulate insulin production (from the Islets of Langerhans within the pancreas), and faster absorption of sugar causes faster and increased release of insulin. A spike in blood insulin is not what we want.

The main purpose of insulin is to regulate (lower) blood sugar when it is above the normal level of about 100 mg/ml (may vary slightly according to the laboratory). It does so by metabolizing sugar and storing it within our cells. But insulin also stores fat and prevents fat from being burned. This is worth an extra thought. When insulin levels are up, you will burn sugar, but you will not burn fat. In addition, you will accumulate and store fat. The way to reduce body fat is to eat your proper fats and keep your insulin levels from spiking due to too much simple carbohydrate intake. We have already seen that certain fats are essential for normal metabolism, hardy cell membranes, resistance against free radical damage, proper brain and central nervous system function, and for hormone secretion—usually unknown items of importance. But we now know from numerous publications and studies that too much insulin is toxic, causing either directly or indirectly the following problems: obesity, type 2 diabetes, heart disease, arteriosclerosis, stroke, certain cancers, osteoarthritis, premature aging, and virtually every degenerative disease that we get as we age.

This warrants further discussion about the function of insulin as well glucagon, which actions are opposite to those of insulin.

Insulin functions:

- Lowers blood sugar to normal levels and keeps it from going too high
- Sends sugar molecules to cells for fuel and for storage as energy
- This process is critical for the brain
- Sends sugar molecules to the liver for storage as glycogen
- Stores sugar as fat, triglycerides, and cholesterol
- I repeat, excess sugar is stored as fat, triglycerides, and cholesterol

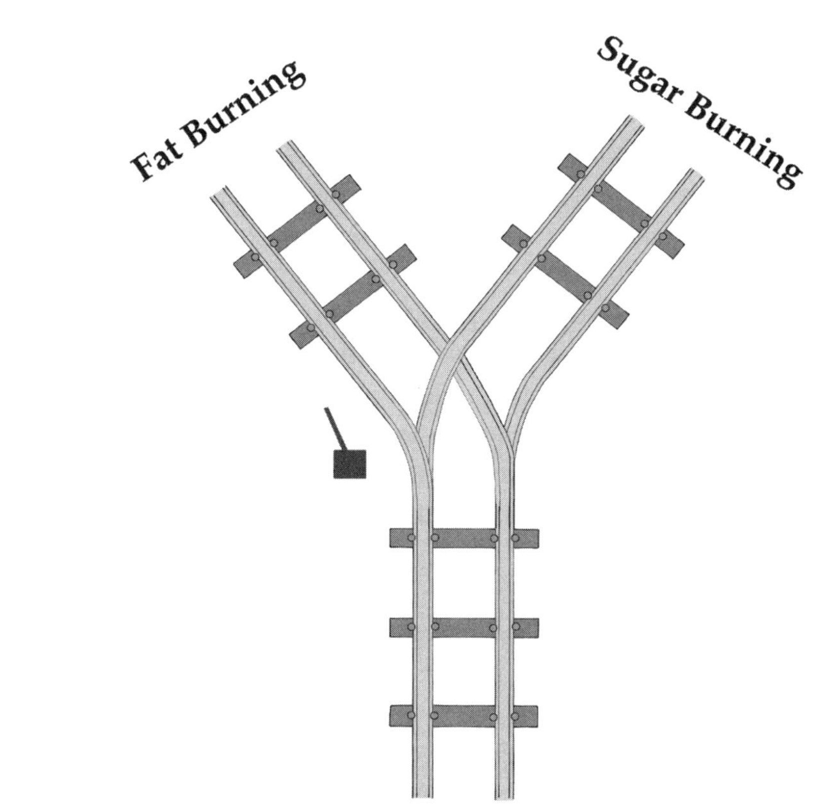

FIGURE 3-1. Insulin determines whether you burn sugar or fat. High insulin levels cause the burning of the elevated sugar, but fat is not burned and is actually accumulated. Like a train track, it's one way or the other. It's either fat or sugar that is burned by the body, and the deciding factor is your insulin level, which is determined by your simple carbohydrate intake.

Glucagon, the antithesis of insulin, functions:

- Raises blood sugar to normal levels and keeps it from going too low
- Mobilizes glycogen from liver into the blood system
- Mobilizes fat, triglycerides, and cholesterol into the blood system to be burned

Insulin is necessary for energy, but the balance between insulin and glucagon is critical for good health. All carbohydrates cause insulin release. Both low blood sugar and low protein intake cause glucagon release, also from the pancreas.

A typical American diet, which usually is a high simple carbohydrate diet, has a very high insulin-to-glucagon ratio—too much insulin and not enough glucagon. This is why Americans have an all-time high obesity problem, and this includes children. Ninety-nine percent of this is not a hormone problem, just a lack of understanding of carbohydrate metabolism and the necessity of limiting the simple carbohydrate intake to just about zero. The insulin-glucagon ratio should be balanced for optimal health and is critical for longevity.

Insulin levels stay elevated longer than sugar levels in the blood, so when the insulin spikes upward from excess simple carbohydrate intake, the blood sugar actually goes too low in a couple of hours—because insulin went too high for too long a period. We then get hypoglycemia (low blood sugar), which causes a slump in energy and a craving for more sugar. We crave for more simple carbohydrates and start a dangerous trend. We then produce glucagon to help raise blood sugar—typically about two hours after the blood sugar drops below normal. Eventually the cells become less sensitive to insulin, and insulin levels must remain up just to keep blood sugar levels effective. This process is bad and is called insulin resistance. We are now on the road to diabetes, obesity, degenerative diseases, stroke, heart disease, and the long list of problems mentioned above.

Causes of Insulin Resistance:

- Excess simple carbohydrate intake
- Stimulants such as coffee, caffeine, tobacco
- Excess thyroid hormone

We cannot live solely on fats and proteins, so what carbohydrates are safe?

We are back to moderation and the balanced diet. When it comes to carbohydrates released into the blood stream, slower is better because it does not cause a spike in insulin release. In addition to limiting our carbohydrate intake to complex carbohydrates, we need fiber, good fats, and protein intake to help control the rapid absorption following their breakdown into sugar, reducing the high spikes and excess insulin response. Remember that protein stimulates glucagon release, reducing hypoglycemia and subsequent sugar cravings.

Protein intake → Glucagon release → Stable blood sugar

Eating no carbohydrates, simple and complex, is also bad because of what excess glucagon does. If someone is obese, maybe the no-carbohydrate approach is OK for the short term. However, it takes protein intake to stimulate glucagon release to elevate blood sugar to normal level—critical for the brain and heart. With chronic carbohydrate deprivation, excess glucagon will cause the body to sacrifice its own muscle, hormone-producing glands, and other body tissue available to maintain a normal blood sugar level. Remember photos of POWs, victims of WWII concentration camps and anorexics? Their emaciation resulted from chronic food deprivation resulting in their bodies drawing blood sugar from their own tissue. So we should always consume a proper amount of complex carbohydrates. Besides, the complex carbohydrate-rich vegetables have wonderful nutrients that we all need, and we should never deprive ourselves of them.

In general, the Glycemic Index is a good guide to follow for our carbohydrate intake. This is a scale that lists foods that are likely to cause too much insulin release. Diabetic patients commonly use the Glycemic Index as a diet guide. High on the list, of course, are sugar, potatoes, white pasta, bagels, white rice, white bread, ice cream, fruit-flavored yogurt, sugared anything, cereal and, yes, beer. Raisins, watermelon, and bananas are high on the list also, but do not have to be eliminated because they have fiber and some valuable nutrients. Remember that moderation and balance are key, except in the case of sugars, in which case none is better than a little. With fruits, the sweetest ones with the lowest fiber content are more apt to stimulate rapid insulin release.

Another measure of dietary sugar intake is Glycemic Load. While Glycemic Index shows how rapidly a food's carbohydrate is likely to turn into sugar, Glycemic Load relates more to various specific foods and their fiber content. This information is important, because some foods, while having lots of carbohydrates, do not create spikes in blood sugar because of their high fiber content. A glycemic load of 20 is high, 11 to 19 is medium, and 10 or less is low. A glycemic index of 70 is high, 56 to 69 is medium, and below 55 is low. David Mendosa, consultant on diabetes, has done exhaustive studies on the subject, measuring blood sugar levels resulting from virtually every food including different name brands and offers a lengthy discussion on this topic on www.mendosa.com. He believes using both glycemic index and glycemic load are necessary for the total picture. On Mendosa's website, just about every food is compared and he offers a helpful newsletter. Some comparisons between the Glycemic Index and Glycemic Load of various foods are as follows:

	Glycemic Index	Glycemic Load
Carrots	80 (high)	1 (low)
Watermelon	72 (high)	4 (low)
Sweet corn	60 (medium)	11 (low medium)
Baked potato	60 (medium)	16 (medium)

With the exception of bananas, most fruits when eaten raw have low Glycemic Loads. Remember that with the Glycemic Index a rating of 55 is low and 70 is high, while with Glycemic Load, a rating of 10 is low and 20 is high, so the actual numbers do not equate.

	High	Medium	Low
Glycemic Index	70	56–69	55 and below
Glycemic Load	20	11–19	10 and below

Vegetables contain carbohydrates, but they are complex carbohydrates. They are more healthful because of the high fiber content and the concentrated nutrients, including vitamins, minerals, phytonutrients, and antioxidants. They are nutrient and fiber-dense. The phrase "nutrient and fiber-dense" is an important concept for the health-goal-oriented dieter. Stick with the brightly colored vegetables for the most nutrients. Eat a rainbow of fruits and vegetables—the more colors, the better the benefit. Colorful pigments are filled with phytonutrients or phytochemicals. They are potent antioxidants and anticarcinogens, thus reducing cancer formation.

Phytonutrients include:

Phytonutrient	Foods
Carotenes	Dark colored vegetables, carrots, squash, spinach, tomatoes, yams, sweet potatoes, fruits like cantaloupe, and oranges
Coumarin	Carrots, beets, celery, citrus
Flavonoids	Blueberries, blackberries, strawberries, raspberries, citrus, peppers, greens, tomatoes, onions, legumes, parsley
Isoflavonoids	Soybeans, other legumes
Lignans	Flaxseed, whole grains, nuts, seeds
Polyphenols	Green teas, red wine, grapes, raisins, mulberry, cranberry
Sterols	Soybeans, nuts, seeds

Your daily vegetable or fruit intake should be at least five portions a day. In Dr. Michael Murray's book, *How to Prevent and Treat Cancer with Natural Medicine* (2002), he recommends ten servings a day, although they may be small. In this way we consume all the essential antioxidants, natural anti-inflammatory agents, and phytonutrients that enhance detoxification and immune functions. Dr. Murray emphasizes that darker-colored vegetables and fruits have more nutrients, as opposed to lighter vegetables such as iceberg lettuce.

Eating a balanced meal is easy: Eat lean meats, vegetables, eggs, low-fat dairy products (if you are not lactose intolerant), nuts, soy products, fruits, and other nutrient-rich foods, including unprocessed carbohydrates such as whole grain bread, brown rice, and whole wheat pasta. In general, when eating carbohydrates try to add protein and fat (good fat, of course, like fish, olive oil, and nuts) to reduce the spike in blood insulin. Try dipping whole-grain bread in extra-virgin olive oil with low fat cheese when you feel you must have bread. The olive oil slows the rapid absorption of the bread, which can act as a simple carbohydrate.

Fiber

What else can we do to prevent blood sugar spikes? The more fiber a food contains, the more slowly we absorb sugars. Fiber is very important. For example, because of its high fiber content, whole-grain bread is better than white bread. Cooking or processing foods usually decreases fiber as well as nutrient content. Also, simple carbohydrates are nutrient-poor foods, and your body hates nutrient-poor foods. Think about this: Our bodies use nutrients to process simple carbohydrates that could have been used to process nutrient-rich foods. So they don't only cause insulin spikes, but they also deplete nutrients required for other necessary processes as well.

The term fiber actually refers to carbohydrates that cannot be digested. The two types of fiber are soluble and insoluble. Soluble fiber dissolves in water and insoluble fiber does not. Fiber is present in all plants we consume, including grains, legumes, fruit, vegetables, nuts, seeds, and roots. The recommended daily intake of fiber for an adult is 21 to 38 grams per day. Americans average about one half that amount, further contributing to the blood sugar and insulin spikes.

An excellent source of soluble fiber is oats and oatmeal (Instant is not as good a source of fiber because it is processed). An added benefit is that oat fiber can lower blood cholesterol levels. Try oatmeal with raisins, berries, cinnamon, and soymilk for breakfast—delicious. Good fiber snacks are nuts, seeds, fruit, and raw vegetables. Get in the habit of reading labels when choosing anything in a package.

Fiber is an excellent colon cleaner. You can rapidly note a positive change in your regularity when taking adequate fiber. If a proper diet is not adequate, many over-the-counter products are available to increase fiber intake.

Proteins

Proteins consists of amino acids. Our greatest sources of protein are meats, seafood, fowl, eggs, and dairy products (especially cottage cheese). Certain vegetables also contain proteins, such as soybeans, nuts, lentils, beans, and grains. However, all sources of proteins are not the same. The goal is to eat quality protein with minimal saturated fats and with a proper balance of the unsaturated fats, Omega-3 and Omega-6 fatty acids. (As we talked about earlier, since we get so much Omega-6 in our diet, this actually means to try to eat a variety of other foods containing Omega-3 fats.) The term "quality protein" makes it timely to mention arachidonic acid (AA), which we get from red meats, egg yolks, and organ meats such as liver. Arachidonic acid is essential to life, but an excess is destructive to long-term health. Arachidonic acid is the precursor to Omega-6 fats, the less desirable eicosanoids. One problem with the meats we eat is that farmed animals are fed the same high carbohydrate, insulin-stimulating diet that overweight, diabetic, and unhealthy people eat and consequently contains much fat. Therefore, when we eat these meats or at least too much of them, we compound our dietary problems. AA resides mostly in the fat found in meats and eggs yolks. At the minimum, we should trim all the fat away and then eat grilled meats. Even so, in low quality meats AA is in the muscle tissue itself, so eat these only in moderation if at all. Eat game meats if available and eat free-range meats and poultry when possible. Lean flank steak is a good choice, as is white meat from turkey and skinless free-range chicken. Of course, seafood is generally a good choice for protein, both fish and shellfish, but leave the skin of fish on the plate. Lean cuts of pork are also low in saturated fats.

As I mentioned at the beginning of this chapter, quality meats are one of the reasons that the Paleolithic people 10,000 years ago were taller than subsequent agricultural generations. These ancient people consumed high quality animal and plant protein instead of meats from animals given high carbohydrate diets plus various hormones and antibiotics. Our ancestors also ate protein as their basic food instead of carbohydrates from grains and sugar. To illustrate how far off some people are from a healthful diet, a classmate of mine was examining an obese patient and found a hidden stash of three Twinkies under her folds of fat! She stated that she might get hungry—an unbelievable but true story.

Regarding quality meats, do not eat aged meats. They contain toxins such as malonaldehyde, which are carcinogenic. Fresh meats are always better for you.

What about egg yolks? They contain many nutrients, so don't eliminate them entirely, providing you do not have an hereditary high cholesterol. (Your physician could provide that information.) Try a whole egg or two plus egg whites for your omelet, or just use egg whites alone. I enjoy egg-white omelets (with one egg yolk) with either soy or regular cheese, tomatoes, mushrooms, and green peppers. I usually include a small portion of oatmeal with berries on the side also. Remember, you should attempt to keep your AA intake low, and egg yolks are a source of AA. If your Omega-3 levels are adequately increased, then avoiding egg yolks may be less important, but you should not push the envelope. Also, as you can see, if you are good about eating few or no simple carbohydrates and you eat good fat and adequate protein, cholesterol intake becomes less important unless you have congenital hypercholesterolemia (a genetic very high cholesterol disease). Moderation is once again the key.

The bottom line in healthful eating is more protein, lots of vegetables (especially leafy green and colorful vegetables), and few or no simple carbohydrates (sugar, potatoes, white rice, white bread, pasta). Good fats are good for you. If you balance the unsaturated fats Omega-3 and the Omega-6, you are likely eating more seafood, particularly non-farmed salmon and shellfish, flax seed, olive oil, and avocado. Healthful hints:

- Eat minimal saturated fats such as those in meat.
- Avoid trans-fats such as partially hydrogenated vegetable oils.
- Read labels when possible.
- Eat whole grains.
- Less processing of any food is always better.
- Eat fruit for your sweet tooth.

A good rule of thumb—one third of your plate should be protein and the remaining two-thirds vegetables with a fruit when desired. Take into account that the protein should be high-quality and the vegetables should be low-insulin stimulating complex carbohydrates, and they should be colorful.

Best Protein sources:

- Free-range meats and/or poultry
- White turkey meat
- Non-fried seafood
- Wild or game meats
- Lean flank meats
- Egg whites
- Soybeans
- Lentils, beans, almonds, cashews
- Cottage cheese

Summary:
Eat a balanced diet.

- Proteins—one-third of your plate
    - high quality
    - low-fat
    - free-range or wild
    - seafood
    - white meat turkey or chicken
    - egg whites, low-fat dairy products
    - soy

- Fats
  - Omega-3 from salmon (not farmed), tuna, shellfish, almonds, walnuts, avocados
  - Monosaturated fats such as olive and canola oil
  - No toxic trans-fats
  - Minimal saturated fats from meats and dairy products
- Carbohydrates (primarily from vegetables)—two-thirds of your plate
  - Lots of vegetables, especially leafy green, colored, raw is better than cooked
  - Minimal, if any, white potatoes, white bread, white rice, pasta (unless whole grain)
  - Minimal sugars
  - Minimal grains unless whole

Keep the fiber up and food processing down.

Hydration

We all have heard time and time again that we should drink eight 8-ounce glasses of water each day. When we realize that every nutrient, hormone, white blood cell, and oxygen-carrying red blood cell is transported in fluid, the importance of good hydration is obvious. An interesting process called blood sludging, discovered by Dr. Horace Knizely, is exactly what the name implies—the blood slows, becomes a sludge, clots, and eventually obstructs small vessels. This process, of course, is the end stage of dehydration, but any degree of dehydration is not good.

Fluid is also necessary for temperature control through perspiration. The process of evaporation of perspiration cools and removes heat. Without water, we can't sweat and therefore can't cool our bodies.

Kidney function requires fluid to filter our blood selectively, which is the body's main method of removing debris from our entire system. Basically, the kidneys keep what we need and excrete the rest, most of which would be toxic if accumulated in excess. With poor kidney function, we accumulate various waste products from metabolism, which is not compatible with life, much less longevity. It would be like never emptying your trash in your house. Ugh! Adequate hydration gives us the margin of safety that we need so that the body is capable of transporting various elements, hormones, and metabolites as needed. So drink your water and be happy, because it makes your body happy.

4 Dietary Supplements and Health Foods

Longevity and good health naturally result in feeling vibrant, energetic, and looking healthy. Nutrient supplementation definitely contributes to these goals. Although the information in this book is not meant to replace your doctor's advice or to treat or diagnose any illness or disease entity, the information I include here comes from various scientific studies conducted worldwide, the citations for much of the research I refer to being available in this book's references, suggestions for further reading included throughout these chapters, and in the back of this book, www.google.com, www.medscape.com, www.hyperhealth.com, www.brighterday.com, and other sources.

This subject is often confusing because of the conflicting reports of various studies such as the following:

The New England Journal of Medicine reported in July 1999 that synthetic multivitamins failed to reduce recurrence of benign growths of the colon after four years.

The New England Journal of Medicine reported in April 1994 that a ten-year double-blind study in Finland on 29,133 male smokers given synthetic vitamins yielded no beneficial effect. In fact, researchers saw an increase in lung cancer of 18%, more heart disease, and an 8% higher death rate.

Other examples are anecdotal. For instance, during the Korean War, one of our medical officers was unfortunate enough to be a POW. He noted that other POWs developed what he diagnosed as a disease called beriberi, a deficiency in Vitamin B1 (thiamine). The thiamine he received from the Red Cross failed to alleviate the symptoms. A Korean guard told him to use rice polish, a natural source of thiamine, which is a discarded by-product when we refine rice. The rice polish alleviated the disease.

The following paragraph is an excerpt from a book by Mary Frost, M.A. (*Going Back to the Basics*, www.ifnh.org): "I had a letter from an Austrian colleague who was suffering from a severe hemorrhagic diathesis. He wanted to try ascorbic acid in (for) his condition. . . . I sent him a preparation of paprika that contained much ascorbic acid and the man was cured by it. Later, we tried to produce the same results with pure ascorbic acid, but we obtained no response. It was evident that the action of paprika was due to some other substance present in the plant." Written by Albert von Szent-Gyorgi, Hungarian-born U.S. biochemist; Nobel Prize winner for discovering that vitamin C cured scurvy.

The American Academy of Applied Nutrition reported in March 1994 an experiment demonstrating the toxic nature of synthetic vitamins. Animals fed unenriched bread lived for an average of fifty-four days. Another group was fed synthetic vitamin-enriched bread, and this group lived for forty-nine days. The synthetic vitamins reduced their life span by 10%.

The evidence goes on and on, indicating that synthetic vitamins are not the same or as effective as whole food natural vitamins (vitamins extracted from whole foods). But what is the definition of "natural"? The FDA defines it as anything that comes from nature and "organic" as anything that contains a carbon molecule (which could even mean DDT or coal tar). Therefore, organics could be synthetic if they contained a carbon molecule, and "natural" could be an extract from coal tar. In fact, thiamine monohydrate (vitamin B1) is often made from coal tar. So we can't rely on either of the terms "natural" or "organic." Therefore, this discussion refers to vitamins and not organically grown foods, which are definitely preferred.

Vitamins often do not provide the health benefits that you expect because most are not derived from whole foods. Most vitamins are small fractions of the vitamin complex in the whole food from which they come. A typical example is ascorbic acid, which we are told is vitamin C. Precisely speaking, it's not. That would be like saying that a steering wheel is a car. The complete whole food vitamin C complex consists of bioflavonoids, enzymes, coenzymes, trace elements, and other factors necessary for vitamin C to be properly utilized. Ascorbic acid is a small part of the vitamin C complex (putting a pinch of rose hips in it may not make it complete either). Studies demonstrate that synthetic or non-whole food vitamins have negative effects on the human body. What we need is a complete vitamin complex, which comes from whole food extracts and not synthetics. Vitamins seem to yield great results for a while. Eventually you begin to feel rundown and often worse than you felt before taking them. When you are consuming only a fraction of a vitamin, your body completes the missing fractions of the vitamin complex from its storages until they are depleted. At that point your health goes downhill because you become deficient in the very vitamin that you are taking. The vitamin you are taking is either excreted or not properly utilized.

A pioneer in the need of taking whole foods instead of synthetic vitamins was the late Dr. Royal Lee. He understood that a vitamin was a complex of ingredients and not just one isolate. Standard Process is Dr. Lee's food supplement line.

Additional excellent companies that produce whole food vitamins are New Chapter and Megafood. New Chapter grows its own foods organically. The company uses a state-of-the-art extraction process that uses no heat, pollution, or chemical solvents. Yields of whole food extractions can be concentrated as high as 250 to 1. A statement taken from its web page at www.new-chapter.com is as follows: "We are a small company owned by families and friends and are based in Brattleboro, Vermont and our organic estate near the Children's Rain Forest of Costa Rica. Since 1982, our mission, our passionate commitment, has been producing the finest probiotic nutrients and herbal formulations in the world. Our purpose is to create the finest products that are truly natural, made of 100% real food and herbs. We have never made products with chemical isolates or solvents and we won't. We culture all our vitamins and minerals and we always will. They are not synthetic—they are food. We are committed to supporting and protecting the environment and our Costa Rican farm is a world model for organic sustainable farming in the rain forest." This is a fine source and other fine sources can be found on the Internet under the key words "whole food nutrients."

Dosages seen in whole food vitamins are not the usual megadoses we are used to seeing because whole food vitamins are many times more effective. Quality, completeness, and being natural are much more important than quantity. Increasing the dose of an isolate creates an imbalance. An analogy would be doing only push-ups or bench presses without exercising your back, which causes an imbalance in muscular development. The result is often an injury such as a damaged rotator cuff. Our bodies see synthetic vitamins as foreign, and much of it makes "expensive urine"—that is, urine containing unused nutrients. Interestingly, synthetic vitamin B turns urine yellow, yet whole food vitamin B does not.

With five to ten million or so years of evolution behind our development, we cannot in a century or less adapt our diets to consuming fractions of foods or altered foods and continue toward good health. In fact synthetic vitamins are often the mirror images of the natural ones. That would be like trying to put a left glove on your right hand. It doesn't fit any more than the synthetic vitamin fits on our receptors.

What are some of the common whole foods taken for their high vitamin content? Brewer's yeast contains biotin; choline; folic acid; vitamins B1, 2, 3, 5, 6; and Inositol (which retards hardening of the arteries and helps prevent cataracts, lung, and bladder cancer and improves nerve function). Brewer's yeast stabilizes blood sugar and reduces insulin resistance. It also has an abundance of amino acids and minerals. It is a wonderful source of nutrients.

"Green drinks" and capsules, such as those containing spirulina and marine algae, are whole food derived both from land and sea that are excellent sources of vitamins, phytonutrients (the other factors in vitamin complexes), and minerals.

Whole rice, unprocessed, contains Vitamins B1, B2, B3, B6, E, and protein. Unprocessed rice includes the bran (the outer hull) and polish (the inner hull), which is where we find that most nutrients have not been removed. The white rice that we usually eat is the kernel, a carbohydrate.

Buckwheat contains many amino acids, plus minerals and vitamin E. The bioflavonoid Rutin is also present.

Spirulina (a blue-green algae) contains about eighteen amino acids, minerals, enzymes, carotenoids and multitudes of vitamins and antioxidants—all whole foods.

I suggest searching the Internet for whole food nutrients for more selections. Your local health food store should also have suggestions. The websites www.hyperhealth.com, www.brighterday.com, and www.whfoods.com are valuable sources of information on various nutrients and references.

This discussion of synthetics versus whole food vitamins leads to other questions: If we eat properly, do we need vitamins? My opinion is most definitely yes. In many cases, a combination of top soils being so depleted of nutrients, various synthetic fertilizers and insecticides being used, and crops being grown without proper crop-rotation leaves our nutrients sorely lacking. What's more, many foods are "fortified" with synthetic vitamins, which can deplete us even further of vitamin cofactors. Even with the goal of excellent nutrition firmly in mind, most people cannot eat ideal foods because of time constraints and limited access to foods containing the various ingredients necessary for optimal body and brain function. In addition food processing removes many valuable nutrients and fiber. Let's not forget nutrient deficiencies caused by bad health habits. On the other hand, vitamin, mineral, and other dietary supplements are no substitute for an excellent diet, organically based when possible.

This information-rich chapter is filled with valuable facts about foods and nutrients. You may choose to simply read it and/or use it as a convenient reference, depending on your needs. You will notice some repetition in the parts of this book regarding nutrition supplements. Repetition has been helpful to me personally in learning about this fairly complex subject.

As one of your first steps toward optimal nutrition, get a good-quality whole food multivitamin, which will contain both fat soluble (A, D, E, and K) and water soluble vitamins (C and B complex). I prefer one that contains minerals as well. Multivitamins come in capsules, tablets, gelcaps, chewable tablets, and powders, so choose whatever form you like best. Kosher supplements are also available, but they may not be whole food derived. Individual vitamins and nutrients with their food sources and their functions are discussed more completely in Appendix I and Appendix II.

Nutrients such as Omega-3, fiber, and amino acids are not vitamins, but they should be considered as important nutrients for your program. However, be sure to take the nutrients listed below in adequate amounts (dosages are not those required for whole-food derived vitamins, which may be much lower). If you wish to take a higher dose of any specific nutrient in addition to a multivitamin, whole food nutrient companies and other quality nutrient companies will include the following (always note side effects of these nutrients, which are usually noted on the bottle):

- *Omega-3 fatty acids:* at least one gram twice daily and up to two grams twice a day, with a possible side effect of diarrhea being the limiting factor. My preference is two grams twice a day. You may have to work up to this dosage. Remember, Omega-3 is necessary for brain and nerve development and maintenance, and it is an effective anti-inflammatory.
- *Vitamin C complex:* most definitely an antiaging vitamin. It is important in collagen formation, reduces glycation, and is an important antioxidant. It accelerates healing of fractures and wounds. It also concentrates in the brain and can alleviate mental retardation. When applied topically, it has bleaching qualities for age spots and reduces fine wrinkles.
- *Folic Acid, a B vitamin:* Remember that this in combination with vitamin B6 and B12 will lower blood homocysteine levels. The recommended dose is 400 micrograms per day in divided doses. Whole-food derived vitamins require much lower dosages because of the increased effectiveness.
- *Vitamins B6 and B12:* The recommended dose is 50 milligrams per day for B6 and 300 to 1,000 micrograms per day for B12.
- *B3 (Niacin, Niacinamide):* important for our circulatory and nervous systems and for lowering cholesterol and lipoprotein A. The usual dose is 100 milligrams per day, but I have seen it prescribed up to 400 milligrams twice a day. (Symptoms of gout are possible with higher doses.) Use "non-flush" niacin to avoid skin flush and irritation. Do not use the timed-release niacin, as it may cause liver disease. Remember, when using whole food vitamins that doses may be lower (not applicable to Omega-3, which is not a vitamin) because of their increased effectiveness. Whole food dosages would, therefore, be much lower.
- *B Complex vitamins:* include biotin, inositol, choline, and hundreds of others.
- *Vitamin A:* a retinoid, is known for its anti-acne and anti-wrinkle activity. It promotes healthy gums and skin and is good for eye health, the digestive and cardiovascular systems.
- *Vitamin D:* a group of fat soluble compounds. Activation requires ultraviolet light. This vitamin is necessary for calcium utilization in bone formation. It increases muscle strength in the elderly. It helps prevent insulin resistance, autoimmune diseases, obesity, and certain cancers. Fifty percent of Americans are deficient in Vitamin D, and in one study low Vitamin D levels are associated with earlier death than those with

adequate vitamin D levels. Exposure to sunlight increases our vitamin D, but most people try to avoid excess sun exposure to reduce the incidence of skin cancers. We are therefore between the proverbial rock and a hard place. We want the Vitamin D, but not the cancers. Again—moderation. Have your doctor check your blood levels of Vitamin D, and take supplements if they are low. 5,000 IU per day may be necessary to reach the ideal levels which are above 30ng/ml.

- *Vitamin K:* is called the anti-hemorrhagic vitamin and is essential for formation of blood clots. It is probably the most underrated vitamin because it also mobilizes calcium from arteries into bone, thus reducing arteriosclerosis, heart disease, osteoporoses, etc., and Vitamin K strengthens bones. It helps prevent cancer of the breast, colon, liver, and stomach and reduces inflammation. Vitamin K2 is longer acting than Vitamin K1, and is more effective in reducing arteriosclerosis of the arteries.
- *Vitamin E:* a group of compounds which include both tocopherols and tocotrienols, antioxidants that promote cellular health for the entire body. Vitamin E is an age-control vitamin, reducing lipofuscin (pigment that accumulates in the brain), senescence (aging of the chromosomes), and glycation. It also reduces eye problems such as macular degeneration and cataracts. As you might expect, I recommend taking the natural complex in its entirety, preferably from a whole food and not just an alpha tocopherol.
- *A balanced amino acid formula:* The importance of amino acids cannot be overestimated. They are the basis of enzymes, protein, hormones such as growth hormone, and virtually the function of our entire body. A balanced combination found at a health food store will do, and they should be taken as instructed on the bottle. Be sure to look at the label, as some may fortify their amino acids with synthetic vitamins.

The following are considered important antiaging nutrients (also discussed in Appendices I and II):

- *Acetyl-L-carnitine (or L-carnitine)* is an amino acid that boosts cellular and mitochondrial energy. L-carnitine is considered a longevity supplement. The FDA has approved its use under the name Carnitor for treatment of congestive heart failure, loss of energy, and other conditions. The newest generation of L-carnitine is glysine proprionyl L-carnitine (GPLC). It is absorbed more easily and is more effective than L-carnitine. The usual dose is 500 milligrams twice daily. It enhances elimination of lipofuscin, a yellow-brown pigment which accumulates in the brain (causing deleterious effects such as loss of memory), skin (liver spots), and is energy producing to the heart and other organs.

Lipofuscin is usually considered an aging problem that should be reversed, if possible. Importantly, it also reduces glycation. L-carnitine may act as a stimulant, so evening dosing may not always be desirable.

- *Carnosine* is a powerful anti-glycation agent and antioxidant. It prevents the cross-linking that leads to AGEs (advanced glycation end products) and actually reverses the cross-linking of AGEs that has already occurred. Remember, AGEs stick to elastin, collagen, immunoglobulins, and other large protein molecules, like enzymes, reducing their abilities to function properly. Scientific studies demonstrate that reducing AGEs results in reduction of formation of wrinkles. The AGEs cross-linking makes our elastin fibers less elastic, causing us to sag. Carnosine reduces production of amyloid beta protein, which leads to harmful plaques in our brains, a key characteristic of Alzheimer's disease. Carnosine also reduces the toxic brain effects of excess copper and zinc, and it protects the brain from ischemia (lack of oxygen). When used in mice, carnosine extends lifespan by 20%. The usual human dose is 500 milligrams once or twice per day. The most valuable and complete article I have read on the subjects of Acetyl-L-Carnitine and Carnosine are in the Life Extension Foundation monthly magazines, issues September 2006 and January 2001, respectively. Contact them at www.LEF.org.
- *Alpha lipoic acid* is water soluble and fat soluble. It is a potent antioxidant. Being fat-soluble allows the molecule to penetrate the cell membrane and enter the cell itself. This nutrient assists in regenerating the antioxidants vitamins E and C as well as glutathione. Alpha lipoic acid also binds and removes heavy metals from the body. The usual dose of this antiaging supplement is 250 milligrams twice daily. It's often sold in capsule combination with L-carnitine and carnosine at your local health food store and online at www.LEF.org or other Internet sources. The product from LEF is called Mitochondrial Energy Optimizer and contains ingredients alpha lipoic acid, carnosine, and L-carnitine.
- *Coenzyme Q10 (CoQ10)* is a powerful antioxidant, but most importantly, the mitochondria in our bodies requires it for proper production of ATP (the energy molecule, adenosine triphosphate). Our body's levels of CoQ10 decrease with age, which reduces energy available for our cells' metabolism. This makes them more susceptible to the free radical damage that promotes DNA damage, mutations, and more CoQ10 loss, thus creating another vicious cycle. Clinical research indicates that patients with congestive heart failure benefit from CoQ10 supplementation. Some fat is required to absorb CoQ10, so take it with a meal containing some fat or with Omega-3 supplements. The recommended dose is 50 to 200 milligrams per day, taken morning and evening. Ubiquinone (CoQ10) must be reduced by the body to Ubiquinol to be active. The

reduced form, Ubiquinol, is now being produced by the parent company, Kaneka Nutrients, and is absorbed and utilized much more efficiently. It is bioidentical, natural, and stable and produced by a biological fermentation process.

- *Dimethylaminoethanol (DMAE)* stabilizes cell membranes, making cells stronger and therefore more resistant to metabolic and free radical damage. Our brain and nerve cells must be especially resistant to such damage, so DMAE is important in maintaining and increasing cognitive ability, as well as for general protection and repair of cell membranes. DMAE is also effective in reducing lipofuscin, and age spots may be reduced with its use. A minimal daily dose of 10 milligrams had a positive effect in one study, though the usual dose is at least 300 milligrams. Take DMAE on an empty stomach.
- *Policosanol* may lower blood cholesterol levels. The recommended dose is 20 milligrams per day.
- *Arginine* is an amino acid that boosts nitric oxide levels in blood vessels. Nitric oxide (NO) relaxes arteries, lowers blood pressure, increases circulation, and may stimulate hair growth in male pattern baldness. It also promotes healthy endothelial lining in blood vessels, reducing arteriosclerosis. Arginine also improves the function of our kidneys and immune system, reduces insulin resistance, and lowers triglyceride levels. Research suggests that arginine may also relieve male impotence and infertility. The recommended dose is 1 to 2 grams (1000 to 2000 mg) taken two to three times a day. Higher doses may cause diarrhea. Arginine is usually found in most amino acid preparations.
- *Biosil* is a unique product to thicken hair, nails and reduce wrinkles. The main ingredient is silicon. Silicon is also necessary for healthy bones and joints. In the form of choline-stabilized orthosilicic acid, collagen production is stimulated. The product is distributed by Natrol, Inc. They report a decrease in fine lines and wrinkles of 19% and an increase in hair thickness of 13% in 20 weeks. The recommended dose is one capsule twice a day.

To mention all supplements would take an encyclopedia, and if you tried to take them all, you would have no room for food. However, I also like Cat's Claw (uncaria tomentosa), which boosts immunity, is an antioxidant, and has been shown in some scientific studies to repair damaged DNA.

At the back of this book you will find a very useful appendix, titled "Choosing Effective Nutrition Supplements," which I wrote with Peter Brodhead, a certified nutritionist. He is an authority on dietary supplements and owner of the most complete health food store in Savannah, Georgia, called Brighter Day (www.brighterday.com). Peter has also written a comprehensive companion appendix, "How to Grocery Shop for Optimum Health."

Some of Peter's favorite brands of nutrient, amino acid, and herb supplements are New Chapter, Jarrow Formulas, Natural Factors (from Canada), Solgar Brand (Solgar is one of few brands offering kosher-certified products), Carlson, Country Life, Enzymatic Therapy, Solaray, Kal, Nature's Life, Amni or Douglas Labs, Nordic Naturals (fish oils), Nature's Way, Source Naturals, Planetary Formulas (Chinese and auruvedic herbs), Natrol, and Blue Bonnet. Other fine manufacturers make nutritional supplements, but those listed in the appendix consistently provide high-quality products.

Another source of nutritional supplements is the Life Extension Foundation (online at www.LEF.org), which also offers an informative monthly magazine. Understand, however, that though this magazine is filled with excellent articles summarizing literature from the scientific world, the Life Extension Foundation and organizations like it also market nutritional supplements, which usual medical and research standards consider a conflict of interest. I do not imply that the information is not true and valuable, but only that we must evaluate information presented in such magazines with a more discerning eye. The numerous references cited in their magazine are certainly to their credit.

Another in-depth source of information about most nutrients is the CD-ROM Hyperhealth (or visit www.hyperhealth.com). I highly recommend downloading this source onto your computer. Finally, I suggest New Chapter at www.new-chapter.com, in business since 1982, and Standard Process at www.standardprocess.com as sources for natural vitamins, nutrients, and herbs taken from whole foods. Standard Process has celebrated its 75th anniversary.

III

Hormones and Aging

5 Hormones and Aging

To achieve good health and long-term activity, we must understand age-related reduction or cessation of various hormones. In the female this cessation is called menopause; in the male it is called andropause. When discussing growth hormone, this cessation is called somatopause. When considering why we grow old, these are large parts of the puzzle. Fortunately, these conditions are also treatable. Menopause and andropause usually occur around fifty years old, plus or minus five years. Clinical somatopause occurs at about the same age, but it is more affected by exercise and diet.

First, let's discuss hormones in general so that you have a general understanding of what they do, where they come from, how we check them, and finally what we can do about hormonal abnormalities.

Hormones are chemicals that originate in one gland and affect another gland, parts of the body, or metabolism of the entire body. Many glands produce hormones. I cannot overstate the power and importance of hormones. Hormonal changes have an immense influence on the shapes of our bodies—just look at what happens at puberty. Later in life we lose muscle mass and our fat distribution is rearranged. Men and women experience different types of changes. For example, among men, muscle loss is more obvious in the shoulders and legs. All people gain size in the midsection—tummy and "love-handles." Abdomens become more protuberant, rears become flat, and libido becomes diminished. In women the lower half of the body gains weight, particularly in the legs, abdomen, and sides. Of course, weight gain affects all of these physiological changes, especially a significant increase in weight.

Balancing hormones helps us maintain a youthful body and mind. Hormones are extremely powerful and influential. Think of the effects of menopause, such as hot flashes. Or consider that a child with a lack of growth hormone will be abnormally small in every feature, while one with excess can be a giant. Remember the bad guy in the first James Bond movies? Also consider that a lack of thyroid hormone (hypothyroidism) can result in significant weight gain and loss of energy. A person with hyperthyroidism (too much of the thyroid hormone) can experience weight loss, exophthalmos (a bug-eyed appearance), too much energy, loss of sleep, and a feeling of being "wired." Thyroid hormone speeds or slows the entire metabolic rate according to whether we have too much or not enough.

Every hormone has great influence, and it is imperative that your physician evaluate your hormone balance regularly. For instance, if you are over forty-five years old and your doctor is checking your blood for hormone deficiencies, you should ask to have your insulin-like growth factor (IGF-1) level checked also (along with a few others to be discussed), as this test indicates your growth hormone production. If your growth hormone level is abnormally low, it will affect all other glands and for that matter all other cells in your body. It obviously has nothing to do with growth in the adult except when rarely in excess, but can have much to do with health. Some growth hormone preparations are available commercially, though you must never use these products without physician supervision. This will be discussed below under the topic of growth hormone.

The thyroid gland produces thyroid hormone, which controls our metabolic rate. Too much causes our metabolic rate to increase, much like running a car in first gear at a high speed continuously. It can cause heat intolerance, sweating, rapid pulse, weight loss, increased blood pressure, anxiety, or nervousness and insomnia, diarrhea, and fatigue, which results from the excess energy. Decreased thyroid hormone causes just the opposite, for example, cold intolerance, weight gain, decreased pulse and blood pressure, mental dullness, lack of energy, dry skin, hair loss, and constipation.

Sometimes a physician will not treat a patient if the thyroid level is at either end of the normal range, even if the patient experiences symptoms. You should ask your physician about your thyroid hormone level and also about the expected normal levels. Know your body and your laboratory results. (Request a T3 free, T4 free, and TSH for your thyroid studies.) Knowing the symptoms discussed above will enable you and your physician to decide if you have a problem. Generally the upper third of the normal range is more suitable than the lower third. Although not entirely comparable, these levels would be analogous to making a D in school instead of an A, especially if one is symptomatic.

Glands and Their Hormones

The pituitary gland produces a variety of hormones: TSH, GH, ACTH, LH and FSH, and ADH:

1. TSH (thyroid stimulating hormone): A hormone released into the blood system, stimulating the thyroid gland to produce thyroid hormone. Pituitary TSH production works on a feedback system: when the thyroid hormone level gets too high, it causes the pituitary to reduce TSH

production, and when thyroid hormone decreases, TSH production increases to stimulate more thyroid hormone.

2. GH (growth hormone): Growth hormone is produced by the pituitary gland. Until adulthood it promotes growth of bones, muscle, and all internal organs. In childhood and as an adult it increases calcium retention, increases muscle mass, and promotes the reduction of fat. Adequate GH levels are necessary for optimal health of all tissues, which is most easily seen in a person's skin.
3. ACTH (adrenocorticotropic hormone): A hormone that stimulates the adrenal gland to produce cortisol.
4. LH and FSH (luteinizing hormone and follicle stimulating hormone): Hormones stimulating the sex organs to produce sex hormones (estrogen, testosterone, and progesterone).
5. ADH (antidiuretic hormone): Affects the kidneys, causing them to decrease urine output, which explains its name.

The thyroid gland produces the thyroid hormones:

1. T4 (thyroxine hormone): requires iodine
2. T3 (triiodothyronine): produced from T4 by removing an iodine molecule
3. Calcitonin: works with the parathyroid hormone to regulate calcium deposits in the bone

In addition to affecting the rate of metabolism, thyroid hormone is also essential for normal physical and mental growth (see the symptoms of TSH excess and deficiency listed below). The final product of the active thyroid hormone process is T3, which is formed from T4. A deficit in dietary selenium (a mineral and an antioxidant) can prevent this T4 conversion to T3, thereby causing a serum T3 that is low. Selenium deficiencies are not uncommon.

Thyroid hormone deficiencies (hypothyroidism) result in:

- Fatigue
- Mental Dullness
- Dry Skin
- Hair Loss
- Weight Gain
- Sensitivity to Cold
- Constipation

Thyroid hormone overproduction (hyperthyroidism) results in:

- Anxiety
- Nervousness
- Intolerance to Heat
- Sweating
- Weight Loss
- Diarrhea
- Fatigue—you wear out from the excess energy
- Heart Palpitations

Adrenal Glands (located on top of the kidneys) consist of:

- Cortex (the outer part of the gland)
- Medulla (the inner part of the gland)

The adrenal cortex produces:

- Cortisol
- Dihydroepiandrosterone (DHEA)
- Sex hormones estrogen and testosterone (although not produced in large amounts as by the sex organs)

The adrenal medulla produces:

- Epinephrine (adrenalin)
- Norepinephrine

Functions of cortisol:

- Suppresses inflammation
- Helps regulate the use of proteins, fats, and carbohydrates
- Suppresses the immune system

Cortisol over-production or cortisol taken as a medication may cause:

osteoporosis with avascular necrosis of the hips and more, water retention, cataracts, deterioration of tissues, and premature aging.

Emotional stress and injury stimulate ACTH production, which in turn stimulates more cortisol. (This hormone production also works on a feedback system—too much cortisol reduces ACTH production, which in turn reduces cortisol production. Then, when the cortisol level becomes low, the ACTH production increases again.) Excess stress causes ACTH overproduction, as do elevated insulin levels (yet another reason to reduce simple carbohydrate intake). Elevated cortisol levels are destructive to tissues, including collagen, elastin fibers, and brain tissue. Elevated cortisol also reduces growth hormone production and is a premier aging hormone.

Cortisol in its man-made form (cortisone) can be used to treat certain diseases, sometimes in high doses. Examples are moderate to severe asthma, autoimmune diseases such as lupus erythematosis, multiple sclerosis, rheumatoid arthritis, severe allergies, and many more disorders. My point is that if cortisol/ cortisone is not being used for therapy, we should try to keep its level low by reducing stress, because chronically high levels damage our organs and tissues.

Excess cortisol causes deterioration of tissues, and sometimes this is intentional. Keloid scars are those that are excessively red and swollen. They may continue to enlarge and may itch or even hurt. Common areas for keloids are over the deltoid shoulder muscles, chest, back, and earlobes, but they can occur anywhere. One of the primary initial treatments is the injection of a synthetic cortisol called Kenalog, which reduces the overactive inflammation and healing process

Epinephrine and norepinephrine, as well as cortisol, are involved in our fright and flight response. When you are frightened, your heart races, you get the shakes, your eyes dilate, your airways to the lungs dilate making breathing faster and better, your pulse races, and you become more alert. These are signs of epinephrine working, and such a response could be most useful. My imagination takes me to the cave man being attacked by some predator where he would need all the adrenalin he could get. However, chronic stress—like stress over your job, marriage, finances, etc.—events that are out of your control, can cause a full-time overproduction of epinephrine that can be very destructive. This overproduction in itself is stressful, causing a vicious cycle of stress, increasing the fright and flight response, which causes more stress. Our lives have become so stressful from our general rapid pace that excess stress is more common than a relaxed or moderately paced life. Most people are in a hurry, and this rush causes anger, impatience, worry, and stress. Chronic stress is not compatible with health and longevity.

It is easily seen how our hormone levels are so interrelated that we can't achieve normal hormonal status simply by taking a single hormone and assuming all is well. Homeostasis can be achieved, but it takes a physician who is willing to follow the patient with appropriate studies to ensure all hormones are at proper levels, and these levels will continue to change as we age.

Hormones we now see discussed in the media are DHEA, pregnenolone, and melatonin:

DHEA levels drop significantly after age thirty. They also drop from excess stress. Since it is a mother hormone, its decline is associated with fatigue, loss of mental alertness, diminished sex drive, weakened immune function, depression, excess fat, and rapid signs of aging. DHEA also affects metabolism. Metabolism is made up of anabolism (building up of tissue) and catabolism (tearing down of tissue). A decline in DHEA is catabolic, which is not what we want as an antiaging plan. Excess DHEA in the female however, yields signs of excess testosterone, such as acne, male pattern baldness, excessive facial hair growth, or masculinization. When women lack adequate testosterone (just as men have estrogen, women have testosterone), it may be related to a deficiency in DHEA. Blood tests for DHEA are available and should be done when taking supplements of the hormone. The usual starting replacement doses are ten to twenty-five milligrams in women and twenty-five to fifty milligrams in men. After six weeks, though, it's necessary to follow up with more laboratory tests. If you take DHEA, do so in the morning, as it may cause insomnia. An in-depth book on DHEA and keeping your youth is *The Metabolic Plan* (2003), by Stephen Cherniske, M.S.

DHEA is produced by the adrenal gland in volumes (many times greater than any other hormone). The adrenal cortex makes DHEA from pregnenolone, and the hormone is a precursor to many other hormones, mainly the estrogens and testosterone. Interestingly, there was no mention of DHEA during my medical training (that I can remember), and it is hardly mentioned in any medical book on my bookshelves. However, over 3,000 papers have been written about this hormone since 1990 in other scientific journals and papers.

Another hormone lately discussed in the media is **pregnenolone**, the true mother hormone and the precursor to DHEA. In *Age-Defying Diet Revolution* Dr. Robert C. Atkins recommends a daily pregnenolone dose of fifty milligrams per day. Fewer studies have been done on pregnenolone as compared to those examining DHEA.

A third hormone often mentioned in the media is **melatonin**, which helps regulate the biological clock and induces sleep. (Occasionally, people will have nightmares initially when taking melatonin.) In addition, melatonin is an antioxidant and considered an antiaging hormone.

Growth Hormone (GH) is produced by the pituitary gland and serves as another perfect example of the power of hormones. Too much production in childhood can produce a giant (acromegaly), and too little can create a little person. Originally GH supplementation was given only to children who were much too small for their ages and with proven deficiencies of GH. In such situations, GH can increase the height of children by as much as five or six inches, if given early enough. Doctors now give it more liberally to children with GH deficiencies because of modern technologies in human-growth-hormone production.

Within the last few years, some physicians have written prescriptions for GH more frequently for older patients (usually fifty and older) with deficiencies of GH. This treatment requires GH injections daily and takes several months to see maximum effects. The most effective method of treatment by far is with daily injections.

In those who are deficient, proper treatment with GH usually results in the following:

- Loss of adult fat, mostly around the middle
- Increased muscle size and strength, especially when combined with testosterone
- Increased libido
- Less fatigue
- More mental alertness
- More youthful skin
- More youthful sex hormone production
- Lower cholesterol, higher HDL, and lower LDL levels
- Significant increase in bone mass density, thus reduction of osteoporosis

GH prescriptions require a knowledgeable physician who conducts proper lab work and follow-up lab work. (The lab draws a fasting blood sample for IGF-1, insulin-like growth factor, which reflects growth hormone levels of GH.) The benefits can be well worthwhile. However, this drug is by no means innocuous and should be the last resort of treatment with GH. Ask your physician or one who specializes in longevity to inform you of any risks. Most problems or complications are from unnecessarily high doses. Anyone with a diagnosis of cancer should not use GH unless under advisement by a physician. In addition, growth hormone is expensive and rarely reimbursed by insurance. However, if you have undergone menopause or andropause plus somatopause (low GH), consider adding GH injections to normal hormone replacement therapy for optimal health.

Growth hormone secretogogues (amino acids that stimulate pituitary production of GH) are another, though less effective, method of treatment and are given by mouth. They can increase GH production and should be tried first before injections. This treatment also requires follow-up with blood tests to determine whether and how well the secretogogues work. The amino acids most often used to stimulate GH production are glutamine, arginine, and ornithine. Although research on sprays and sublingual secretogogues is underway, I have seen no medical studies demonstrating their effectiveness. These secretogogues can be found in your local health food store.

The liver converts growth hormone (a product of the pituitary gland) into IGF-1. In people about thirty years of age, IGF-1 levels are around 300 to 350 and dwindle year by year after that. The normal range for IGF-1 varies for each age, but if it is about 150 or so, increasing GH levels by secretogogue supplementation can help many people.

Now that we know that GH is considered an antiaging hormone, how else can we increase our levels of this hormone? Exercising is one method, and it can be effective. But resistance exercising (weight training) rather than aerobic exercising is necessary for GH stimulation.

Sex hormones include estrogen, progesterone, testosterone (remember they are made partly from cholesterol), follicle stimulating hormone (FSH), and luteinizing hormone (LH). First, I should defuse the myth that estrogen is the female hormone and testosterone the male hormone. The truth is that men and women have them both—it's just the ratio that is different. Men have more testosterone and women more estrogen, but both sexes require both hormones. The bottom line is that each hormone is strongly responsible for the male and female shapes, size, voices, emotions, and hair patterns.

Follicle stimulating hormone and luteinizing hormone (FSH and LH), from the pituitary gland, stimulate the ovaries and testicles to produce the sex hormones, estrogen and testosterone. Levels of these hormones should be included in a proper blood work-up for hormone status.

Estrogen is produced in the ovaries and, to a lesser degree, in the adrenal glands. Some estrogen is also produced (aromatized) by metabolism of testosterone. Thus, testosterone is a step toward the formation of estrogen.

Function of estrogen:

- More fat deposit in the hip and leg department
- Less muscle in shoulders and arms (mostly)
- Breast development
- Hair distribution
- Higher voice
- Development of the reproductive system
- Libido

Progesterone (also called progestin) is produced by the ovaries during the last part of the menstrual cycle and by the placenta in pregnancy.

Testosterone is produced in the testes and in smaller amounts by the adrenal cortex.

Function of testosterone:

- Less fat in hips and legs (except in those with poor dietary habits)
- More muscle
- Male pattern baldness
- Larger larynx and thus deeper voice
- Development of reproductive system
- Libido

Estrogen and testosterone are very powerful hormones. For example, we have all seen body builders who are on high doses of anabolic steroids (forms of testosterone) resulting in abnormally large muscles. Unfortunately, they also get reversal of the hormone-related patterns they would want for longevity, such as hair loss, liver disease, acne, atrophy of the testes, and other undesirable symptoms such as large breast (gynecomastia). This is from testosterone being aromatized into estrogen.

Hormones are very influential in good health, and in that sense they are the true fountain of youth. If you feel your hormones may be out of balance after reviewing the various symptoms of hormone deficiency mentioned in this chapter, a good gynecologist (in the case of females), endocrinologist, internist, or other heath care provider can evaluate the situation. If you need supplementation, insist upon treatment with hormones that are biochemically identical to those found naturally in the human body whenever possible, especially in the case of progesterone. An example of non-bio-identical hormone use is treatment with Premarin (an extract from pregnant mare urine—hence its name), which is a substance containing over thirty compounds foreign to the human body and that may cause inflammation and increased incidence of breast cancer.

Local compounding laboratories can synthesize estrogen and progesterone from plant sources that are molecularly and biologically identical to those produced normally in our bodies. Opinions vary regarding the need for biochemically identical estrogen. As an example, see the upcoming section on page 77 by Barry Schlafstein, M.D., who has credible scientific evidence that the non-bio-identical hormone causing problems is progesterone rather than estrogen. However, compounding pharmacies can provide a better balance of estrogens (estradiol, estriol, and estrone).

At around fifty years of age, women go through menopause, a potentially miserable experience that should be treated with hormones mimicking a woman's normal monthly cycle. Otherwise, women experience continuous PMS-type symptoms, hot-flashes, bloating, and increased heart disease and begin to age faster. You will not experience bloating, fluid retention, and hot flashes when you have the correct balance of estrogen, progesterone, and testosterone. For a proper balance of the female sex hormones during menopause, you should seek help from your physician, usually a gynecologist, endocrinologist, or an age-management specialist. And don't be discouraged if it takes several months to achieve a proper balance, because everyone is different, as are everyone's hormonal needs. As you may expect, blood tests may be required. Do not hesitate to request a second opinion and more lab work if you think it's necessary for an evaluation of any menopausal or andropausal symptoms.

Symptoms associated with andropause are getting thick around the trunk, pot belly, increased fat, decreased muscle mass, thinning skin, decreased libido, and impotence. As seen in menopause, andropause is also related to dementia, cardiovascular disease, and even osteoporosis. Andropause thus should be treated as vigorously in men as menopause is in women. Both sexes should get repeated blood tests when being treated until the hormones in question reach acceptable levels, and patients are happy with their physical status. Concerns about testosterone supplementation in men include the following:

1. BPH (benign prostate hypertrophy) may result from improper treatment.

2. Those with prostate cancer or cancer cells influenced by testosterone should not take testosterone, as their disease may be exacerbated.
3. Some believe testosterone supplementation may increase the incidence of prostate cancer, but evidence indicates that there is no cause-and-effect relationship.
4. Other problems seen, usually from excess testosterone, are acne, breast enlargement, and hair loss. Avoidance of these side effects requires correct dosage, proper route of administration, and usually other medication to prevent conversion into estrogen and/or DHT (dihydrotestosterone).

Several methods of testosterone administration are available:

- Testosterone cyprionate—this can be injected by either the patient or doctor on a weekly basis. This treatment has certain advantages over the creams and gels, such as less conversion to DHT (dihydrotestosterone), thus fewer side effects such as hair loss and prostate hypertrophy (causing frequent urination, urgency, and deceased urine stream).
- Testosterone Patches. Androderm and Testoderm are trade names of this supplement.
- Testoderm, on the other hand, is applied daily to the scrotum while Androderm should be applied anywhere but the scrotum.
- Androgel is a gel to be applied to skin other than scrotum, once a day.
- Formulated creams can include DHEA, pregnenolone, or other ingredients.

Remember that topical application causes more DHT production.

My preference of all the above is the testosterone cyprionate weekly injection. A gel or cream is more convenient and the blood level doesn't fall at the end of the week, but, as mentioned, much more is converted into DHT with its inherent side effects of hair loss, acne, and BPH. This is important!

> Important: Discuss any possible side effects that occur during testosterone supplementation with your doctor or pharmacist and always get a good physical exam (particularly a prostate exam) before starting these hormones.

With any testosterone product, one must look for some testicle atrophy. If it occurs, the regimen is to combine the testosterone with Chorionic Gonadotropin, which will stimulate the testes to produce additional testosterone and also prevent testicular atrophy.

As men grow older, they convert (aromatize) more of their testosterone into estrogen. This process can be avoided with products like Arimidex, which prevents this aromatizing process. The usual dose is 1/2 mg. two to three times a week. Occasionally, this is the only product needed to maintain hormonal balance in a male—initially anyway. It's interesting that a sixty-year-old man often has more estrogen than a similarly aged female. If one has BPH, the physician may prescribe a drug to reduce DHT (dihydrotestosterone), such as the brands Proscar or Avodart. Laboratory tests and a physical examination are needed to assess a patient's needs, and results of treatment should be coordinated with the patient's signs and symptoms.

So, to sum up, the male hormones regimen often needed includes:

1. Testosterone cyprionate weekly injections (my preference).
2. Chorionic gonadotropin injections to prevent testicle atrophy and augment testosterone production, which may require one or two injections with a very fine needle toward the end of the week by the patient.
3. Arimidex tablets to prevent conversion of testosterone into estrogen.

Estrogen, progesterone, and testosterone for women come in numerous products and combinations, including various commonly prescribed birth control pills. Treatment with non-bio-identical hormones and at incorrect doses may result in lack of menopausal symptoms such as hot flashes, but that doesn't necessarily indicate a reduction of other adverse effects of menopause, such as dementia, coronary artery disease, or osteoporosis. With hormone replacement therapy, blood tests must confirm blood hormone levels to ensure achievement of proper levels.

Regarding estrogen, compounding pharmacies using bio-identical hormones usually use a 10:10:80 formula of estrone, estradiol, and estriol or a 20:80 formula of estradiol:estriol. The body breaks estriol down into estradiol and estrone. To my knowledge, no commercial products provide this combination of bio-identical forms of estrogen, which is a strong case for using a compounding pharmacy for these products.

Approximate hormonal doses for the menopausal woman are:

Estrogen: 1 to 5 milligrams a day, the average being 2.5 to 3.5 milligrams
Progesterone: 50 to 100 milligrams a day taken at night
Testosterone: 1 to 8 milligrams a day, the average is 3 to 4 milligrams

The regimen of hormone replacement therapy should generally include testosterone. Many signs of deficient testosterone in men are the same as estrogen deficiency in women (as well as testosterone deficiency in women):

Dementia
Increased coronary artery disease
Osteoporosis
Decreased libido
Increased body fat
Decreased sense of well-being.

Therefore, a proper balance of hormones (primarily estrogen, progesterone, and testosterone) is necessary to achieve optimum hormone replacement therapy. All of the above-mentioned hormones (and necessary tests) must be prescribed by a physician.

Some suggest that females take estrogen and testosterone by cream application and the progesterone by mouth. Oral estrogen lowers growth hormone levels, measured by the blood IGF-1 test, by about 20%. Note that in males it is best to take the testosterone by weekly injections because topical application causes excessive conversion to DHT (dihydrotestosterone). If a female taking testosterone cream notices an increase in hair growth, saw palmetto should be taken at 160 milligrams once or twice a day to reduce conversion of testosterone to DHT.

The problems seen associated with menopause are:

1. Vasomotor instability, such as hot flashes, sweating, palpitations, and flushing
2. Coronary artery disease
3. Mood lability and increased anxiety
4. Dementia with loss of memory and cognitive ability
5. Osteoporosis
6. Urological changes such as vaginal dryness or pain during intercourse
7. Changes in sleep patterns

Benefits of hormone therapy (estrogen, progesterone, and testosterone) are:

1. Reduction of incidence of coronary disease
2. Decreased osteoporosis
3. Reduction in dementia, Alzheimer's disease, and increased cognitive ability
4. Reduction of fat and better weight distribution
5. Better mood, increased libido, and elimination of hot flashes
6. Better quality of life

With estrogen replacement therapy (ERT) or hormonal replacement therapy (HRT) (meaning estrogen, progesterone, and testosterone), blood cardiac markers are improved. These results are good news because coronary artery disease is the leading cause of death in women over fifty years old. These improved markers would be increased HDL (high density lipoprotein), decreased LDL (low density lipoprotein), and LPa (lipoprotein[a]). We see improved artery lining (endothelium) and increased artery diameter. In fact, studies demonstrate a 35 to 50% reduction in cardiac disease with estrogen therapy. However, some experts doubt whether patients should be started on estrogen therapy if they already have coronary artery disease.

After menopause, bones lose 1–2% calcium per year, and by eighty years old women experience a 50% loss in bone density without estrogen replacement therapy. The net gain on estrogen replacement therapy (ERT) after three years was 7–8% in the vertebrae and 4% in the hip in the PEPI study (Postmenopausal Estrogen/Progestin Interventions) in the *Journal of the American Medical Association*. These results provide a strong reason to consider HRT.

Estrogen therapy (ERT) and hormonal replacement therapy (HRT) result in a two-to-four-fold increase in deep vein thrombosis (blood clots), but patients on statin drugs (drugs to lower cholesterol, such as Lipitor or Mevacor) and an aspirin a day had a reduction in deep vein thrombosis by 50% below the baseline.

Most interesting is the reduced risk of mortality of 50% in women receiving HRT relative to control groups in studies by both Sellers and Willis.

The following section is written by a friend and very talented gynecologist regarding the aging woman and the function of female hormones.

Barry Schlafstein, M.D., a prominent obstetrician-gynecologist in Savannah, Georgia, has written the following explanation about bio-identical hormones.

The highly publicized Women's Health Initiative (WHI) Study has created a stir in the medical community, the media, and the lay public alike, and deserves some attention. The issue at hand is essentially that of the role of female reproductive hormones in the menopausal woman. It is important to understand that these hormones, estrogen, progesterone, and to a lesser extent testosterone, are cyclically produced during a woman's reproductive ages, from her early teens to her late forties/early fifties. The primary function of this hormone production is to prepare the reproductive organs each month for pregnancy. Production of female reproductive hormones occurs with greatest efficiency from a woman's late teenage years until her early forties.

While these hormones primarily affect the reproductive organs, specifically the inner lining of the uterus and the glands and ducts of the breasts, they also affect secondarily virtually every other organ system of the body to a lesser extent; including the bones, heart, brain, urinary tract, and skin. These secondary effects are of great importance to a woman's long-term health, and will be discussed in greater detail later. The goal of menopausal hormonal replacement therapy is to achieve the benefits to these secondary organ systems, while carefully avoiding improper or over stimulation of the primary reproductive organs.

What we know from the WHI trial is that taken alone conjugated equine estrogens—those derived from pregnant mare urine, such as Premarin—are safe. What may be a problem is simultaneously taking medroxyprogesterone acetate (MPA), also known by the brand name Provera, the benefits of hormone therapy are diminished. This problem certainly requires a closer look.

Provera (MPA) is a synthetic molecule biologically similar to naturally occurring progesterone. All substances with progesterone-like activity but not biologically identical to progesterone are called progestins. Of the many progestins Provera is the most commonly prescribed. When Provera is ingested orally in pill form, or injected intramuscularly (Depo-Provera), the molecule eventually enters the body's blood stream. Because of Provera's structural similarity to progesterone, these molecules seek and then bind to progesterone receptors throughout the body. At the level of the uterine lining, Provera molecules bind to these receptors and activate them, thereby providing balance to estrogen's stimulatory effect on the lining of the uterus and preventing an overgrowth (hyperplasia) or uterine cancer, thus, achieving a favorable progesterone-like effect. In fact, because of its potency, Provera is excellent in this capacity, which is in large part why it became the most popular and widely used progestin in this country.

This primary effect of Provera, protecting against overgrowth of the uterine lining, was instrumental in the early evolution of menopausal hormonal treatment. When hormonal therapy was first being prescribed to menopausal women, estrogen was given alone. Women who had not had prior hysterectomies ran a seven to ten fold increased risk of hyperplasia or cancer of the uterine lining (endometrial carcinoma). However, adding the progestin completely eliminated the risk. Again, in this capacity Provera seemed a good choice. Because of its low cost, its high potency, and small size, doctors could prescribe this easily ingested pill.

If this were the entire story, then all would be well with the more traditional synthetic menopausal hormonal treatments. The problem with MPA (Provera) is that although the molecule has a favorable progesterone-like effect at the uterine level, such is not the case in virtually every other organ system of the body. In fact, Provera produces an unfavorable effect on other organ systems such as the breasts, cardiovascular system, central nervous system, and the bones. In these other organs MPA does indeed bind with the familiar progesterone receptors. But instead of activating these receptors (to provide the natural balance for estrogen), the MPA molecule blocks or jams the receptors. This highly potent molecule thereby prevents any naturally occurring progesterone, or even estrogen, from binding to the appropriate receptors and eliminates any beneficial or favorable effect that these natural hormones would otherwise have.

The results of the WHI trial confirm the deleterious effect of MPA. Again, in this trial menopausal women could safely benefit from conjugated equine estrogens (Premarin) taken alone. But when MPA was added (Prempro), the safety and benefits of therapy were completely eliminated. Two other retrospective epidemiologic studies suggest the addition of the progestin MPA to estrogen alone may increase the risk of breast cancer, although the increased risk has not yet been statistically proven. In these studies, taking estrogen alone revealed no increased risk of breast cancer over controls (patients not taking any hormone).

All of this information demonstrates that the widely used synthetic progestin, Provera, is not an ideal choice for menopausal hormonal replacement. In fact, Provera is a rather poor choice for hormonal replacement. But does this mean that all hormonal replacement, including bioidentical hormones, is a poor choice?

To answer this question, we must look further at the natural role of the female reproductive hormones in the body.

Female reproductive hormones include estrogen, progesterone, and to a lesser extent testosterone (produced in much larger amounts by men). A woman naturally produces these hormones from menarche—that is, the start of reproductive years as a teenager, until menopause, the completion of the reproductive years in her late forties or early fifties. During peak reproductive years, from the late teens through the thirties, healthy women produce a balance of these hormones in the ovaries. This hormone production coincides with monthly ovarian egg production (ovulation), and is vital for effective preparation for pregnancy. Estrogen facilitates a thickened, lush uterine lining able to support a potential embryo. Progesterone converts the thickened uterine lining into a secretory lining, able to bathe and sustain an early implanted embryo within the uterus. As the uterus grows with pregnancy, progesterone allows uterine muscle to expand without causing contractions, which would otherwise prematurely expel the growing fetus. At the same time the ducts and glands of the breasts proliferate monthly because of this balanced natural hormonal stimulation. To a lesser extent, these same reproductive hormones have a secondary effect on virtually all of the non-reproductive organs and tissues of the body, including the cardiovascular system, the central nervous system, the bones, the urinary tract, and the skin.

Ovarian hormone production is balanced and efficient during these peak reproductive years. This balance changes during times of extreme mental or physical stress, including starvation or excess physical exertion, as the body reflexively shuts off ovarian egg production, and alters the coincidal hormonal production. At extreme ages of reproductive potential, ovarian function also is less efficient and hormonal production is imbalanced. Consider, for example, a woman in her late forties. Before her ovaries cease functioning (menopause), they will essentially malfunction. Eggs ripen in the ovary, but don't fully mature. Estrogen is produced, but it is not properly balanced by progesterone. This condition, also known as perimenopause often results in irregular, heavy, and painful menstrual periods, mood swings, headaches, breast tenderness, and other familiar symptoms characteristic of hormonal imbalance. Perimenopause results from progesterone deficiency, while menopause results from complete lack of hormone production. At menopause, menstrual periods cease, and symptoms include hot flashes, night sweats, sleeplessness, insomnia, memory loss, anxiety, depression, weight gain, and loss of libido.

The best treatment for perimenopausal symptoms is to shut the malfunctioning ovaries off, by providing just the right amount of estrogen and progestin to induce suppression. The best way to do so is via an ultra-low dose oral contraceptive, containing twenty micrograms of ethinyl estradiol combined with one of the newer and much safer progestins. As yet no oral contraceptive containing bioidentical estrogen and progesterone exists. To achieve sufficient strengths for complete ovarian suppression, a bioidentical pill would need to be about the size of a golf ball, and clearly that would not be a practical or desirable product. Fortunately, plenty of information supports the safety of the current low dose oral contraceptives, and I hope we will have an effective bio-identical oral contraceptive pill in the near future.

Because menopause treatment requires much lower amounts of hormone, bioidentical hormones can be used. If used in balanced, low dosages, these compounds mimic the body's natural physiological responses and safely produce the desired effects. In contrast to synthetic agents, bioidentical hormones bind and activate receptors appropriately throughout the body. Forms of natural estrogen, progesterone, and testosterone are commercially available, and in many cities and towns local pharmacists will compound natural hormone replacement therapies upon request. Some pharmacies now even specialize in compounding hormonal therapies. These preparations are all plant derived (phyto-hormones) from natural precursors found in soybeans and yams. When compounded, the dosage can be titrated to the individual's specific need.

Ideally, bioidentical estrogen includes estrone, estradiol, and estriol in a 10/10/80 proportion. While this preparation can be compounded, currently there is no commercially available preparation in this appropriate proportion (estradiol is commercially available). Short-term estrogen use will diminish menopausal vasomotor symptoms such as hot flashes and night sweats, improve vaginal lubrication, decrease vaginal bacterial infection, and improve libido. Proven long-term benefits of estrogens include improved cardiovascular health by lowering cholesterol levels, improved memory and cognitive functioning, a decrease in the incidence of Alzheimer's disease, improved bone calcium metabolism with prevention of osteoporosis, improved bladder function and continence, decreased genitourinary tract atrophy, and improved skin elasticity.

Oral micronized progesterone, a bioidentical phyto-hormone, is commercially available in the form of Prometrium. Bioidentical progesterone can also be compounded. Natural progesterone provides biological balance to estrogen and augments the beneficial effects of estrogen. Just as progesterone causes smooth muscle to relax, thereby allowing the uterus to expand in pregnancy, it also causes smooth muscles in the blood vessels to relax, causing vasodilatation and improved blood flow to the body's organs. Menopausal women often complain of difficulty sleeping, which is a direct result of progesterone deficiency. Natural progesterone has a sedating and relaxing effect on the central nervous system, allowing better sleep. In fact, compounded natural progesterone's sedating effect is so pronounced that most compounding pharmacies add precautionary labels warning that the medication may cause drowsiness if taken during the day. Of course, drowsiness is exactly what the menopausal woman wants to occur as she is going to bed at night. Therefore, be sure to take bioidentical hormones in the evening. No synthetic progestins will have this effect; rather, because of their receptor-blocking action in the central nervous system (CNS), they will further impair sleep. Finally, adding a small amount of natural testosterone will increase sexual desire, may generate an overall feeling of well-being, and enhance energy levels.

Certainly we need trials like the WHI that specifically evaluate the safety and efficacy of bioidentical hormones. To date the WHI trials have only compared conjugated equine estrogen alone to a combination of conjugated equine estrogen and the synthetic progestin, MPA. Until such trials include bioidentical hormones, women of menopausal age along with their physicians must make individual decisions regarding hormonal replacement. My mentor, the late Carson B. Burgstiner, M.D., had a wonderful expression to help me make sense of this vast array of current hormonal therapeutic possibilities, and all of the seemingly conflicting information on this topic. He said, "Maintain natural physiology, and you will prevent disease and pathology." Never have such words had more relevance.

Some final thoughts on menopausal hormone replacement therapy. Although conjugated equine estrogens are natural in that they come from the urine of pregnant horses (PREgnant MARes urINe, hence the product name PREMARIN), they are not bioidentical to the estrogen present in adult human women. Hence we prefer our patients to use plant derived phyto-estrogen.

The dosages of HRT (hormone replacement therapy) required to achieve benefit to the secondary organs (to prevent bone loss, prevent cardiovascular disease, and preserve memory) are much lower than those required to treat the acute symptoms of menopause (hot flashes, night sweats, vaginal dryness, loss of libido). I, therefore, prescribe the lowest dose that will achieve these long-term benefits and then titrate up to treat the acute symptoms. I usually start patients at 1.0 mg. to 1.25 mg. of bio-estrogen, 2.0 mg. of testosterone, and 100 mg. of progesterone daily. Younger patients, in their forties and early fifties and women who have surgical removal of the ovaries along with hysterectomy prior to menopause, often require larger dosages of bio-estrogen in the range of 2.0 mg. to 2.5 mg. daily.

Blood and saliva tests also measure and monitor hormone levels in the body. As a woman, your symptoms are your best bio-assay, and the bioidentical hormones can be titrated up or down in response to these symptoms.

Bioidentical hormones can be taken by mouth (orally) or in the form of topical creams (transdermally). Oral preparations are much less messy and easier to use for patients with healthy livers. In fact, most of my patients use oral HRT. When taken by mouth though, the hormone makes a first pass through the liver after it is absorbed through the gastrointestinal tract. This first-pass phenomenon can cause dangerous elevation of blood clotting factors in patients with unhealthy livers. Transdermal delivery avoids this first pass through the liver; by the time compounds reach the liver, they have already been metabolized peripherally, so no elevation in liver blood-clotting factors occurs. Therefore, anyone with a history of liver disease should use the topical cream preparations. If you do use a topical, dab a very small amount on the face under the eyes; it is excellent for preventing wrinkles!

Salivary Testing of Hormone Levels

A sex steroid hormone molecule, such as estrogen, testosterone, or progesterone, affects the body by influencing the function of the nucleus within the cell of a given organ, such as the bone, heart, brain, breast, or uterus. The hormone molecule must first diffuse across a tissue cell membrane and bind to an intracellular receptor protein before transferring into the cell's nucleus, where the hormone affects bodily function. The fat soluble sex steroid hormone molecule is only able to diffuse across a cell membrane in its unbound state, and only in this unbound state can a hormone molecule be active. To circulate in the blood stream, which is water based, the hormone molecule must attach to a water soluble protein carrier. For a sex steroid molecule, the primary carrier protein is sex hormone binding globulin (SHBG). When traveling the blood stream bound to SHBG, the hormone molecule cannot cross a cell membrane and is rendered inactive. At any given moment only 1%–2% of the body's sex steroid hormone is in the free or active state, while 98%–99% of sex steroid hormone is in the inactive state, bound to its protein carrier. Thus SHBG acts not only as a transporter, but also as a reservoir for the sex steroid hormones.

Just as sex steroid hormone molecules circulate in the blood stream bound to SHBG, and only the free unbound molecules cross the cellular membranes of the various tissue organs such as the bones, heart, brain, uterus, and breast, so it is with the salivary glandular membrane. Once again, only free unbound hormones will cross the cellular membrane and enter into the saliva. Thus, collecting saliva and measuring hormone levels directly reflect active intracellular hormone levels. While blood or serum levels represent the total hormone content of the body, including free and SHBG-bound hormone levels, only the free, active hormone levels are useful when managing and adjusting hormonal replacement therapy. In fact, blood levels themselves can be misleading. Consider the following: Women who eat generally healthy diets, low in fat and starch content, and who exercise regularly have elevated SHBG levels (weight loss will increase SHBG levels). Checking blood hormone levels alone in such patients will yield deceptively high results, thus tempting clinicians to under-treat thinner women. Conversely, SHBG levels drop in women who eat generally unhealthy diets, high in fat and starch, and who do not regularly exercise (weight gain will lower SHBG levels). Blood hormone levels checked alone in these patients will appear falsely low, and clinicians will tend to overtreat heavier women. While it may be of academic interest, when adjusting treatment, we do not need to know how much hormone is in reserve, circulating in the blood stream bound to SHBG. However, we do need to know how much hormone is active and functioning within the body's cells. Salivary testing yields the level of active intracellular hormone and is therefore more useful than blood testing when tailoring a patient's postmenopausal hormone replacement regimen.

Salivary testing will generally cost the patient $125–150, and is rarely covered by insurance plans; therefore, we are selective when recommending such testing. We specifically measure salivary levels of estradiol, estriol, estrone, testosterone, and progesterone. Levels of synthetic progestins, such as MPA and the estrogen and progestins in oral contraceptive pills, are not detected with salivary testing or conventional blood testing. Therefore, if a woman presents on no HRT, or is on synthetic HRT, checking salivary hormone levels is useless. After she has been on a bioidentical hormonal replacement therapeutic regimen for several months, we can then measure salivary hormone levels. Such measurements are useful if the patient is not achieving her desired clinical effect, or if she has adverse symptoms. Levels may also be checked simply if the patient so desires, and does not mind incurring the expense. Salivary hormone testing can then lead to therapeutic adjustments according to the patient's symptoms.

6 Laboratory Tests

When requesting lab work, you and your doctor may consider several tests.

1. Standard blood tests include a complete metabolic profile (CMP), a standard test for liver and kidney function. These tests are ordered routinely for most patients and include:

   a. Hemoglobin (Hgb) and Hematocrit (Hct)—These tests determine your blood's oxygen-carrying capacity by measuring how much hemoglobin and how many red blood cells you have.
   b. White Blood Cell (WBC) Count—A differential may be added to determine the various types of WBCs present. Results of this test often tell the doctor if a patient has an infection and what type of infection it may be and/or how severe it is. It can also detect allergies and leukemia.
   c. Platelet Count—This is important because platelets initiate blood clotting. A decreased platelet count creates a bleeding tendency, as does a lack of other clotting factors. Excess platelets may cause excessive clotting.
   d. Fasting Blood Sugar (FBS)—This test is performed in the morning before any food is eaten (only water is allowed) and indicates presence of elevated blood sugar, diabetes, or even hypoglycemia. If your FBS is elevated, your doctor will probably order a blood sugar test two hours after a meal and possibly a glucose tolerance test.

Additional tests will provide additional important information.
For instance:

2. Lipid profile—This will measure your levels of total, HDL and LDL cholesterol, triglycerides, LPa (lipoprotein A) and, if requested, will even break down these findings into various fractions of HDL and LDL.

3. Homocysteine test—If elevated, this may be an indicator of heart or vascular disease and/or heart disease risk.
4. Thyroid function tests—TSH, T4 free, T3 free. These indicate if your thyroid gland is producing too little or too much thyroid hormone and help determine the cause.
5. C-Reactive protein (CRP)—a standard test for the presence of inflammation within the body; elevated CRP often indicates heart disease and chronic conditions involving inflammation.
6. Estrogen and progesterone—Consult your physician for normal values, which are determined by a woman's monthly cycle and age. Both are low in the postmenopausal female.
7. Testosterone, both total and free—ordered for both males and females.
8. Luteinizing hormone (LH) and Follicle Stimulating Hormone (FSH). These tests measure levels of hormones from the pituitary gland, which stimulate production of estrogen and testosterone.
9. Insulin-like growth factor-1 (IGF-1)—This is to determine your growth hormone levels. Normal levels are related to age. Consult a knowledgeable physician if your levels are below 125. I would prefer levels of 175 or more.
10. Hgb A1C—This test measures how much glycation damage you have from excess simple carbohydrate intake. This measurement indicates simple carbohydrate intake for up to three months prior to the test.
11. DHEA—This measures blood DHEA levels and may indicate the need for oral DHEA.
12. Insulin—This should be done after fasting for twelve hours. It may indicate presence of insulin resistance and the need for reduction in simple carbohydrate intake.

Your physician or health official should interpret these laboratory results. Other levels, such as cortisol, other hormones and even vitamin levels, may be checked according to your needs.

IV

Aging and Your Skin

7 Aging and Your Skin

What happens to skin during aging? To understand aging and proper skin care, we must discuss important and pertinent aspects of our skin.

The function of the skin is to protect us from external elements such as heat, cold, moisture, and dehydration. It also keeps everything inside that should stay inside and acts as a barrier between inside and outside. Within the skin are various glands, such as sweat glands for cooling and sebaceous glands for lubrication. The skin is also our largest and most exposed organ and is in fact our largest sensory organ. In short, we have many reasons to nurture, maintain, and protect our skin in addition to the fact that healthy skin makes us more attractive.

Anatomy of the Skin

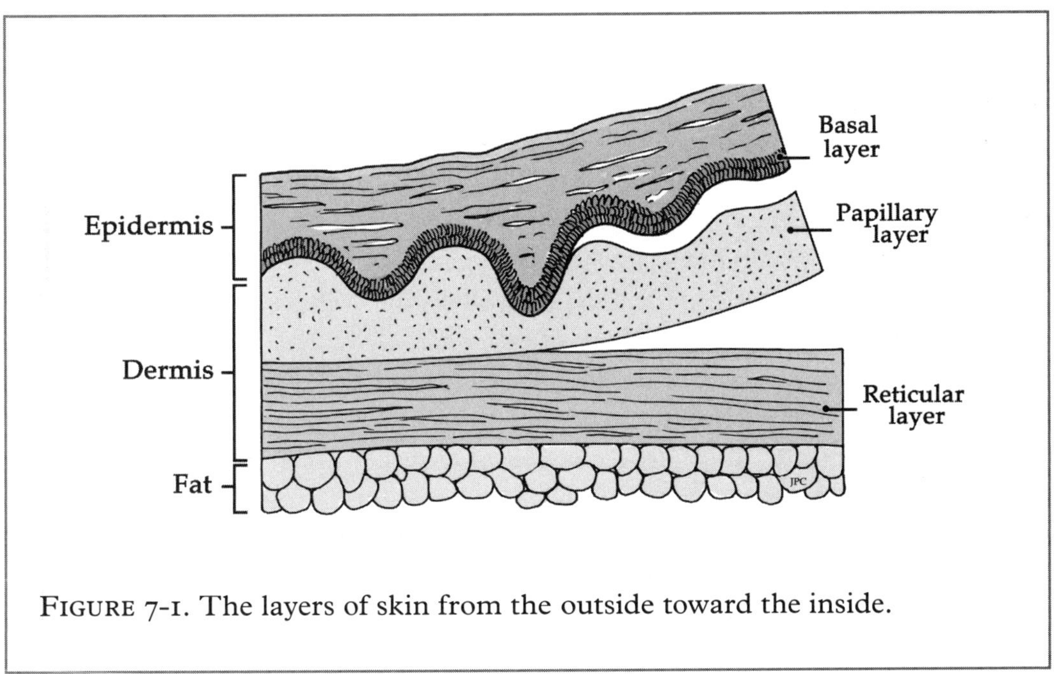

FIGURE 7-1. The layers of skin from the outside toward the inside.

Skin consists of several layers. The epidermis, which is the outermost layer, consists of three layers: keratin, the outer layer; the middle layer; and the basal layer or inner layer. The keratin layer is the most superficial layer and is the layer that we touch when we touch the skin. It continually sheds and is replaced. The basal layer is between the epidermis and dermis and is the layer from which cells of the epidermis are produced. The melanocytes, the pigment-forming cells, are found in the basal layer.

Underneath the epidermis is the dermis, and under that is the subcutaneous layer, or fat. Most of the blood supply is in and below the dermis in the subcutaneous layer. Many problems occur from the reduced blood supply that accompanies increased age, excess sun, and smoking. Most importantly, less blood and nutrients reach the skin, and cellular debris is removed more slowly. This reduction in blood supply makes it difficult for skin to thrive, and it withers and becomes dehydrated just like an unfertilized or un-watered plant. Much more happens beyond that obvious problem, however. Telangiectasia, commonly known as spider veins, are caused by small vessel abnormalities within thinning skin. These spider veins indicate environmental injury of some sort, such as irradiation—for example, excess sun exposure—or even surgery or trauma. These telangiectasia actually do not solve the problem of reduced blood supply to vital parts of the skin. The usual treatments for spider veins are laser, injections of a sclerosing agent (causing coagulation and scarring), or individual coagulation of each capillary—a tedious job.

Cigarette smoking is one of the more common causes of reduced blood supply to the skin due to vasoconstriction, a process of shrinking or constriction of the capillaries and smaller vessels. Smoking definitely takes its toll on the youthful appearance of skin. Just look at chronic smokers, and you will note smoker's wrinkles around their mouths as well as wrinkled, leathery skin.

Another change occurring with increased age is the loss of rete pegs—the hills and valleys between the epidermis and dermis shown in Figure 7-1. Rete pegs help hold the two layers tightly together. As we age, the loss of rete pegs causes the connection between the epidermis and dermis to flatten and does not hold the epidermis tightly to the dermis. It's easy to see how the outer layer becomes more fragile and easily rubbed or knocked off.

Within the dermis and epidermis, the collagen and elastin fibers maintain the natural youthful shape and elasticity of our skin. As we age, collagen production decreases and elastin fibers lose elasticity. Glycation end products (AGEs) attach to elastin fibers, and we inevitably begin to sag.

Unfortunately, elastin fibers do not regenerate significantly, so we must protect them as much as possible. The speed of regeneration is greatly affected by how we care for ourselves. So, our skin is another important factor in our appearance and reflects our overall health.

Several visual changes occur in our skin as we age.

They are:

- Thinning of both the dermis and epidermis
- Wrinkles
- Rough skin
- Leathery skin
- Pigmentation problems and age spots
- Sagging
- Large pores
- Increased skin fragility (from loss of the rete pegs)
- Inflammatory skin growths
- Cancer

As a result of these changes, the keratin layer becomes thicker, irregular, and roughened with increasing age. Nonsmokers who limit their exposure to the sun and tanning beds may never see the later stages of skin aging.

The first wrinkles that we develop come from expression and muscle activity: such as smile wrinkles, frown lines, crow's feet, eyelid wrinkles, and furrows on our foreheads.

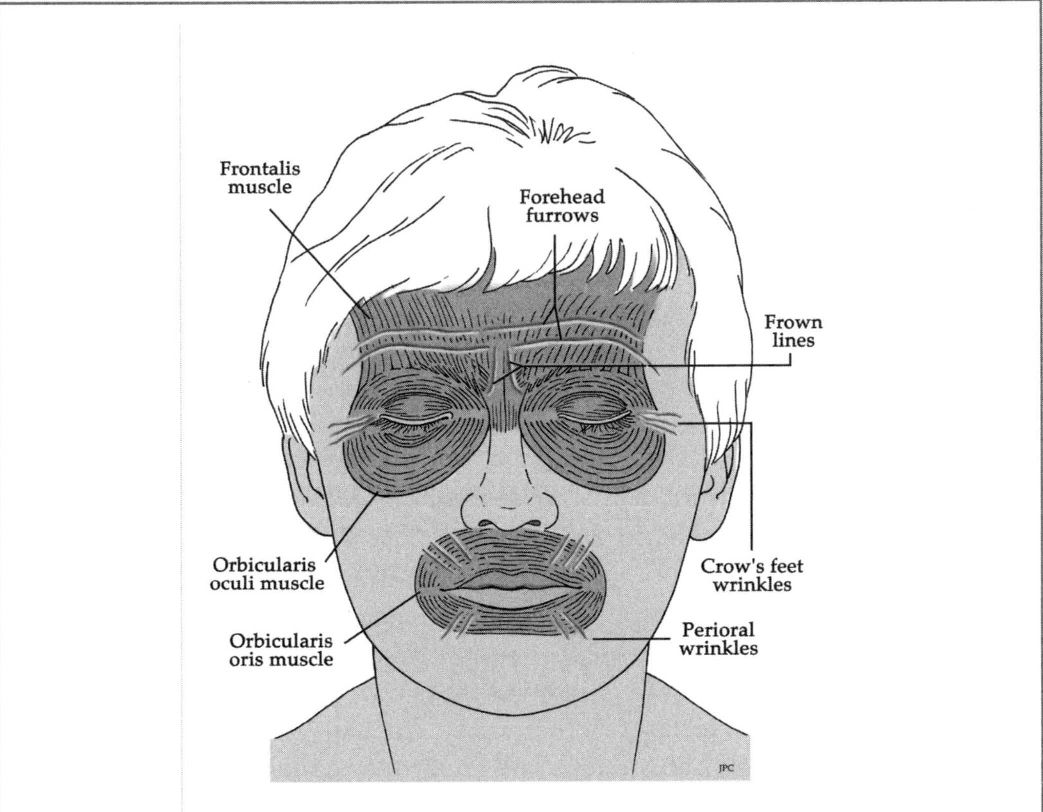

FIGURE 7-2. Notice that these wrinkles are perpendicular to the action of the underlying muscles.

Wrinkles from thinning skin, environmental damage, and deterioration due to smoking and other factors are the fine lines seen in the middle of the cheeks and areas other than those of expression. When advanced, these lines often look like multiple small crosses (or crosshatches, as some patients call them). These wrinkles appear in the previously mentioned leathery skin and for the most part can be avoided for many decades with appropriate skin care. I have in fact seen many patients in their seventies and even eighties who have none of these types of wrinkles. Loss of rete pegs also results from environmental abuse, and in these cases, the skin becomes fragile and is easily injured by even the most minor bump or scrape.

A word of caution: sun damage is cumulative. The sun baking we did as teenagers manifests itself as visible skin damage about ten to fifteen years later, but damage continues to accumulate with our sun exposure over the years. The good news is that any time we stop exposing our skin to excess ultraviolet damage, we will help our overall skin health, and some sun damage can be reversed with proper skin treatment and care.

The melanocytes in the basal layer and the blood supply are responsible for the color of our skin. The melanin pigment from the melanocyte gives us protection from the sun. The pink hue in skin is from red blood cells in the small vessels and capillaries within the skin, and the dark or brown tint is from the melanin. As we age, there are fewer red blood cells and less youthful pink color in our skins due to the reduction in blood supply. Reacting to sun damage, the melanocyte most often produces uneven or excess pigment, which we see as pigmentation irregularities, sunspots, and age spots. Also, with aging and more sun exposure our skin becomes darker in areas that continue to get exposure to the UV light. A good example of this transformation is to compare the outside of your arm to the more protected inside of your arm or comparing skin areas covered by bathing suits compared to more exposed areas. These areas are almost always paler, less wrinkled, less marked with pigmentation spots and freckles, and younger looking.

Other pigmentation changes are due to pregnancy (often called pregnancy mask). They are related to hormone changes, perhaps in combination with excess sun exposure.

The Story Our Skin Tells

Our skin tells an interesting story, depending on complexion and pigmentation. Here are a few examples:

Consider a darker skinned person with multiple small freckles and spots on the outside of the arm, but on the inner arm the skin is much lighter without spots. This person's face would also be dark and somewhat leathery with pigmented spots and a somewhat saggy neck. The skin on the upper chest would be the same as the outer arm. What story does this person's skin tell? He/she has an outdoor occupation or is a sun enthusiast or indulges in some sport such as tennis, golf, hiking, or gardening, and does not use a sunblock and hat effectively for protection. This person will look much older, much faster.

Another example is the older person with almost baby skin: not dark, no spots and, almost no wrinkles. This person has had little exposure to the sun, or at least limited exposure, and uses a sunblock effectively. He/she is also an indoor person, possibly a scholar or writer, or a busy business person with few outdoor hobbies.

Finally, consider the older gentleman with an old-fashioned farmer's tan: very dark arms and neck, white legs and, usually, a lighter face because of regularly wearing a hat.

Just as pigmentation reveals information about activity, expression lines such as frown lines, crow's feet, and smile lines tell us a little about personality. Sad eyes, for example, often reflect history, but we must keep in mind that the playing field is not level in this regard, and some of the above differences may simply be due to anatomy and genetics. Often patients have told me that they look unhappy or angry yet feel happy. In these cases, my job as a plastic surgeon is to make them look the way they say they feel.

The degree to which people vary is almost infinite, but sun damage happens to everyone, and the degree of damage susceptibility from environmental hazards varies according to Fitzpatrick skin type, which is classified as follows:

Fitzpatrick's classification:

Skin Type	Color	Reaction to UV	Reaction to Sun
Type I	Caucasian; blond or red hair, freckles, fair skin, blue eyes	Very sensitive	Always burns easily, never tans; very fair skin tone
Type II	Caucasian; blond or red hair, freckles, fair skin, blue or green eyes	Very sensitive	Usually burns easily, tans with difficulty; fair skin tone
Type III	Caucasian; dark hair, white to light olive skin, brown eyes	Less sensitive	Burns and tans moderately
Type IV	Caucasian; Mediterranean, olive skin, dark eyes	Not very sensitive	Burns minimally Tans moderately
Type V	Asian, darker skin and eyes	Not sensitive	Rarely burns Always tans
Type VI	African	Not sensitive	Never burns Always tans

The lower the number on this classification scale, the more aware one must be about UV damage and the more likely one is to have skin areas prone to cancer.

Skin Cancer

Precancerous skin lesions are reddish or pink, scaly, possibly irregular in shape, and possibly faintly eroded (if viewed under some magnification). Your physician must examine these lesions to rule out the possibility of skin cancer. Dark pigmented, often warty-looking spots are age spots and are almost uniformly benign, though unattractive.

The most common skin cancers are:

- Basal cell carcinoma
- Squamous cell carcinoma
- Melanoma

Excess sun exposure is by far the most common cause of these cancers.

Basal cell carcinoma is the most common and slowest growing of the skin cancers, making up about 90% of them. They are usually found on the face, ears, or neck, but can be found on any area of excess sun exposure. Typically they are small nodules or lumps, pink and waxy or pearly in appearance, but may also be ulcerated. They can be treated with minor excisional (to cut out) surgery. Any lesion or sore that will not heal in a month should be considered a carcinoma of some sort and should be evaluated by your physician.

Squamous cell cancers are more invasive than basal cell types. They commonly develop on the lower lip, on the edge of the lower eyelids and the extremities, but can occur anywhere. They grow rapidly and may show more erosion and can metastasize to other areas of the body if not removed. They are typically irregular in shape, pink, scaly, or ulcerated.

Melanomas are the most malignant of the skin cancers and are fortunately the least common. They can be very deadly, very fast. They often occur in areas that have received severe sunburns and may appear in moles that have been present for decades. They have even occurred in the retina of the eye. Typically the melanoma is a dark, multicolored, mole-like lesion that is changing in character—perhaps enlarging or irregular in shape, irritated, or itching. These characteristics alone are motivation enough to use sunblock and reduce sun exposure. Unfortunately, melanomas are becoming more common, almost like an epidemic, possibly a result of baby boomers wearing smaller bathing suits and looking for that dark tan as young adults. I lost three friends to melanoma in the first six months of 2004.

I have seen media coverage about five-year studies supposedly demonstrating the ineffectiveness of sunblock in preventing skin cancers. Do not believe it. These studies are inaccurate, incomplete, and ridiculous, as it may take ten to twenty-five or even thirty years for skin cancers to develop due to sun abuse.

Proper use of a sunblock, a hat, and long sleeves do work, but they are not complete substitutes for reduced sun exposure.

I'm not, however, suggesting that any of us abstain from sun exposure. We get vitamin D from the sun and must enjoy our sports and the outdoors, but remember that sun baking is definitely harmful. Consider a tan an injury. The best prevention is a good sunblock with protection from UVA, UVA1, and UVB rays. I also recommend a good hat, along with good quality sunglasses to protect the eyes from UV damage.

Glasses that protect us from UV light also reduce eyelid wrinkles, the incidence of cataracts, and possibly even melanoma of the retina. In addition retailers now sell shirts and other clothing advertised as offering additional UV protection.

Those of Irish descent or with very fair complexions and fair hair and eyes (see Fitzpatrick classification 1 and 2 on page 93) should be particularly careful because they are more susceptible to injury and damage from the sun. Those with darker skin have higher concentrations of melanin, which absorbs more ultraviolet rays.

In my practice I have also noted in a few fairly young patients a relationship between daily use of glycolic acid creams and the development of unexpected skin cancers. This relationship is not surprising as continuous exfoliation exposes us to more UV damage. Remember that the sunshine is a powerful oxidant. Proper use of antioxidants, anti-inflammatories, and nutrients, both topically and by mouth, plus a good sunblock should help solve this problem and allow us to enjoy the benefit of topical glycolic acids or peels, which is more youthful looking skin. Also, glycolic acid is used in my practice to enhance the penetration of other age-control topical nutrients.

In a Nutshell

A good discussion of skin types has to include age and environmental damage, including the various skin cancers. We've reviewed basic skin anatomy and what happens with aging and environmental injury—not always a pretty picture, but we are not helpless in avoiding and reversing even some severe damage. Remember, when using glycolic acid peels, always follow with topical creams or serums with antioxidants, anti-inflammatories, and nutrients.

8 Skin Care and Treatment

One of my great interests is in the treatment and age reversal of skin. How can we make skin look healthy and youthful by topical treatments, those applied directly to the skin? Through much time, effort, and with the help of the right biochemists, we have proven it can be done. Such treatments involve altering the cells that produce the skin we see, so they are not Band-Aid treatments like simple superficial peeling. As a result, skin cells are healthier and their product—the overall skin—is healthier too. When cells change from looking like healthy grapes when young to resembling shriveled-up raisins from environmental hazards, we cannot expect their products to be healthy. Good overall health and appearance are difficult to distinguish.

Nutrients and various other beneficial ingredients can definitely be absorbed through the skin. That is the first fact that you should understand. For instance, nicotine patches help people stop smoking. Hormone patches, nitroglycerine patches, patches for seasickness, narcotic patches, and others treat patients via skin absorption. Also, serums, gels, and creams are available, both by prescription and over-the-counter. However, these patches, serums, gels, and creams must be in a form that allows penetration into the layers of the skin. The means for accomplishing absorption is called transport or delivery systems. Ineffective transport systems will obviously not result in effective treatment because the desired ingredients remain on the surface and do not penetrate into the epidermis or dermis.

On the other hand, what good is an effective delivery system with ineffective ingredients? The goal of skin care is to provide necessary ingredients to repair and protect cells from the environment, which is no simple task. Virtually all skin already has damage due to our constant exposure to various environmental hazards, including poor dietary habits (truly a dangerous hazard).

For a skin care product to provide maximum rejuvenation, it must contain the following categories of ingredients in forms suitable for topical application:

- Phytonutrients
- Vitamins
- Minerals
- Antioxidants
- Anti-glycation agents
- Anti-inflammatory agents
- Substances that stimulate production of collagen, elastin, and ground substance (material between the cells)
- Substances increasing blood supply
- Pigment stabilizers and other ingredients to de-pigment age spots
- Multipeptide combination ingredients for wrinkles
- Mild exfoliants
- Ingredients for DNA and cell repair
- Omega-3 and Omega-6 fatty acids

Without getting bogged down with details of every possible ingredient that performs the jobs in the above list, I will mention a few that are especially beneficial. The comments that follow pertain principally to topical applications to the skin.

The items in the above list and the discussions about them below need not be committed to memory, but they may be of interest to anyone serious about skin care and repair.

The New Youth Skin Treatment System includes the categories listed above necessary for skin rejuvenation and repair. Therefore, they are effective, and long-term use of these products results in continued skin improvement.

Vitamins

Vitamin is an apt name because these are necessary for life, as in "vital." Vitamins mostly come from the foods we eat, but can be supplemented topically via creams, gels, and/or serums. The fat-soluble vitamins are A, D, E, and K. The water-soluble vitamins are B complex and C. You do not need to know the names and properties of the various vitamins to take care of your skin, but if you are interested, the following brief discussions can be used as reference guides.

Vitamin A

Vitamin A is an effective vitamin to protect against viral and bacterial infections as well as some cancers. It is our immune-boost vitamin. Analogs (chemical cousins) of vitamin A are retinol, Retin-A, retinyl palmitate, and the oral acne medication, Accutane.

Another form of vitamin A is beta-carotene, which is a powerful antioxidant and is necessary for healthy skin. Beta-carotene gives plants and animals many of the pigments that result in beautiful colors. As a matter of interest, the carotenoids are a family of six hundred or more pigments that create yellow and orange colors of various vegetables and plant life. Broccoli, carrots, and spinach are loaded with beta-carotene. These colors are often masked by green chlorophyll, as in broccoli. In autumn, when the chlorophyll is oxidized in leaves, we see the transformation of the fall foliage from green to rich yellows and oranges that are the result of beta-carotene.

Beta-carotene is necessary for the formation of vitamin A. It reduces formation of cancer (anti-carcinogenic), boosts our immune system, and protects our blood from abnormal clotting.

Vitamin B

B vitamins are a family or complex of water-soluble vitamins. They are involved in many tasks such as converting nutrients into energy, functioning of the immune system, and enabling proper balance in our hormone systems, cell repair, and more. B complex vitamins include the following:

- B1 (thiamine) is essential for energy production and, when taken orally, a healthy heart and nervous system. Deficiencies appear in patients with Alzheimer's disease, in alcoholics, and in people with various behavior disorders.
- B2 (riboflavin) helps convert nutrients into energy. Our 100 trillion cells survive by converting nutrients into energy, so without this function there would be no life. Vitamin B2 activates and regenerates glutathione, a powerful antioxidant for our constant battle against free radicals and other toxins. Required for energy production in the skin, B2 is necessary for skin repair and health.
- B3 exists in two forms: niacin and niacinamide. Some people who take vitamins orally may recognize niacin as the vitamin that causes us to flush for a few minutes. People take it to decrease LDL (bad) cholesterol and triglycerides in the blood and raise HDL (good) cholesterol levels. Some also believe it helps prevent senility by its ability to stimulate circulation. Importantly, when taken by mouth, No-Flush Niacin (with inositol hexanicotinate) is the safest systemic form of niacin that fulfills our need for niacin without the annoying but harmless flushing. Avoid the timed-release form as it may be toxic to the liver.
- B5 (pantothenic acid) is an important topical vitamin for optimal skin repair. B5 is used to convert fuel into energy and is essential for healing wounds, including those from burns. (As you may remember, severe sunburn is a common cause of aggressive cancer, melanoma). B5 is also important to our immune system and is an effective anti-inflammatory agent. Hence, B5 helps minimize skin aging. An important antioxidant, B5 causes blood vessels to dilate thereby stimulating new cell formation. It also reduces scar formation, and as mentioned previously, it functions as an anti-inflammatory agent.

Remember how important inflammation is in various diseases, including cancer? Vitamin B5 rapidly penetrates into the skin and helps protect us from exposure hazards. It is also an excellent moisturizer.

- B6 (pyridoxine) is a cofactor (an important chemical necessary for an enzyme to work) in the manufacture of protein. It is also essential for skin health, for optimal immune system function, and for combat against many degenerative disorders. It should be taken with a balance of all other B vitamins. Deficiencies of magnesium and/or zinc can cause an inability to activate B6, which explains the need for certain minerals.
- B12. For the sake of completeness, it must be mentioned that B12 is necessary for both our nervous and circulatory systems. It is not effective in skin products. Many people are deficient in B12 because of a difficulty of absorbing this vitamin. Deficiencies result in pernicious anemia, depression, dementia, tingling and numbness of fingers or toes, and much more. Most often we see deficiencies among vegetarians and the elderly. High doses (1,000 micrograms) are necessary for treatment by the oral route.

Vitamin C

Vitamin C (ascorbic acid) is a very powerful antioxidant necessary for our connective tissue and the manufacture of collagen and healthy skin. It also helps keep vitamins A, B, and E from deteriorating in the body. Perhaps because of its ability to repair cell membranes and protect us from damaging free radicals, vitamin C also prevents certain cancers. The most effective vitamin C for topical application is ascorbyl palmitate and magnesium ascorbyl phosphate (MAP). However, there is some concern that the ascorbyl palmitate is carcinogenic (causes cancer).

We cannot make this vitamin in our bodies because we lack an essential enzyme for the process, so we should also take adequate vitamin C by mouth. Vitamin C exists in many fruits and vegetables. The recommended daily allowance (RDA) of 60 mg per day is inadequate, except in very healthy individuals with superb diets. The two-time Nobel laureate Dr. Linus Pauling popularized the importance of vitamin C supplementation and believed the daily intake should be between 5,000 and 10,000 mg. Those with gastritis, ulcers, or esophageal reflux should take the ester form of vitamin C, often called Vitamin C Ester or by the trade name Ester C, which can be found in most pharmacies and health food stores. Better yet, one should take vitamin C complex from whole food products as discussed under Dietary Supplements in Chapter 4.

Many forms of topical vitamin C exist, though unfortunately many have a short shelf life. The most effective forms are MAP and ascorbic palmitate, and these have a shelf life of about two years. MAP reaps the antioxidant benefits without the irritation of other, more acidic vitamin C formulas. Vitamin C also helps preserve skin cells, reduces hyper-pigmentation (hyper means more and hypo means less), and improves the skin's ability to retain moisture. It is important for age control of the skin.

Vitamin E

Vitamin E (tocopherol) is a powerful antioxidant. When taken by mouth, it is also an anticoagulant and reduces the adhesiveness of platelets. (Platelets are responsible for initiating a blood clot by sticking or clumping together.) Because of this, I routinely have patients stop taking any oral forms of vitamin E for two weeks prior to elective surgery. Otherwise, they bleed excessively, which prolongs their recovery. However, vitamin E is important because of its ability to reduce heart disorders and certain cancers. Our diets often leave us vitamin E-deficient, and food refining or cooking can destroy this vitamin. It is suggested that one take the complete Vitamin E complex, which includes alpha, beta, and gamma tocopherol in doses of 250 to 1,000 units a day divided into two doses and taken morning and night. It's best to take as a whole food vitamin and not a synthetic, and dosage, as mentioned, will be significantly lower.

Remember that the above-mentioned vitamin discussion is primarily for use as topical creams or serums for skin nutrition, repair, restoration, and protection, but also some general characteristics for oral use are mentioned to help readers understand the value of various vitamins.

Minerals

Minerals mentioned in this section are the various elements needed in the creams, gels, and serums for optimum skin care. Minerals contribute to the utilization of the multiple other ingredients, such as bio-nutrients necessary to complete various vitamin complexes. They are also important for repair and maintenance of the many structures that make up the skin.

- Calcium helps maintain the epidermis, the top layer of the skin. It is important in cell membrane integrity. The cell membrane is like our skin in the sense that it separates certain elements inside the cell from those outside. An example of one of the cell membrane functions is the sodium pump. Potassium has a much higher concentration inside the cell than outside, so the cell membrane's sodium pump forces sodium out of the cell and potassium to the inside. Calcium contributes to this phenomenon. As well, it nourishes both the circulatory and the nervous system by its role in cell membranes, and it promotes bone integrity and enhances our immune system. It is essential in skin care and treatment.
- Copper works as a catalyst to help utilize certain vitamins. This mineral also assists in the formation of collagen.
- Iron assists in enzyme functions, and is also necessary for immune functions. It is necessary for the oxygen capacity in hemoglobin, but this is

not related to topical application. Interestingly, hydrochloric acid in the stomach is required for iron absorption, so individuals who take antacids routinely should have their blood hemoglobin measured occasionally.

- Magnesium is vital for adequate enzymatic activity.
- Zinc, another essential mineral for our skin, is involved in more than a hundred different enzymatic functions in the body. Zinc contributes to wound repair because of its role in enzyme enhancement and integrity of the cell membrane, and it is necessary for protein synthesis.

It should be clear that if your skin is to remain, or become, healthy and beautiful against the ravages of the environment and the usual consequences of the aging process, it needs help from absorbable creams, serums, and similar products specially formulated for that purpose.

A large variety of products are on the market, ranging from very fine down to a total waste of your money. Investigate and compare them, buy the best for yourself, and then stick rigorously to a regimen to feed your skin beneficially just as one eats on a regular basis to nourish the body. While comparing commercial products, be sure to use the general guide on page 97 to make certain the products you consider leave no gaps in the essential categories of nutrients required for healthy and beautiful skin.

Over a period of years I have explored many cosmeceutical products available to the public, and I have found them wanting in one respect or another toward my goals for skin restoration. Perhaps an important vitamin or mineral was omitted, or the ingredients were not synergistic. Rarely do products address the glycation problem with necessary anti-glycation ingredients. Sometimes the balance of components is not quite right. The field of skin care is a frontier, and standards must be uncompromising. For those reasons I developed my own line of cosmeceuticals known as New Youth Skin Treatment System. My objective was to bring together everything I know as a health enthusiast and professional which I believe to be essential for optimal skin care.

If you find on the market a combination of products to make your skin the healthiest and most beautiful it can be, skip the rest of this chapter. Otherwise, the following material will explain why I am so enthusiastic about the skin-care products I, with other biochemists, have developed for my patients and others who want to reverse skin damage.

New Youth Skin Treatment System

I formulated New Youth with the aid of several biochemists. The line has been my passion since 1996. You might say that for a specialist with my affinity for thwarting age that New Youth is my baby.

I'll start by reemphasizing that healthy cells produce healthy skin. Thus, you may think of skin as their product. Concealing skin defects or simply peeling and bleaching the skin with a few chemicals never made sense to me. The problem is not just superficial. Manufacturers have not approached skin care focusing primarily on repair at a cellular level. This focus, however, has always been the New Youth goal.

Savannah is a coastal city with a beach and is near many coastal resort areas, such as those in Florida and Hilton Head Island. These areas are also known for fishing, boating, golf, and tennis. Since living near the coast often leads to damaged skin from excessive and unprotected sun exposure, early in my practice I received requests for cosmetic surgery as opposed to reconstruction, and by the late 1970s many patients wanted surgery for facial rejuvenation, which involves primarily eyelid surgery, facelifts, and laser or chemical peels.

Early on it was clear that one could surgically tighten the skin and return the shape to that of a younger person, but with badly damaged skin, the result was like a cake without the icing. I tried many available skin care products on my patients but found that the ones that worked best also caused continuous flaking, redness, and/or irritation. In addition, I saw several patients with skin cancers who were not typical skin cancer patients. They were younger, not necessarily light-complected, and had multiple cancers on their faces only. When multiple skin cancers appear, they usually occur on the arms and chest, too, so these isolated lesions were unusual. Upon obtaining good histories, I learned the common denominator was the use of glycolic acid-containing products, most of which were bought over-the-counter. After I pondered the problem for a while, it seemed that the facial cancers resulted from acid or microdermabrasion treatments without proper protection and nutrition. These treatments basically removed some of the skin's outer protective layer, the keratin layer, exposing the skin to more ultraviolet rays, which would be equivalent to removing some of the ozone layer. It was bad in the long term, even though initially the skin looked refreshed.

The sun's ultraviolet rays cause oxidation and thus the release of free radicals, which causes damage to the cell membranes as well as important cell structures, such as the mitochondria and DNA. This internal cell damage results in leathery, aged skin, DNA mutations, and even skin cancers. Externally, it damages the fibroblasts between the cells that produce collagen. Furthermore, UV rays damage the elastin fibers within the skin and accelerate sagging. When this damage occurs, we see many of the aging disorders of the skin, including basal cell and squamous cell cancers and even the very aggressive melanomas.

I presented my observations to biochemists specializing in skin formulations, and soon after, development of an effective skin product program began with skin rejuvenation on a cellular level as our goal. Initially, one of the biochemists, Michael Warshaw, was already working on a skin product that was primarily an anti-inflammatory agent. In fact, he had been using it on women receiving radiation treatment for breast cancer. He found his formulation reduced the redness and swelling resulting from radiation treatment, although to my knowledge he never conducted a supporting double-blind study. We began formulating our age control and management products in 1996, focusing on the anti-inflammatory component of his product along with numerous antioxidants, vitamins, minerals, and ingredients specific for skin and cell repair.

The products were intended for my own patients, so we spared little expense on the ingredients. With a proper transport system, the skin absorbs these ingredients, so I wanted them to be the finest quality. We focused on products that could make a visible difference. We wanted products that not only repaired and protected the skin, but also returned it to a healthier state, as healthy skin looks youthful.

To complete the New Youth story, other lessons were learned the hard way. Initially, most of those using the products were friends or patients, and I needed their honest opinions. As you would expect, many batches of products were disposed of along the way. For one thing, the quality of the ingredients was not the whole story. If the ingredients were wonderful but not absorbed, what good was the product? Also, the ingredients should have been odorless, or at least have a pleasant one, and some of the key ingredients did not smell very pleasant. The product could not feel too greasy or oily, and it had to layer well so women could use it with makeup, definitely an important factor. The product also had to look good and have a long shelf life. If it was adversely affected by ultraviolet light, it must be put in bottles that block UV light. We found that some of the ingredients we wanted could not be mixed with other ingredients because of pH requirements or other incompatibilities. Sometimes we thought the product was fine, only to hear various complaints from users.

Because of unusual but fortunate connections in Moscow several years ago, I gave lectures there and demonstrated certain surgery techniques in a Moscow hospital to plastic surgeons from Russia and surrounding countries. This experience evolved into selling the New Youth products in Moscow, which turned out to be a wonderful testing ground. We requested feedback and got a few complaints that required changes and additions. But eventually the business grew in Russia, and now the business has numerous employees and is moving into neighboring countries.

At one point we had four different laboratories for production across the United States and Italy. Have we completely reached our goals? The answer, as in plastic surgery, is no. There is always room for improvement. We continuously strive to be better. To be among the best, one must be persistent and make changes when necessary. In life, I often think of Richard Bach's *Jonathan Livingston Seagull* (1970), which outlines different plateaus of excellence. With New Youth we continue to pursue new levels of excellence by adding new ingredients that are beneficial.

The New Youth Skin Treatment System offers a number of benefits:

Reduction of pigmentation spots and freckles
A more youthful skin color
Reduction in fine wrinkles
Reduction in number and size of large pores
Better blood supply to the skin
Thicker dermis and epidermis
Smoother skin
Tighter skin
Healthier skin
More protection from sun exposure and other oxidants

The New Youth starter kit consists of a number of products:

Cleanser: A gentle pH balanced cleanser which also removes makeup completely.

Activator: A mild salicylic acid wash with minimal hydroquinone to help with pigmentation problems, to prevent acne breakouts, and to enhance absorption of other products.

Fade Serum: A strong pigmentation reducer and stabilizer, containing lactic acid and four pigment stabilizers.

Anti-inflammatory Cream: A cream containing multiple vitamins, anti-glycation, antioxidants, minerals, skin and cell repair ingredients, immunity enhancers, and anti-inflammatory agents. In addition, it contains marine algae extract, which has whole-food nutrients and is necessary for valuable phytonutrients, and peptides for fine wrinkle reduction.

Age Control Serum: A different combination and high concentrations of the same ingredients as the cream with more B vitamins for daytime protection and cell repair.

Retinol Silk (Microencapsulated Retinol): A timed-release and fat soluble formulation for absorption into the deep layers of the skin.

Moisturizer SPF 30: An immediately effective mechanical and chemical blocker of UVA, UVB, and UVA1 containing nutrients, antioxidants, vitamins, and anti-inflammatory agents. Its protective effects are immediate as opposed to chemical blocks.

Regarding the current products as they are today (as they are continually improved), applying one cream or solution over another ("layering") is preferable. Just as all vitamins and nutrients cannot be put into one pill, all necessary ingredients for maximum skin health cannot be in one jar of cream. Layering yields the best and fastest results, especially for outdoor people or those over forty. Actually, anyone over the age of twenty will benefit from using a good skin care product.

The New Youth regimen is as follows:
Each morning—

1. Wash your face with the Cleanser.
2. Apply the Activator to a cotton pad and scrub your face lightly.
3. Apply a few drops of the Fade Serum to the entire face.
4. Apply a few drops (one squirt) of the Age Control Serum. You can mix it with the Fade Serum in your palm and then apply to your face if you prefer.
5. Apply a very small amount of Moisturizer SPF 30 for protection.

Each evening—

1. Wash your face with Cleanser.
2. Apply the Activator as described above.
3. Apply the Fade Serum and let dry.
4. Apply Anti-inflammatory Cream.
5. Apply the Retinol Silk. Use the entire capsule on your face and neck. For more aggressive therapy, use it twice a day, but start with once a day for a few weeks.

Product Descriptions

Cleanser: This unique cleansing liquid includes a blend of meadowsweet and lactic acid combined with polysaccharides from honey extract. This combination provides excellent moisturizing, increasing skin surface renewal. Lemon bioflavonoids and rosemary extract stimulate and tone the skin, while the fragrant essential oils of orange, geranium, and eucalyptus refresh the senses. The product thoroughly cleanses and removes excess oil, environmental impurities, and makeup.

Activator 3.3 w/HQ: This exclusive product is a liquid that contains the active ingredient, hydroquinone 2%, which fades age spots and evens out pigmentation due to natural aging and environmental damage. It provides natural proteins, botanical extracts, and minerals to keep the skin elastic and hydrated. It contains salicylic acid to enhance penetration of other products and to reduce acne breakouts. It is a mild exfoliant, stimulating the skin's natural repair process of new cell growth.

Anti-Inflammatory Cream: This was our first product and has, of course, been improved from its beginning many times. It is a strong warrior against free radicals and contains numerous ingredients, including marine algae extracts with all of their phytonutrients, natural antioxidants, anti-inflammatory agents, minerals, nutrients, and vitamins. This is a strong anti-glycation cream also. Other important ingredients are squalene oil that contains moisturizing agents found in both plants and animals. It contains green tea extract and calendula, which are both anti-inflammatory and effective antioxidants. It also contains more than twenty other antioxidants to neutralize different types of free radicals. It contains cat's claw, which boosts the immune system and has been demonstrated in studies to repair DNA. Its vitamin C comes in three forms. The list goes on and includes many more antioxidants, anti-inflammatory agents, vitamins, minerals, nutrients, and cell repair ingredients.

Age Control Serum: This product is similar to the Anti-Inflammatory Cream but contains some ingredients not compatible with those in the Cream above. It also contains higher concentrations of the B complex vitamins for more protection from environmental hazards during the daytime, as well as for additional cell repair ingredients.

Fade Serum: This product is our strongest fighter of abnormal pigment formation. It contains 2% hydroquinone, along with three more synergistically acting ingredients that are pigmentation stabilizers, namely, kojic acid, morus root, and bearberry. It also contains lactic acid and superoxide dismutase (SOD), a strong antioxidant. It is a non-prescription product that is more effective than many prescription bleachers and is less irritating.

Retinol Silk: This is a microencapsulated, time-release formation of retinol 0.015% that penetrates rapidly into the deeper layers of the dermis. It is as effective as prescription-strength products, but it causes less irritation and inflammation. It enhances cell turnover, exfoliation, and blood flow. It thickens damaged skin and increases collagen production, thereby resulting in tightening of the skin and softening of fine lines and wrinkles.

Moisturizer SPF 30: This is a microfine zinc oxide mechanical blocker of UV, UVB, and long wave UV1. It is transparent on the skin. It also contains retinyl palmitate (a weaker form of retinol), ginseng, ginkgo extract, vitamins C and E, and green tea.

The following is more information on sunblocks: For protection, we need to reduce our sun exposure and use a sunscreen or sunblock, which can be mechanical, chemical, or both. Mechanical sunblock contains either zinc or titanium, which actually absorbs UV radiation before the skin has to deal with it. Microfine zinc oxide (Z-cote, an ingredient in New Youth Moisturizer SPF 30) is a broad-spectrum mechanical sunblock that offers photo-protection for UVB, UVA, and extra long wave UVA1. It is transparent when used in small quantities but still retains effectiveness. It is photostable, it does not react with other ingredients, and it is safe. Titanium is also produced as a microfine product and may be equally effective. Both zinc and titanium have the advantage of immediate activity. Some products contain both ingredients. Get in the habit of looking at the ingredients used by sunblocks and all other products.

Sun protection factor (SPF) relates to UVB radiation only. Most of the available published literature on the topic proposes that a SPF of 15 is adequate; however, my recommendation is that a minimum of 30 SPF is necessary. An SPF of

15 means that it offers fifteen times the protection compared to using no sunblock at all. An SPF of 30 provides thirty times the protection and so forth.

A study in Australia found a total of twenty-one allergic reactions to sunscreen chemicals observed in nineteen patients over eight years. There were nine positive photopatch (a test for allergies to topical applications) reactions to oxybenzone, eight to butyl methoxy dibenzoylmethane, three to methoxycinnamate, and one to benzophenone. However, it found no allergies to either zinc or titanium. Interestingly, no subjects reacted to para-aminobenzoic acid (PABA), a chemical sunscreen. Nevertheless, this chemical has been removed from most sunscreens because of its possible link with autoimmune diseases such as lupus erythematosus. In this study, chemical sunscreens were the most common cause of photo-allergic contact dermatitis.

In addition to the starter kit, the New Youth line includes other beneficial skin care products.

Personal Peel: This is a glycolic wash product to be used two to three times a week, if needed. It is the strongest non-neutralized glycolic acid peel allowed for over-the-counter sales by the U.S. Food and Drug Administration (FDA). Its oxidation tendencies should be reduced by the multiple antioxidants in the other New Youth System products. This is an important concept. Personal Peel exfoliates and softens the outer layer of the skin, allowing the other products to penetrate faster.

Use of this product should produce:

- Smoother skin
- Reduction of unsightly pores
- Less inflammation than other peels due to anti-inflammatory ingredients
- Reduced pigmentation and age spots

Perfect Eyes: A few drops applied twice daily reduce fine wrinkles, especially around the lower lids and corners of the eyes. Maximum results take about thirty days.

Acne Spot Treatment: This is a salicylic acid product that penetrates rapidly and dries out inflamed acne lesions without leaving marks. When dry, it leaves no film and accepts makeup. It comes in a small roll-on top container that fits easily in a pocket or purse, and it lasts for months.

Microdermabrasion Cream: This fine textured microdermabrasion cream is to be used on either the face or body. Dermabrasion involves planing (smoothing) of the skin, as a physician sometimes does mechanically with fine sandpaper or wire brushes with an anesthetic of some sort. A cream is obviously a more comfortable means for achieving the desired effect and can be used at home. This product is excellent for skin truly resistant to other topical home treatments. It is also effective for age spots on the arms and legs. It works best when followed by the Peptide Body Lotion, and if the goal is to remove age spots, also use Fade Serum.

Peptide Body Lotion: This lotion consists of peptides for wrinkle control, rice bran for the wonderful B-vitamins, and other nutrients for smoother, moist skin.

Although New Youth products can be used separately, they are designed to be used as a system. As with any skin care products, the response in users varies. If you experience too much irritation initially or any other complaint such as mild acne, those initial reactions are a form of detoxification. People with the most damage or the most sensitive skin sometimes have the most vigorous adverse reactions to any topical treatment, including irritation and/or mild flaking. These reactions do not mean that you cannot continue using the product, but only that the application of the product must be altered if the problem becomes worrisome.

You may need to adjust the New Youth regimen in the following situations:

1. If you experience too much irritation with a product below, try any of the following modifications:

    Retinol Silk—Reduce application to once every other day for a while and then increase gradually.

    Activator—Rarely causes irritation, but reduce use for a few weeks if necessary.

    Personal Peel—This product will cause some irritation initially. If it is excessive, reduce application to once a week and then gradually increase. Some clients eventually use it every day, but I worry about too much exfoliation.

    Fade Serum—Rarely causes irritation. Reduce frequency of use if necessary.

2. If your skin is too oily, reduce the amount of the product used. This decrease may be necessary primarily with the moisturizer SPF 30 and in rare cases, the Anti-inflammatory Cream. Only a very small amount of product is necessary. Also, try using more Activator and/or Personal Peel.
3. On the other hand, if you only see minimal results, use more Activator and/or increase Retinol Silk to twice a day. Add the microdermabrasion cream to the regimen twice a week.

For pigmentation problems, the Fade Serum, Retinol Silk, and Activator are a combination necessary for optimal results.

Some of my patients and clients have been using these products almost since their introduction in 1996 and continue to use them daily. We continue improving the products as more is learned about cell stimulation and rejuvenation. This is our effort in an unending new frontier, which is what makes this project so interesting.

In a nutshell, for healthy, beautiful skin:

1. Limit your sun exposure
2. No smoking
3. Healthy living
    a. Diet—Limited simple carbohydrates.
        Lean protein intake with lots of fish for its Omega-3 oils.
        Limit your fat intake with no trans-fats, minimal saturated fats, and with lots of monosaturated fats and polyunsaturated fats.
        Eat lots of brightly colored vegetables and fruits.
        Stay away from refined foods whenever possible.
    b. Light to moderate exercise, which will be discussed in a later chapter.
    c. Nutritional supplements, also discussed in a later chapter.
4. Use proper skin care that attacks the core of the problem and not just appearance
5. Daily use of sunblock
6. Attention to hormonal imbalances

V

Exercise, Why and How

9 Exercise Programs for Age Reversal

Exercise is an essential ingredient in any age reduction and rejuvenation plan. Our next step in age reduction and creating a healthy lifestyle is finding an exercise program that works for you. The program you choose must fit your needs, personality, physical ability and goals, and it must take into consideration limitations you may have from physical injuries in your past as well as your current health status. Exercise related injuries are very common and are usually caused by trying to achieve too much too quickly or without proper warm-up. So you should exercise safely to avoid injuries.

Effective exercises are many and varied:

- Gardening is an excellent form of exercise.
- Walking, preferably fast with a light weight in each hand if possible
- Jogging is effective when combined with some stretching and resistance exercises.
- Exercise with videos or DVDs
- Aerobic classes
- Yoga
- Pilates
- Martial arts
- Swimming
- Hard-core weight lifting
- Tennis, racquet ball, basketball, or other group sports are also good exercise.
- Any combination of the above

If you have health problems or if exercising is new to you, consult your physician and possibly a professional personal trainer.

You must choose sports and exercises that are right for you, and these choices will change the more fit you become. Once you achieve a goal in a particular program, you may want to venture out into other worlds of physical fitness.

Most important is to record your progress in becoming physically fit. Check your weight, percent of body fat (usually done at a gym or fitness studio), strength, and how much improvement you are making toward your goal. Also, plan for each exercise day. This way you can add a small amount of weight or distance as appropriate for your plan.

It's important to know that you can improve muscle size, strength, stamina, and balance at any age. People in their eighties and even nineties can improve their physical condition dramatically. Our muscles and brain were meant to be used. Remember the old adage "use it or lose it?" Believe it about your physical and mental abilities, because it's true.

However, keep in mind that exercising with extreme intensity over a long period of time can cause symptoms of chronic fatigue. These signs will be fatigue, sore throat, mental slowness, slight loss of memory, insomnia, and increase in injuries. When exercising intensely, get more rest and sleep and make sound nutritional choices.

Simple rapid walking for thirty minutes a day improves cardiovascular function, blood pressure, and blood lipid profile (cholesterol HDL and LDL). Jogging would naturally increase the intensity of your exercise. It is harder on joints such as knees, hips, and back, however, but it would increase your cardiovascular fitness. By itself, walking gives one a good stretch, though jogging does not. In either case, do some gentle stretching, but especially do so with jogging. As we have seen throughout this book, moderation is the key to just about everything, so start slowly and work your way up.

Numerous exercise videos and DVDs are commercially available. Some of the highest-rated ones include the Firm series. Most of the Firm DVDs are excellent. They received high ratings for strength/toning. To purchase the DVDs, check www.firmdirect.com. Other good exercise videos are Kathy Smith's Functionally Fit Peak Fat Burning DVD and Kathy Smith's Kickboxing Workout. You may also want to try Tae Bo by Billy Banks. The Curves DVD is for women only. To purchase it, check www.curvesinternational.com. For The Blitz—check www.timetoblitz.com.

There are many good DVD's and tapes, but you can't go wrong with any of the above programs. Find the ones that better fit your needs and stick to them religiously.

For yoga and/or Pilates, you must seek out a class, individual instructor, or instructional DVD, but a personal trainer might be best to get you started. The problem with a class setting is that classes are designed to serve everyone at once, though we know that people differ widely, both in ability and in limitations. Often I have seen beginners start classes and try to keep up without knowing the right technique or true goals of the exercise. And I've rarely seen a class in which the participants really received enough individual attention. Classes are less expensive, however, so if that is your choice, please go at your own pace, and don't compare yourself to others.

As for yoga, don't simply try to get into the positions demonstrated by the instructor. The goal in yoga is to stretch muscles in each position so that you feel only the slightest tension. The stretches are coordinated with slow, relaxed breathing. This way the muscles don't react to too much tension or to movements performed too quickly, which may create a reflex rebound response causing the muscles to tighten. Do each yoga exercise gently whether in a class or using tapes. With proper yoga technique over a period of time, you will achieve better flexibility and strength without injury.

Martial arts classes provide a great workout, improved stamina, speed and strength and instruction in self-defense. With the martial arts you must visit each gym (called a dojo) and decide which one is right for you. I was involved in the martial arts beginning as a youth and have truly enjoyed it. It is an exciting frontier with so many different moves, weapons, and techniques. It does take time, however. Be sure to look for a class with students who are about your age.

Weight lifting ranges from simply doing resistance training to body building or power lifting. You have seen how resistance training has many benefits to the body, from increased strength and stamina to increased growth hormone. There are many home gyms—the Total Gym, Bowflex, and various universal gyms to name a few—and all are great, if you use them. It's also hard to beat a set of dumbbells and a table on which you can do a variety of exercises, in combination with elastic bands and floor exercises such as crunches and stretching.

For the lower abdomen, forget the usual crunches though. Routine crunches exercise your upper abdomen muscles and often make your lower abdomen push out even more. For a flat abdomen, it's best to do specific hip raises, which also raise your hips and legs. Keep the knees bent somewhat and focus on pressing the lower abdomen into the mat during the exercise. Tilt the hips forward then back to neutral position, and do not focus on raising the legs. The legs are just weight for the hip (or pelvis). Do this exercise on a mat with your hands under your buttocks to keep from hurting your back. Focusing on keeping the lower back flat against the mat is the key. Last, but not least, is an exercise ball. If you must do crunches, do them on an exercise ball. Many additional muscles must coordinate to keep your balance. Exercise balls are tremendously versatile. Try doing push-ups on the ball, and you will get the idea. As with the abdomen, many more balancing muscles are needed. Any store with a sporting good department sells exercise balls, and they come with instructions and sometimes instructional DVDs.

My favorite weight-lifting technique for strength and endurance, if you prefer weights, is to warm-up on all of your planned exercises, and then do three sets of each exercise. Begin with about twenty repetitions (reps); then do another set of twelve to fifteen. Then for a final set do about eight to ten repetitions, increasing the weight slightly with each set of reps. Go only for a very slight burn. If the weight becomes too easy, then with each exercise session increase the weight very slightly. Before long you will be lifting heavy weights with no injuries.

You can do a number of basic weight-lifting exercises. They include:

Chest Exercises

Push-ups—in addition to using your arms, also let your shoulders move forward when pushing yourself up. Keep your elbows in as much as possible to work the triceps muscles. One of my favorite techniques is to do push-ups on an exercise ball. This exercises all of the small balancing muscles as mentioned above. With push-ups you can only lift your body weight, but you can do more repetitions. Push-ups work more muscles (especially on an exercise ball), for example, the abdominal, leg, thigh, lower chest, and even neck muscles.

Flies—lie on your back on a table or exercise ball with a dumbbell in each hand held out to the side. Bring the weights upward and to the front, with arms somewhat straight. Do at least three sets; first with twenty reps, then with twelve to fifteen, finally with eight to ten reps. More reps with lighter weights allow your muscles and joints to warm up properly.

Bench presses—use the same three-set approach mentioned above. Bench presses can, however, be harmful to your shoulder rotator cuff. The trick to avoiding injury is not to allow your elbows to go behind you when bringing the weight back to the chest, and keep the weight low on your chest, toward your feet.

Arm Exercises

Triceps muscles—these are worked both with push-ups and bench presses. Think about how the triceps work, and you will understand this. Any arm extension against resistance works the triceps.

Bicep Muscles—these are exercised with back exercises (to be discussed next) and with arm curls. When doing curls, keep the proper form without jerking the weight up using your body, and keep your elbows in.

Back Exercises

Let's divide this into upper and lower back for descriptive purposes.

Lower back—face the weight machine, usually cables of some sort above and in front of you, and pull the handle toward you and downward. This exercise requires an apparatus higher than yourself. Both Bowflex and Total Gym have this apparatus available. Or simply do chin-ups. The main muscles you are working are the latissimus dorsi muscles, commonly called the "lats," and shoulder blade muscles.

Upper back—these muscles require you to pull weights straight toward you and from your front. An example would be to face toward a cable or weight machine. In either the sitting or standing position pull the weight toward you. Another exercise is to bend forward at the waist, and lift the weight from the floor out to your side like a reverse fly. If necessary you can rest one arm on the bench by exercising one arm at a time. Rowing is also an excellent back exercise.

Shoulder (Deltoid) Muscles

You can divide this exercise into those working the anterior (front) and posterior (rear) shoulder muscles. The rear part works more with the back muscle exercises and the front works more with the chest exercises. While standing, bring your dumbbells from your side straight out to the horizontal position. If you do this exercise while bending forward, you will strengthen the posterior deltoids; recline, and you will strengthen the pectoral muscles as well as the anterior deltoids.

Leg Exercises

Squats and lunges are thought to be the main exercises for the front of the thigh (quads). There is no need to do deep squats. The only additional thing deep squats may accomplish is an injured knee. A good alternative is the lunge. Basically, with or without weights, take a step forward and allow the forward knee to bend at ninety degrees, which works the quads (top of the thigh) and the buttocks. Then change legs. Some people walk across the room doing these lunges.

The rear of the thigh (hamstrings muscles) are more difficult to exercise, and you have to be innovative. While standing, attach a weight to one foot (strap devices are available), bend your knee, and do a curl bringing your foot toward your buttocks. Your local fitness stores may provide these straps.

As with the chest, arm, and back exercises, do three sets of leg exercises going from twenty reps down to fifteen, then eight to ten reps. With each set, use enough weight to cause only a slight burn.

If you want to build size, forget about limiting the burn and just do all you can do, period. However, you risk injury when lifting to your limit. When doing a set with fewer reps, you would require more weights and vice versa. If you work only to the slightest muscle burn, you can do all body parts about three times a week. You will then build muscle, balance, and stamina, and you will lose fat.

You can do aerobic exercises on the off days. Reserve at least one day a week for total rest from exercise. Listen to your body. If you are getting fatigued, have a sore throat, or feel you are not as mentally sharp, slow down or take a few days off.

A visit to the health food store for the supplements creatine and branched chain amino acids may be worth your time. These supplements help speed muscle recovery, and I have found they give me more strength with better endurance. Talk to your professional health food store management about these supplements.

My opinions regarding exercising come from about fifty years of exercising and lots of reading and first-hand experience with injuries. But many effective and very different plans are worth exploring. I encourage you to find the one that best suits you, but doing aerobic and resistance exercises should be part of your plan. Remember that resistance exercises also increase your growth hormone levels.

Health Benefits of Exercising

By Theodore M. Beiter, M.S., and Robert G. Lefavi, Ph.D., Armstrong Atlantic State University
Nutritional additions by E. Ronald Finger, M.D.

Although how you choose to exercise is up to you, exercise itself is a vital factor of reversing the aging processes of your body and mind. No discussion of slowing the aging process would be complete without assessing the effects of exercise on aging. Several diseases normally emerge during the aging process, and exercise has specific effects on them.

Preventable Diseases Associated with Aging

According to the Centers for Disease Control (CDC), a relatively small number of diseases account for a large percentage of deaths each year in the United States. The leading cause of death is diseases of the heart, including ischemia (lack of blood flow, usually due to a blocked artery) and thrombosis (weakening of a blood vessel wall causing a plaque and an associated blood clot). In fact, heart diseases accounted for nearly 30% of all deaths in 2001. Stroke, chronic lower respiratory diseases, diabetes, influenza, and hypertension accounted for another 18.3%. Combined, these maladies were responsible for nearly 50% of deaths in the US. These diseases not only threaten life itself, but they also contribute to poor quality of life and poor overall health. These diseases are more prevalent in older age groups, so as we age we are more likely to be diagnosed with one or more of them. Perhaps it is most appropriate to use the term "diseases of aging" to describe these problems.

Age is certainly not the only factor contributing to development of these life-threatening conditions. Nutrition, smoking, genetics, and amount of exercise all play a role. All these contributing factors, except of course genetics, respond to discipline and a solid desire to improve oneself, though exercise behavior may be the easiest to control.

The Primary Culprits

The CDC estimates that over 10% of the population suffers from heart disease. Certainly, some types of heart disease appear to have genetic origins and afflict young people, as about 4% of people aged eighteen to forty-four years old have some form of heart disease.

However, the incidence of heart disease increases with age, as evidenced by the fact that nearly 13% of people between the ages of forty-five and sixty-four have heart disease. Without question, however, adults in their later years feel the impact of heart diseases most. Those aged sixty-five to seventy-four make up one-quarter of all patients with diagnosed heart conditions, while those over seventy-five years old make up over one-third of this group. These data suggest that genetic predispositions are exacerbated by lifestyle choices, or that lifestyle contributes to heart disease. McGill and McMahan indicate that modified lifestyles, especially an increase in physical activity, have strongly reduced the incidence of heart disease over the last decade. The bottom line is that people who perform regular exercise are less likely to develop heart disease.

Cerebrovascular diseases, including stroke, are the third leading cause of death in the U.S. These diseases display a similar pattern to that of heart disease in that people are more likely to have strokes as they age. In fact, people over age seventy-five are twenty-seven times more likely to have strokes than those aged eighteen to forty-four. A recent article in the *Journal of Physical Education, Recreation and Dance* describes a study conducted by the Cooper Institute (a well-respected center for exercise research) demonstrating a connection between exercise and incidence of stroke. The researchers classified a group of older men into three levels based on fitness, as determined by a fitness test on a treadmill. The original group consisted of 16,878 men between the ages of forty and eighty-seven. These men were divided into three subgroups: high-fit, medium-fit, and low-fit. Within ten years of the original screening, thirty-two men died of stroke. Compared to the low-fit group, men in the medium-fit group were 65% less likely to die from stroke, while men in the high-fit group were 72% less likely to die from stroke. As with heart disease, people with a higher level of fitness were less likely to have a fatal stroke.

Diabetes

CDC statistics indicate that around 13.4 million adults have been diagnosed with diabetes. The American Diabetes Association (ADA) estimates that an additional five million people have diabetes but have not been diagnosed. Diabetes occurs in three types. Type 1 diabetes, often referred to as childhood-onset or juvenile diabetes, occurs when a person produces too little insulin or none at all. It accounts for only 5% to 10% of all cases of diabetes. Type 2 diabetes, often called adult-onset diabetes, occurs when the body's cells become resistant or intolerant to insulin, as discussed under carbohydrates in Chapters 2 and 5. In Type 2 diabetes when one becomes insulin resistant, the blood insulin level remains elevated, encouraging free radical production, glycation, and cell damage that further result in many health problems mentioned in Chapter 2 under Glycation and Free Radicals and Antioxidants. The third type of diabetes is gestational diabetes, which occurs when blood glucose levels become abnormally high during pregnancy. The ADA estimates that about 4% of pregnant women experience this problem.

Insulin transports glucose into cells. Glucose is one of the main sources of energy in cells. Without it, cells may not have enough energy to survive. Problems occur in diabetics in part because glucose levels build up in the blood when glucose is not transported into cells by adequate amounts of insulin. Damage to the eyes, kidneys, nerves, and/or heart may occur over time if blood glucose levels remain high. In all three types of diabetes, cells do not receive enough glucose to function normally. Diabetes itself contributes to other life-threatening problems such as heart disease, kidney disease, stroke, and high blood pressure. The ADA estimates that the risk of premature death doubles in people with diabetes. As with other chronic disorders, the incidence of diabetes and diabetes-related problems increases with age. For example, people between the ages of twenty-five and sixty-four are almost five times more likely to have diabetes than are people eighteen to twenty-four years old. Those aged sixty-five to seventy-four are diagnosed eight times more often than people in this younger age group. Diabetes occurs less often among active people. Exercise can help mediate the effects of diabetes by controlling blood glucose levels and reducing insulin intolerance.

In another condition related to diabetes, something the ADA terms pre-diabetes, blood glucose levels rise above normal but do not reach the very high levels typical of diabetes. The ADA estimates that forty-one million Americans have pre-diabetes. Although not every one of these individuals will develop diabetes, these people are probably already damaging their cardiovascular systems. Controlling blood sugar during pre-diabetes may prevent the development of type 2 diabetes. In two experimental studies, increased levels of exercise combined with dietary changes were the most effective ways of preventing or delaying the onset of type 2 diabetes.

The term diabetes is usually reserved for patients who require some type of medical treatment. However, many variations of the disease exist. For example, some patients experience elevated blood sugar and insulin levels only after meals and snacks. In other words, these individuals have abnormally high blood sugar levels for only a few hours each day. Hence, the unfortunate statistics of diabetes would also apply to these people, but to a lesser degree. Diabetes, like heart disease, stroke, and other age- and lifestyle-related diseases, is therefore usually caused in large part by the choices we make. Our goal in this chapter is to offer you the knowledge and encouragement to enjoy a healthy lifestyle and avoid or delay these serious age-related diseases.

Exercise and Diseases of Aging

What we see from the available research is that physical activity reduces the occurrence of three of the top ten leading causes of death in the United States. It is likely that exercise also reduces the incidence and/or severity of several of the other top killers, including cancer, Alzheimer's disease, influenza, and chronic lower respiratory infections. In one twenty-year study, overall mortality declined with increasing levels of physical fitness. Despite overwhelming evidence that exercise reduces the risk of chronic diseases, statistics from the CDC show a decline in physical activity with age. Interestingly, these declining exercise rates closely mirror the increasing rates of heart disease, stroke, and diabetes identified in the National Health Interview Survey conducted in 2002. So, a link exists between disease and age, namely that as we age we are more likely to develop a chronic disease. Another connection exists between exercise and chronic disease, namely that individuals who exercise regularly are less likely to develop chronic diseases. Regular exercise not only helps prevent chronic diseases, but also greatly improves quality of life and overall health.

Quality of Life as We Age

Though considerable research has confirmed the beneficial effect of regular exercise on the quality of life, one must ask the important question, What is good quality of life? It is not just the absence of chronic diseases, and it is not simply an objective measure of physical abilities or independence. Objective measures cannot be the only thing used to gauge life quality, because different people have different values, resilience, and emotional capacity. Health, however, seems to be one of the objective factors affecting quality of life, especially in cases where health problems interfere with daily function. Still, daily function is not the only factor to think about when considering health and quality of life. The complex factors influencing quality of life make measuring it a largely subjective endeavor, as we each assess life quality according to our own needs and values. Therefore, many studies have collected data using self-assessment surveys and have identified an important connection between quality of life and exercise. W. Jack Rejeski, Ph.D. and Shannon L Mihalko, Ph.D. evaluated many studies and summarized their findings. They found that for many older adults, participating in physical activity improved life satisfaction. In fact, participating regularly in fun activities seemed to have the strongest connection to happiness. To be most beneficial to health, the activity should also have a tangible benefit, such as social interaction. For example, taking part in a group activity such as a class or planned outing provides even more satisfaction for most people. Rejeski and Mihalko also found that regular physical activity improved people's perceptions of how well their bodies were performing—another major factor in quality of life.

So, to maintain a regular routine of physical activity that improves your quality of life, find a kind of exercise that you enjoy, since fun activities and good group interactions help you stay with your exercise program. A third factor that encourages consistent exercise is regular feedback—that is, when exercise is fun, that fun experience itself increases our quality of life.

Exercise and Overall Health as We Age

Unlike the subjectiveness of quality of life, overall health can be measured objectively. Overall health includes absence of disease, absence or control of symptoms associated with disease, and the ability to function normally and independently. In addition to preventing and controlling chronic, life-threatening conditions such as heart disease and diabetes, exercise promotes excellent overall health by helping people function normally and feel independent.

As changes occur in our bodies as we age, muscular strength, balance, and disease-fighting capabilities all decrease. Due to these and other physiological factors, injuries, mental health disorders, infections, and other health problems all happen more often as we age.

In a recent article, the American College of Sports Medicine (ACSM) described the relation between exercise and aging. The paper focused on areas of aging that can be directly influenced by exercise. The ACSM concluded that regular exercise effectively prevents or controls many diseases and disabilities associated with aging and slows the normal decline accompanying the aging process. In addition, the ACSM points out that the health benefits of exercise can occur before changes in weight or body composition become apparent.

Regular physical activity has many very favorable physical effects on our bodies. Endurance or aerobic training gives us better cardiovascular function, some important measures of which are called VO2max, cardiac output, and the arteriovenous oxygen differential (the difference between the oxygen level in the artery and vein). All three of these important cardiovascular measures are significantly improved by regular aerobic exercise. VO2max is the maximum amount of oxygen used by the body in one minute. It gives us important information because oxygen is essential for the aerobic production of energy (aerobic means "with oxygen"), which is the main way our bodies create energy during daily activities. Cardiac output measures the volume of blood pumped by the heart in one minute, and the arteriovenous oxygen differential tells us how effectively muscles use oxygen delivered to them by the cardiovascular system. In general, an increase in VO2max, cardiac output, or the arteriovenus oxygen differential indicates an increase in maximal cardiovascular performance—that is, the heart becomes stronger and more efficient! Increases in maximal cardiovascular performance are accompanied by an increase in a related measure called submaximal performance—that is, for any given workload the percent of maximum is less.

So, what does all this scientific gibberish mean? It means that someone with a low VO2max will have shortness of breath while climbing stairs or walking some distance before a person with a higher VO2max. Increases in cardiovascular performance carry with them a reduced risk of chronic diseases like heart disease, diabetes, and hypertension.

Additional good news is that resistance training (weight training) slows the loss of muscle mass and strength associated with aging. Other benefits of endurance and resistance training include improved bone strength and postural stability. Stronger bones reduce the occurrence of osteoporosis, while improved strength and postural stability reduce the likelihood of falls. Together, stronger bones and fewer falls result in fewer fractures and surgeries.

Improved mental ability, lower rates of depression, and higher self-esteem are all associated with regular exercise as well.

Exercise and Heart Function

What happens if you just diet and hope for the effects of good genes? Not much. Cardiovascular function improves only with regular exercise, and the aging process itself has the opposite effect on cardiovascular performance. In fact, VO2max decreases between 5% and 10% per decade of life after age thirty. In a comprehensive study performed by Bortz and Bortz, the decline in VO2max averaged 0.5% every year from age thirty-five to age sixty, and after age sixty-five it declined rapidly. This decline in VO2max results from a lower cardiac output and the smaller arteriovenous O2 differential associated with aging. Cardiac output declines because the maximum heart rate (the number of beats the heart can make per minute) and stroke volume decline. Stroke volume (the amount of blood pumped with each heartbeat) declines with age because of age-related reductions in blood volume and in additional measures called early ventricular filling, ejection fraction, and left ventricular contractility. These reductions in cardiac function are not just an explanation of why we do not see octogenarians competing in the Olympics, but they also have implications for everyone during normal lifetime activities.

A reduction in cardiac stroke volume means that the heart must contract more times per minute to produce the same amount of blood flow. Every year after age twenty-five our maximum heart rate declines by about one beat per minute. The associated decrease in stroke volume and lower maximum heart rate mean that the heart must operate at a higher percentage of maximum cardiovascular function to achieve a certain goal. This situation is exacerbated by the increase in blood pressure that most people experience with age.

So the bottom line is that the heart must work harder as we get older. Therefore, compared to a younger heart, an older heart works much harder to deliver adequate blood for daily activity. For example, a healthy twenty-five-year-old woman may require a heart rate of ninety beats per minute to accomplish her holiday shopping. That would be approximately 45% of her maximum heart rate. Her fifty-year-old mother might require the same amount of cardiac output to do her holiday shopping, but will need a heart rate of ninety-five beats per minute, or 56% of her maximum heart rate. The mother would therefore be using a higher percentage of her maximum heart rate. Aging results in lower maximum cardiovascular function, but a higher percent of maximum function for any given workload.

It is also important to realize that body weight and percent body fat tend to increase with age and those increases correspond with higher levels of disease. The good news is that regular endurance training can reduce body weight and our percent body fat. Reducing the body fat increase associated with aging also reduces fat inside the abdomen—the kind of fat most associated with increased heart disease.

Finally, regular exercise (even to a light to moderate degree) lowers blood pressure. Also, high-density lipoproteins (HDL the good cholesterol) increase, while triglycerides and low-density lipoproteins (LDL, the bad cholesterol) decrease, creating a more favorable ratio of HDL to LDL.

Hit the Weights: The Benefits of Resistance Training

We've briefly mentioned the benefits of weight training, but how does hitting the gym really help? Lack of regular strength training causes a decline in muscle mass associated with aging. Older individuals tend to have smaller, less dense muscles and higher levels of intramuscular fat. This loss of muscle mass and the associated loss in strength relates to a decrease in physical function and impairment of daily activities. The ACSM considers a slower walk and inability to lift an object weighing ten pounds as significant impairments to daily activity. Muscle loss results from two causes. First, many older individuals do not eat enough protein and so do not consume the amino acids necessary to repair and maintain muscle mass. Second, without regular use, muscles do not absorb amino acids, even if they are present in the diet. Furthermore, resistance exercise increases our growth hormone levels, which makes us more muscular and leaner.

In addition to reducing daily function, loss of muscle mass and strength indirectly causes a higher risk of heart disease and diabetes. The reason this is true is that this decline of muscle mass and strength causes a decline of lean body mass (muscle tissue), which reduces the resting metabolic rate. This lower metabolic rate along with reduced activity levels results in increased body weight and the percent of body fat. Higher body weight and increased body fat strongly predict heart disease. Other problems related to lower lean body mass are lower bone density, lower insulin sensitivity, and lower aerobic capacity. These changes are associated with osteoporosis, diabetes, and cardiovascular disease, respectively.

So, poor physical conditioning is a vicious cycle in which every body part that is out of harmony negatively affects every other part.

Through strength training, you can increase your lean body mass, thus increasing your resting metabolic rate. An increase in lean body mass also promotes greater functional independence and a lower rate of chronic diseases, trends opposite of those generally associated with aging. Research by K. E. Yaresheski indicates that, with exercise, rates of muscle mass increase are similar for younger and older people because increased muscle mass allows more efficient use of ingested amino acids. If you add endurance training, the increase in lean body mass causes an increase in resting metabolic rate. Again, the end result is a lower body weight and percent body fat, though in some cases body weight may in fact increase, as muscle weighs more than fat. At any rate, regular exercise can greatly improve body composition. Weight training also increases insulin usage and decreases the risk of osteoporosis by increasing activity level, muscle mass, dynamic strength, and bone density.

Exercise, Aging, and Mobility

Regular exercise training can help with postural stability, which helps us avoid falls. Researchers have found that postural stability declines steadily with age and that this decline corresponds with an increase in falls as we get older. Inactivity and age are not the only factors that decrease postural stability. Medications, vision, environment, postural hypotension (low blood pressure upon standing), and changing cognitive status all contribute to falls. Regardless, individuals who exercise regularly fall less often, and are less often injured if they do fall.

One component of postural stability is balance. Good balance requires constant sensory input and muscular adjustments to maintain a position. Studies have shown that practicing Tai Chi significantly improves balance among older adults compared to those who do not exercise. In fact, a couple of minutes a day standing on one foot also improves balance. More time spent doing these activities is always better.

Joint flexibility is another important benefit of regular exercise. Flexibility depends on bone, muscle, and connective tissue strength, which diminishes with age. Exercise counteracts this age-related diminishment in flexibility by increasing strength of the bone, muscle, and connective tissue. Two areas in which flexibility tends to decline with age are the knees and hips. In a survey of more than 800 men over age sixty, exercise was associated with a reduced incidence of knee osteoarthritis and knee replacement surgery. That means men who exercised regularly at some point in their lives were less likely to have knee osteoarthritis and knee replacement surgery. Regular exercise therefore seems to have a positive effect on flexibility.

Exercise, Aging, and Mental Function

Regular exercise improves more than physical health. Although the connection is clear between exercise and reduced risk of conditions like heart disease and diabetes, studies have shown us that regular physical activity also improves cognitive function, reduces symptoms of depression, and increases perceptions of control and self-esteem. One possible explanation for this connection is that improved cardiovascular function maintains an adequate supply of oxygen to the brain.

The connection between exercise and prevention of depression is well established, as studies have shown that people who exercise regularly experience fewer depressive symptoms. In some of these studies, depressive symptoms decreased in people who began exercising and increased among those who stopped exercising. This connection is relevant because the incidence of depression increases with age. Findings of a study by Dimeo show that walking thirty minutes per day reduces depressive symptoms. In fact, in this small study, eight out of twelve people diagnosed with depression reduced their symptoms by walking every day for a ten-day period. Impressively, five of the twelve reduced their depression symptoms so effectively that they were no longer considered clinically depressed. A regular exercise program therefore improves flexibility, strength, postural stability, and overall health, all of which improve people's sense of having control over their lives. One side effect of regular exercise that may reduce depressive symptoms is that it increases our feelings of self-control. Participation in an exercise program is voluntary, so people who exercise are exerting control over their own lives. This sense of control in part contributes to better mental health.

Overall, aging is associated with decreased physical function and mental health and an increased risk of illness. Increased activity levels counteract these effects of aging and can reduce or delay age-related illnesses. As we mentioned, the factors causing these declines in health may be genetic or environmental and therefore out of our control, but other essential contributing factors are the numerous lifestyle choices discussed throughout these chapters. Certainly, one of the most important choices you can make is choosing a healthful level of physical activity.

VI

Plastic Surgery

10 Relationship Between Plastic Surgery and Our Health

Total body health and appearance cannot be separated. A person who looks better also feels better and is more attentive to his or her health. What could be more discouraging than looking into the mirror and thinking, "Who is that old (or overweight) person?" Thoughtfully conceived and performed plastic surgery can help correct certain problems. For me, there is nothing like seeing elated patients thrilled with their new appearances. Typically, they become interested in nutrition, supplements, exercise, and often life itself.

Plastic surgery has been the rage in some countries in South America for decades. In Argentina, for example, people often walk around with nose splints and facial bruising, and in Brazil plastic surgeons are on almost every block in some areas. So what about the United States? I can remember when people considering plastic surgery wanted total anonymity. Once, early in my career, two women in their fifties came to me from another city, each wanting a facelift. You may find this hard to believe, but they told their husbands that they were going on a cruise. When they returned, they told me that their husbands said the cruise did them so much good they should go on one every year!

All this secrecy is now history, and it seems as if almost every magazine has some article on the subject. These days we have television shows devoted entirely to plastic surgery, although some have little relationship to reality. Also the Baby Boomers are not ready to look or feel their age. I don't blame them—neither am I. The problem is that there is almost a plastic surgery frenzy now, and people must understand several considerations completely before making changes for aesthetic reasons.

- Not all plastic surgery is necessary.
- Not all plastic surgery is done well.
- Plastic surgery must be tailored to the patient and not the other way around.
- There is no place for assembly-line surgery.
- Poorly conceived plastic surgery can be much worse than no plastic surgery at all.

- Complications can and do happen occasionally. There are risks involved.
- It is the patient's obligation to learn about a desired procedure, so that he or she can have some input in various decisions.

On the other hand, the results of excellent plastic surgery are so uplifting that they can completely alter your self-esteem and confidence. It's impossible to put a value on that. How can we get that feeling? First, you must know your options and which one fits you, what to expect, what to do to find a good plastic surgeon, and how you can personally affect your results.

Just what is plastic surgery? To clear up a point, there are actually some people who think it has something to do with plastic! Well, the word *plastic* comes from the Greek word *plastikos*, meaning something like *change in form* or *to mold.* Plastic surgery began as reconstructive surgery for cancer, war injuries, burns, and birth defects. Over time it expanded to include aesthetic or cosmetic surgery. You might consider aesthetic surgery as a type of antiaging surgery or age-reversing surgery, as well as pure cosmetic surgery, such as breast augmentation or meloplasty (facelift).

Regarding cosmetic (aesthetic) or age-reversing surgery, my first goal (and that of any excellent plastic surgeon) when patients consult me is to ask about their particular problems. Then I describe to them what physical changes we can expect with surgery or nonsurgical treatment and with age if we live long enough—after all, living as long and well as possible is the plan. My next step is to explain the various options that can bring about their desired changes. The problems are often what surgical candidates have disliked about themselves since the day they first looked in a mirror.

FIGURE 10-1. Female age 20 to 30. Minimal wrinkles, sagging, or deflation.

What do we see with increasing age? Typical changes with age are summarized in Figures 10-1 to 10-5. Note the changes between ages twenty to thirty and fifty to sixty, especially the volumes or shape of the face. In youth, our lower face is V-shaped, but as we get older it becomes more square. Note the more rapid changes seen in the smoker in Figure 10-4.

Figure 10-2. Female age thirty to forty. Patient develops a few wrinkles around the lids. The first stages of a nasolabial fold and tear trough is seen. Early age-spots begin to appear. See Figure 10-6 for description of terms.

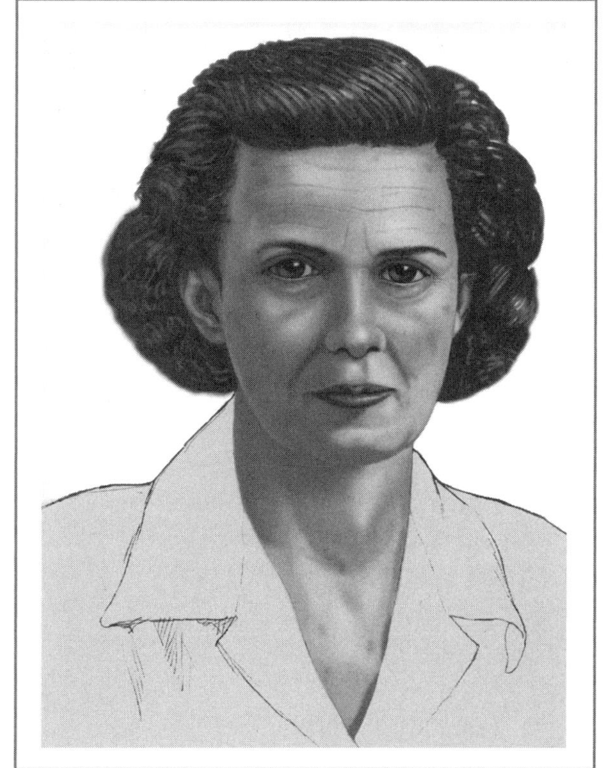

Figure 10-3. Female age forty to fifty. More perioral and periorbital wrinkles appear, and the tear trough starts about this time. The face begins to shift downward.

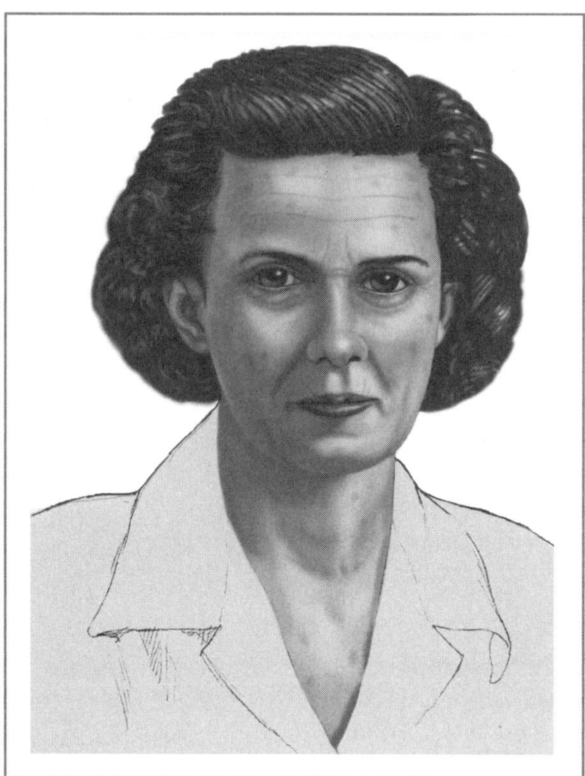

FIGURE 10-4. Female age forty to fifty, smoker, excess sun. All signs of aging increase, especially the wrinkles around the mouth. Elasticity decreases causing more sagging.

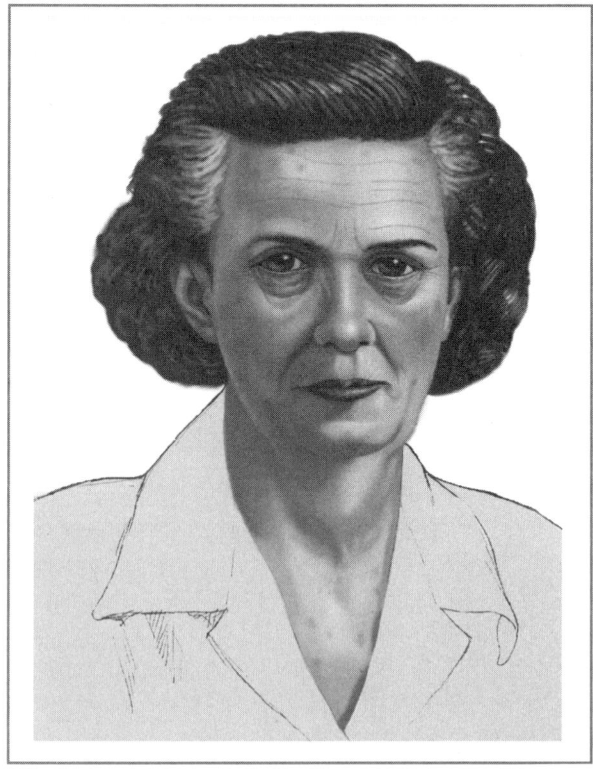

FIGURE 10-5. Female age fifty to sixty. The lower face becomes more square. The neck sags and the jowls increase in severity. The "cheek-bones" become smaller, and the middle part of the face deflates.

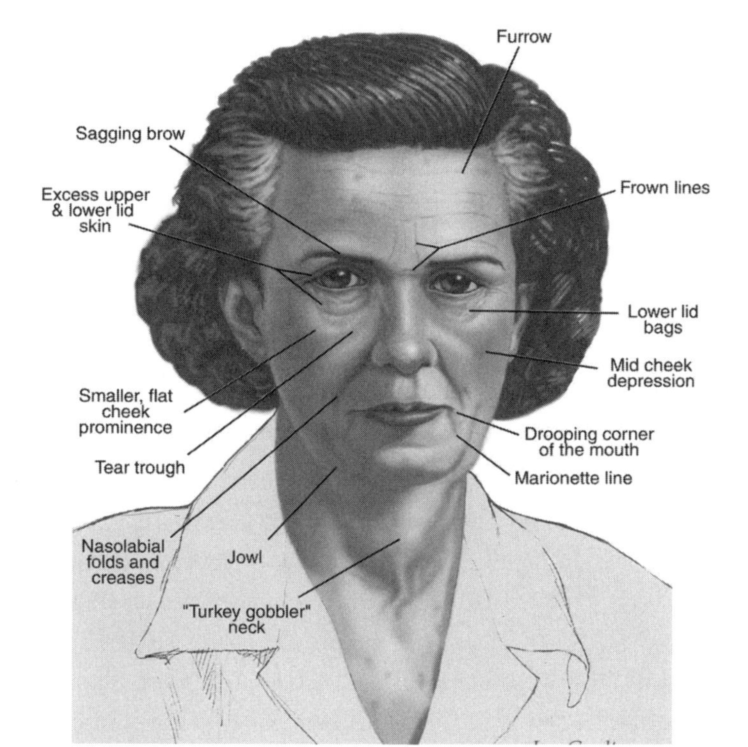

FIGURE 10-6. Various terms of aging are identified as follows:

Forehead furrows
Frown lines
Upper and lower eyelid wrinkles and excess skin
Lower lid fat pads (bags)
Tear trough
Cheekbone (malar protuberance)
Infraorbital depression (hollow under the eyes)
Mid-cheek depression
Nasolabial fold and crease
Sagging oral commissure (corner of the mouth)
Marionette lines
"Turkey gobbler"
Jowl

Because of the effects of sun damage, smoking, and the results of other forms of environmental hazards (and let's not forget gravity), our appearance will age and may age more than we expect. The body's hormonal system also strongly influences shape and appearance, as do frequent up-and-down changes in weight.

All these factors, including aging itself, cause actual changes in the various masses or volumes of our faces, which in turn change the shapes of our faces as well as our bodies. Think about this. Sagging is not just because of loss of elasticity. As we age, the fat in our face diminishes and our skin loses its support and thus sags. And muscle atrophies. That may sound terrible, but if you understand the process, it's a little easier to explain what needs to be corrected. In addition, because of hormonal changes, glycation, and muscle activity (for example, facial expression), volumes change. The facial fat actually loses volume, mostly from muscle activity. Unfortunately, we gain fat in the body.

Regarding the face and neck, the drooping from volume loss actually pulls the skin of the face down. The volume in a more youthful cheek area is higher, thicker, and larger in diameter. Over time, this volume becomes thinner and smaller and the lower part of this cheek mass diminishes, leaving a depression in the middle of the cheek (the mid-cheek depression). Some of drooped volume becomes the jowl, which everyone hates with a great passion. Some of this volume also moves into the nasolabial fold. In fact, most patients who seek consultation for facelifts complain, "I hate my jaw line (jowl)." "Can you also do something about my turkey gobbler neck?" And, "What about correcting these creases?" pointing to their nasolabial creases and folds. (Please refer to Figures 10-1 to 10-6).

The crow's feet just lateral to the eyes and frown lines are also high on the list of complaints, as are the horizontal forehead furrows. Other less conspicuous age changes often go unnoticed until a plastic surgeon points them out, and then the response is usually, "Yes, fix that, too."

The youthful fullness of the cheeks under the lower eyelids gravitates downward, as do most changing bodily structures over time, leaving the space between the eyelid and the cheek much wider than before, creating hollowness under the eyes. This depression extends into a dark shadow obliquely across the cheek and is called the "tear trough." As you can see, the sagging face is much more than just sagging skin from loss of elasticity. It is important to reinflate these lost areas of fullness during a facelift in order to achieve a natural, youthful-looking face. We do so by repositioning the droopy fat to its original place. In addition, the patient's own fat may be grafted (transferred) from other places to re-volumize the deflated areas, or products like Sculptra and other fillers (discussed below) may be used.

It's not enough simply to tighten the neck and remove or liposuction the jowl. That can make the patient look "face-lifted," pulled, and even older as features flatten out under too much skin tension. The look thus created comes especially from just tightening or over-tightening the skin (or the wrong layers of the skin) and expecting this procedure to move the volumes back to their youthful positions.

These fat areas, masses or pads, must be directly suspended back to their original youthful areas. Lifting these masses brings the skin up without making it look stretched. In many cases, the face only needs fat-grafting or injections with one of the fillers, such as Sculptra, Perlane, Juvederm, or Restylane, without actual surgery.

Although plastic surgery is an effective antiaging strategy, please understand these words of wisdom:

1. No one needs plastic surgery or cosmetic surgery. It's your choice. Don't let the doctor or anyone else talk you into it. With few exceptions, surgery will not save a marriage or a job or make someone who knows you like you more—not for long, anyway. It can, however, instill self-esteem and make you like yourself more, provided you don't have psychological or emotional issues preventing that from happening, in which case a psychiatrist may be helpful.
2. Plastic surgery has limitations. Talk to your plastic surgeon about these limitations realistically. A natural-looking facelift will take about ten years or more off your appearance. A very crooked nose will not usually become perfectly straight. Asymmetrical breasts will not usually become perfectly even. Not very wrinkle disappears.
3. Plastic surgery does not stop the clock. When someone asks, "How long is my facelift good for?" I usually say, "Would you believe forever?" The patient's answer is always "No." But it does. If I take ten years off your face, at ninety you will look about eighty years old (probably younger). One very nice woman asked me if she would need another facelift in the future. I said, "You are sixty now, and I will probably make you look about fifty. When you are seventy and you look sixty, I doubt if you will like it then any more than you like looking sixty now." She laughed and scheduled her surgery. Results vary from person to person, as some people may even look twenty years younger while some will look less than ten years younger. But the important feature to request is to look natural, if that is what is important to you. Actually, I have had an occasional patient who actually wants to look tight, pulled, and "facelifted." Personally, I find this appearance unnatural and unattractive, but you must discuss your own preferences with your plastic surgeon. It is you who must be made happy, not your plastic surgeon.
4. People often look like monsters for a few days or even weeks after plastic surgery. Expect it. You will see bruised, swollen eyes, faces, necks, abdomens, and breasts according to what was done. You will wonder why in the world you underwent surgery. You may get depressed and may develop "cabin fever." Be patient and listen to your surgeon when he or she discusses the postsurgical course.
5. You will have to refrain from smoking before and after any type of flap work—for example, a face lift, a tummy lift, or breast reduction or uplift. This means zero! Not a single cigarette. And you should also avoid passive smoke. Discuss this matter with your surgeon, as it is very important.

6. Some medications make you bleed excessively. More bleeding means longer recovery, more bruising, or possibly a hematoma (an accumulation of blood). Stay off these medications for at least two weeks (I prefer three weeks for my patients prior to and one week after surgery). Most of these medications are anti-inflammatory agents, and some are foods and herbs, such as:
   a. Aspirin or aspirin-containing products. (Ask your pharmacist or doctor which products contain aspirin.)
   b. Ibuprofen (Motrin, Advil, etc.)
   c. Aleve, Naprosyn
   d. Omega-3 oils, fish oils
   e. Salmon, tuna, mackerel
   f. Vitamin E or multivitamins containing vitamin E
   g. Herbs such as ginkgo biloba, ginseng, garlic and many more. To be safe, stop using all herbs.

For aches and pain, take Tylenol and/or glucosamine. You may also take Celebrex, Darvocet, Ultram, or Ultracet, which are prescription medications. However, do not take Ultram or Ultracet if you are also taking a serotonin reuptake inhibitor antidepressant such as Prozac, Zoloft, etc., as this combination may cause grand mal seizures. Always note precautions on medication bottles.

Finally, be careful not to put yourself in the hands of a plastic surgeon who is excessively self-oriented, that is, he or she claims to be the best and no one else knows how to do anything properly. Also be wary of a plastic surgeon who has faced multiple lawsuits and has had several adverse verdicts. Ask to see pre- and postoperative photos of previous cases with the same problem as yours that were handled by the doctor you are considering having operate on you. And make sure he or she is certified by the American Board of Plastic Surgery. Get second opinions. Do your homework diligently!

Some of the following discussions about specific techniques are technical and may be a bit tedious reading, so if you have no interest in a chapter pertaining to a specific procedure, then skip over it and go on to the next chapter that does interest you. However, all the procedures have similarities. For instance, they all involve planning, cutting, sewing, bleeding, bruising and recovery time—with the exception of non-surgical procedures.

11 Eyelid Lift (Blepharoplasty)

The following format will be used for all procedures:

Age
Physical Problems of Aging
Expectations
Treatment Techniques
Limitations
Postoperative Course

Age

Some people have congenital hooding of the eye and are candidates for an upper lid blepharoplasty as early as twenty years old. Those with average eyelids who are attuned to their appearance began to notice a need for a lift in the mid to late forties. However, another group of people will wait until their sixties when they find that their upper lids actually rest upon their lashes. Any of these people would benefit from this surgery. The oldest patient on whom I can remember performing a blepharoplasty was in her late eighties, and the youngest was twenty-one.

Physical Problems of Aging

The aging problem we see with the upper lids is excess skin, fat, and sometimes looseness of the orbicularis muscle that encircles the eye area. Upper lids can differ widely from one person to another and thus must be treated on an individual basis.

Lower lids have different problems. They have excess skin, but not as much as in the upper lids. Mild to profound "bags" may appear within the lower lids. These bags are actually herniated fat located in three separate pockets. Finally, the edge of the lower lid at the lashes itself may sag, turn out, or droop, a condition called an ectropion, which occurs in older patients, often those with lots of sun exposure. It's usually worse among men. Ectropion must be surgically corrected and can be difficult to repair. The problem ultimately causes dry eyes from excess exposure to the air because of inadequate eye coverage by the upper and lower lids, as these are now further apart in addition to inadequate tear production. In some cases, the lower lid actually turns outward and the inside of the lid becomes dry as well. This problem warrants special attention when doing a lower lid lift because ectropion may occur from the procedure itself due to excess skin removal or excess bleeding, or temporarily because of postoperative swelling.

Expectations

Upper Lids: Excess skin will be removed, but some smaller wrinkles must remain or the eye will not close. The surgeon will establish a crease about 1/3 of an inch above the lashes (the supratarsal crease), which is a desired feature. Fullness above this crease should be reduced.

Lower Lids: Expect fewer wrinkles, but the area will not be as smooth as the upper lids. The procedure should reduce or eliminate under-eye bags and improve, sometimes dramatically, dark circles below the lower eyelid. People talk to your eyes, not your face. An eyelid lift alone in the proper patient can make a person look dramatically better and younger (see Photo 11-1 and 11-2).

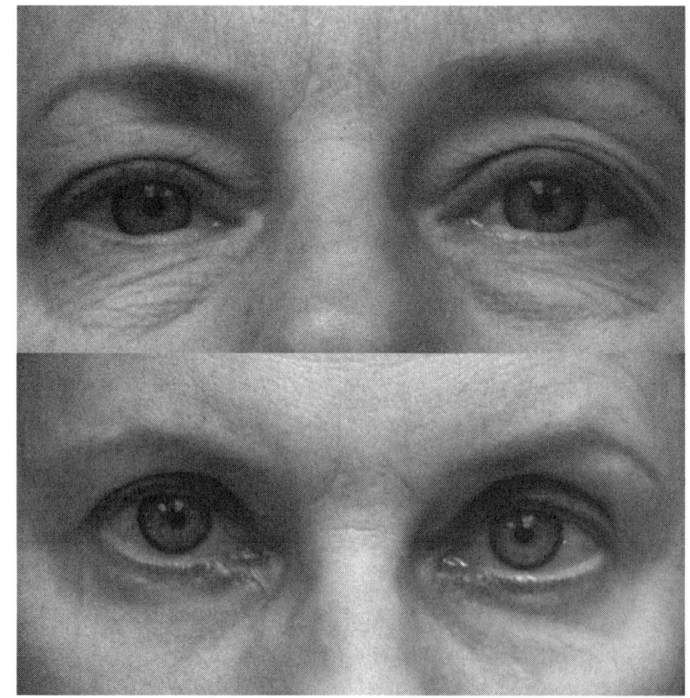

PHOTO 11-1. Before and after photos of a patient after upper and lower lid blepharoplasty. Note the main problem was the redundant skin in her upper lids. She also had minimal fat pockets in her lower lids as well as some extra skin, both of which were corrected.

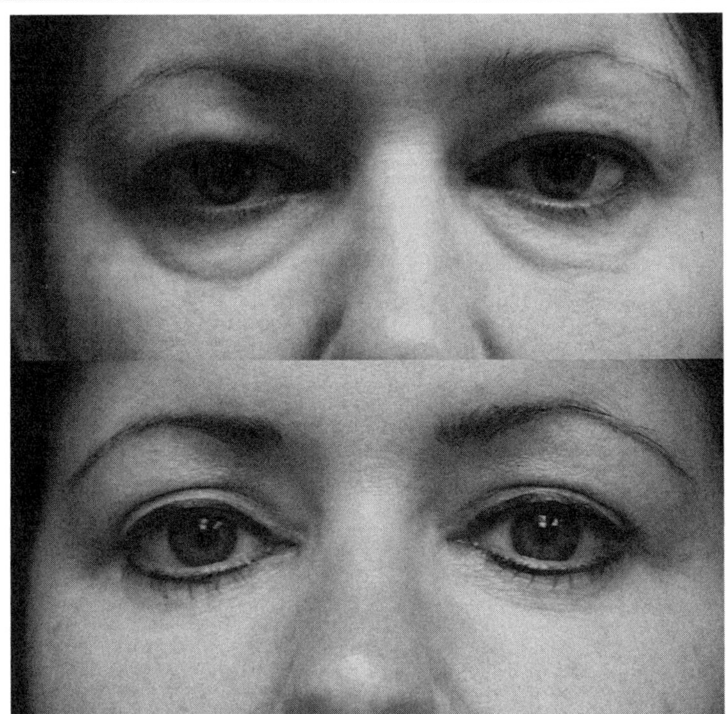

PHOTO 11-2. Before and after photos of a patient who underwent an upper and lower lid blepharoplasty. Her problem was excessive skin of the upper lids to the point that it rested on her lashes. Also she had significant extra fat pockets and skin in her lower lids. Note the natural appearance of her eyelids postoperatively.

Treatment Techniques

Upper Lid Surgery (Figure 11-1): This requires only a simple description because there is little controversy about how this procedure is performed. Some surgeons will make the incision with a carbon dioxide laser, while others prefer to use a scalpel. I have used both and found no difference in the outcome, except that the laser takes longer to perform. Theoretically, the laser should create a little less swelling postoperatively, which may save you a day or so of recovery time, but the laser also leaves no room for error. I prefer the scalpel, as it offers a little resistance to the surgeon's hand, allowing more control. I recommend carrying the incision out beyond the lateral edge of the eyelids, as illustrated in Figure 11-1. Otherwise, drooping of the eyelid occurs below the outer part of the eyebrow.

For very fine wrinkles without much excess skin, your surgeon may prefer to use a CO2 or Erbium laser as a resurfacing tool without making an incision, though I have found that this method requires a longer recovery period and is not adequate in patients with lots of excess skin, though the skin does shrink

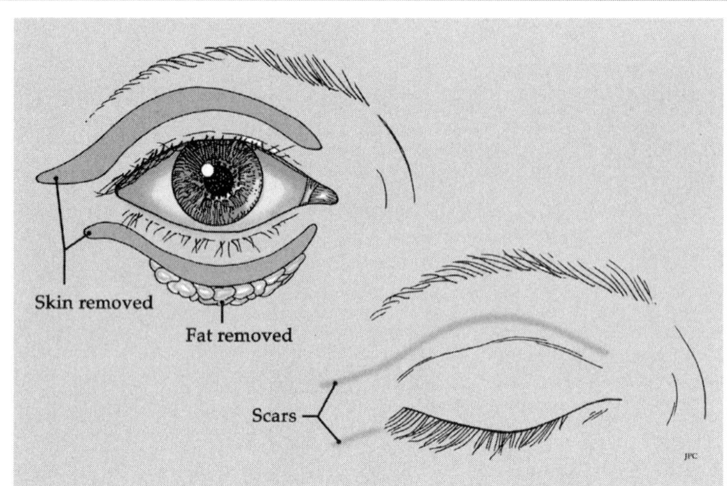

FIGURE 11-1. The figure on the left represents the skin and fat to be removed. Often a strip of underlying muscle is also removed.

somewhat. The Fraxel Laser requires less recovery, but necessitates several treatments and there is a limit to how much skin will be removed.

Lower Lid Surgery: This procedure is not as simple as the upper-lid blepharoplasty. Surgeons must take great care not to remove too much skin, as this applies too much tension to the lower lid and may pull the lower lid down into an ectropion (a lower lid that has been pulled too low and turns outward). Typically, the surgeon makes the incision in the skin just below the lashes, extending outward from the corner of the eye for about 1/4 inch or so (Figure 11-1).

For removal of fat pads (the bags) only, without skin removal, the surgeon may make the incision inside the lid with a scalpel or carbon dioxide (CO2) laser. I prefer to create the incision with the laser in the lower lid. The incision inside the eyelid, called a "trans-conjunctival" approach (the conjunctiva is the lining inside of the lid), is preferable in the younger patient with bags but very few wrinkles due to excess skin.

If there is significant excess skin in addition to under-eye bags, the skin must be removed through the described skin incision just below the lashes. The surgeon then makes a small hole through the underlying muscle and removes the excess fat, usually from all three pockets. Also, if necessary, the surgeon can spread the fat out and suture it into the tear trough (see Figure 10-6), which is the dark circle area under the lower lid. If this is done, it also gives an appearance of a slight facelift centrally, as if the cheek were moved upward slightly. For a very deep tear trough, the surgeon may add a silicone implant (no, it isn't harmful) to this area, resulting in a dramatic improvement for some patients. Alternative procedures to fill the tear trough are injectable materials or fat grafts. Each surgeon has his or her preferences.

Sometimes a droop appears in the outer (lateral) corner of a patient's eyelid (the lateral canthal tendon is where the upper and lower lids come together into a tendon-like structure), which may cause the entire lower lid itself to droop. This droop may cause a lower lid ectropion or just a sad-eyed look. Correction requires a suture tacking it to the outer bone around the eye, called the lateral orbital rim (you can easily feel this bony structure with your fingers). The lower lid blepharoplasty is thus more involved than the upper lid lift, but if done well, can be equally as gratifying.

Anesthesia

Upper and lower lid blepharoplasty can be done under local anesthesia with light sedation or under general anesthesia. At the patient's request, I have also done the upper lid blepharoplasty under local anesthesia with no sedation at all. Performing the lower lid procedure with only local anesthesia could be uncomfortable, however.

Limitations

Blepharoplasty will not remove every wrinkle. The incisions will extend out beyond the lids themselves, which is necessary to help correct the "crow's feet" wrinkles. Scars are inconspicuous, usually difficult to see at all. After the surgery the crow's feet will be improved, but not entirely eliminated.

Postoperative Course

Surgery always causes swelling and bruising. Count on it. It takes several months for everything to look its best, but you will look presentable seven to fourteen days after surgery. Be patient. Wear dark glasses and use makeup when necessary. The peak of postoperative swelling is usually on the second day, so use ice packs, soaks, or whatever cooling measures your doctor suggests. It's best to keep the eyelids cold and slightly wet for two days (three days is better) and to keep your head elevated on at least two pillows. Try not to look down with your face unless absolutely necessary. Obviously you must do so to eat, but keep it at a minimum, because looking down will make your face swell more. You can look down right now and feel your face fill up with blood—this is not what you want postoperatively.

Risks

Risks of these procedures include the following:

Visible scars
Ectropion (turning out) of the lower eyelid
Inability to close eyelids completely
Distortion of each or both eyelids
Delayed healing
Swelling
Bruising
Infection (rare)
Dry eyes (always tell your doctor if you have experienced this problem before the surgery)
Blindness (a complication I have never seen, but it has been reported)

12 Facelift (Meloplasty, Rhytidectomy)

Historically, the term *facelift* refers to the area from the cheek down to the middle of the neck. When you discuss facelift procedures with your plastic surgeon, you must know what he or she is referring to and what is available, so an explanation is in order. Many decades ago, the first facelift was a simple removal (excision) of excess skin in front of the ear, but this approach was unsuccessful, as it only moved scars forward and created minimal, if any, lift. Surgeons then began dissecting (cutting and elevating) the skin much more forward and eventually even tightening the underlying muscle with sutures. This procedure allowed for much more elevation of the tissues. The scars created from the incisions extended above the ear into the hair and behind the ear into the scalp. This approach however still addresses only the side of the cheek, jowl, and the neck. Eyelid and forehead surgery were then added, as well as correction of the central part of the face (called the mid-face). So a patient may be getting a facelift (which means cheek and neck), a mid-facelift, a forehead (brow) lift, and an eyelid lift (see Photos 12-1 and 12-2).

Age

Problems definitely change and increase with age. The youngest patient I have performed a facelift on was a twenty-seven-year-old man and, amazingly, he actually needed one. Usually, however, the majority of patients are in their middle forties to late fifties, extending into the late sixties or mid-seventies. To keep the face looking natural and not pulled, the facelift will remove an average of about ten to fifteen years from the patient's appearance, though some people who have taken care of themselves will get even more benefit. As mentioned, my goal has always been to give my patients a natural look and not the stretched appearance we have so often seen.

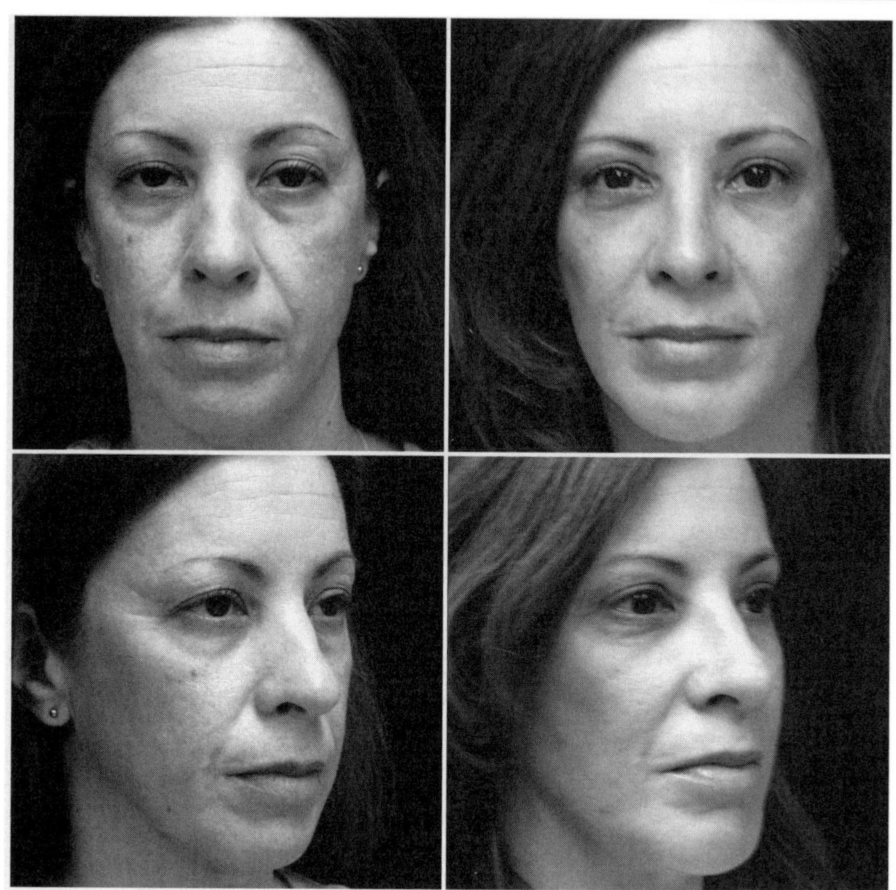

PHOTO 12-1. Before photos are on the left and after on the right. She underwent a facelift, mid-face lift, both upper and lower eyelid lifts, and a chin implant. The goal of a natural appearance without the "wind-tunnel" or pulled look was achieved.

Physical Problems of Aging

Refer to Figures 10-1 through 10-5 on pages 130–133 for examples of changes that typically occur with age. Everyone looks different, so we can expect that treatment must be individualized.

Listed again below are the areas that are affected by age (see Figure 10-6):

Forehead: furrows, frown lines.
Eyelids (upper and lower): excess skin and often fat, ectropion (turning out of the lower eyelid).
Upper cheek area: "cheek bone" diminishes.
Lower cheek area: jowls, increased fat.
Mid-face: sags, leaving tear trough, nasolabial fold and crease. Volume, thus size, is lost.

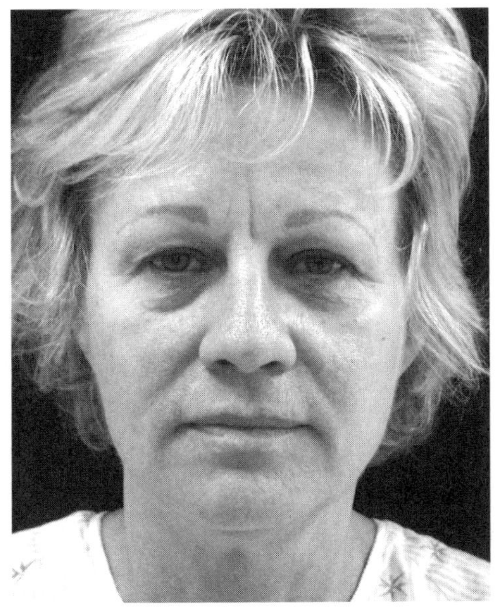

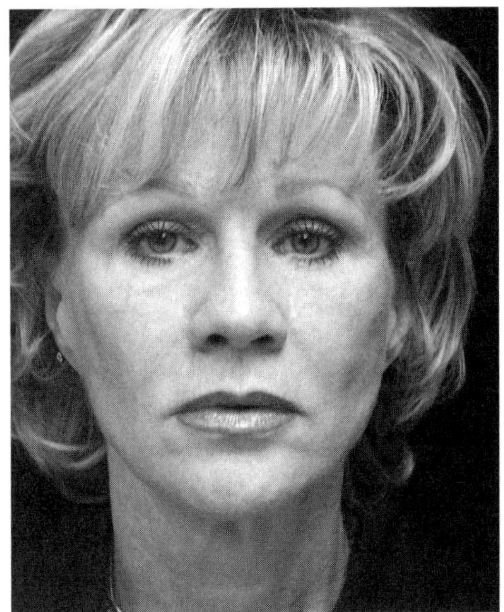

Photo 12-2. Pre- and post-op photos of a patient who had a brow lift, face-lift, and mid-face lift and upper and lower eyelid lifts.

Mouth: corners sag.
Upper lip: acquires multiple wrinkles, becomes longer between nose and lip and becomes thinner, turning inward. Teeth are no longer visible in repose.
Lower lip: multiple wrinkles, thinner, with marionette lines below the corners of the lip.
Jowls: sag and often extend into the neck.
Neck: the dreaded "turkey gobbler." May lose the jaw line a little or completely.
Nose: continues to grow and sag, as do the ears.

Expectations

Facelifts done properly on healthy patients can be extremely gratifying for both patient and doctor. They can return self-esteem to someone who has not had it for years or who had never been fortunate enough to have it at all.

One can expect the cheek mass area to be much fuller and more youthful. The tear trough (see Figure 10-6) will be reduced, although not always completely eliminated unless fat is grafted (transferred) or the patient is injected with a product like Sculptra, Restylane, Perlane, Radiesse, Juvederm, etc. to re-inflate the deficient areas.

The nasolabial fold is stubborn. A facelift can improve but not eliminate it. The procedure can only minimally improve marionette lines unless the surgeon injects something into them, such as the patient's own fat or other injectable solutions or gels such as Restylin, Perlane, Radiesse, Juvederm, Sculptra, etc. This is also a very difficult area.

Remember, about 10, maybe 15 years will be taken off the appearance with facelift surgery, so a person who is 60 may look 45 to 50. The good news is that the facelift will greatly improve the neck, and the jowls usually disappear. Jowls should be history! That alone makes someone look much younger and better. The above-mentioned injectable fat or solutions and a good skin care program will enhance the results of facelift surgery.

For the lip problems, a patient can have an upper lip lift, an excellent procedure, which leaves a small, hardly visible scar under the nose (see Figure 12-1).

Multiple lip wrinkles require a resurfacing carbon dioxide laser, Fraxel laser, and/or an injectable filler of some sort. My choice for fillers would be Sculptra for generalized volumizing of the skin above the lip, followed by, if necessary, one of the hyaluronic acid fillers, such as Restylane or Juvederm.

The result is improvement rather than complete correction, but this improvement can be substantial and sometimes even breathtaking.

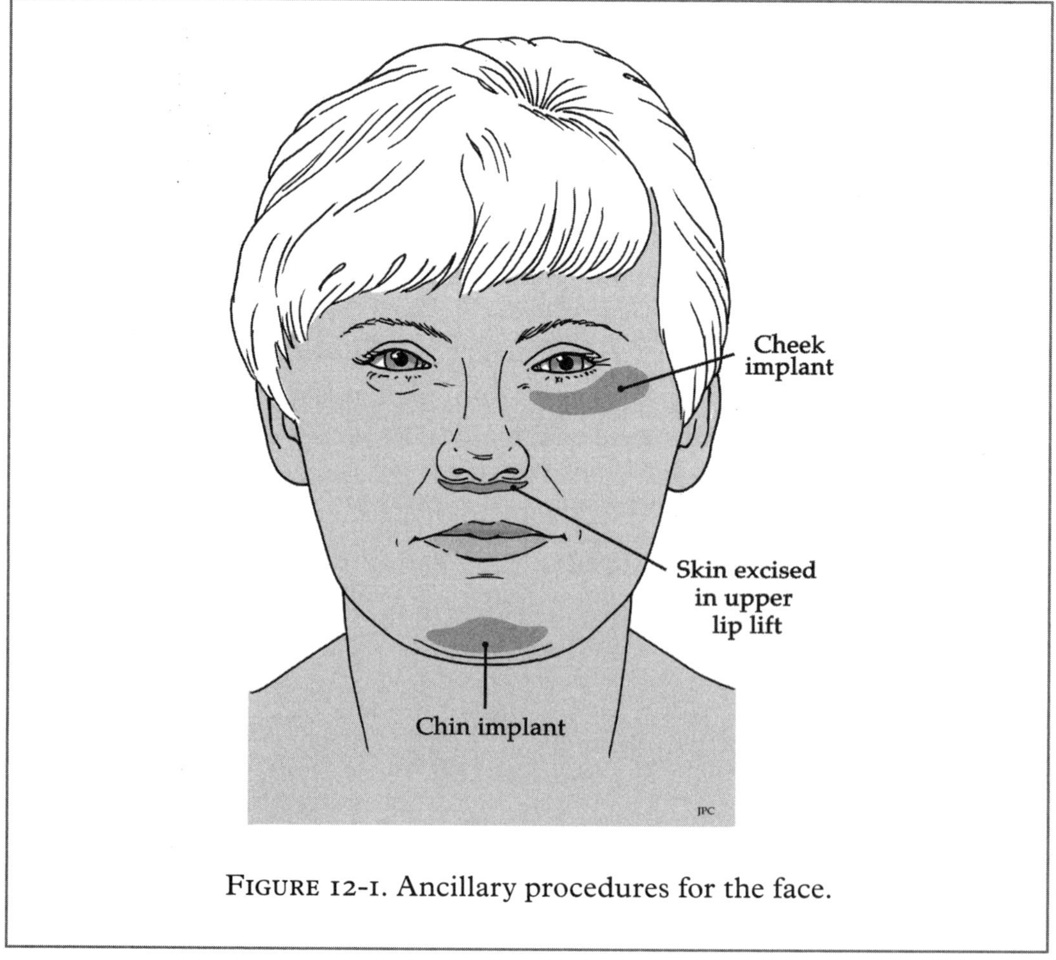

Figure 12-1. Ancillary procedures for the face.

Treatment Techniques

The incision for the facelift starts in the hair above the ear. It goes down to the top of the ear, then in front of the ear and actually inside the ear. It then continues around the earlobe, on the back of the ear and into the hair behind the ear (see Figure 12–2).

You can read about many various procedures, such as superficial musculo-aponeurotic system (SMAS), mid-face, subperiosteal, and endoscopic procedures. One thing to remember is that facelift procedures continue to evolve, and if we had a perfect way, it would be the only way. I look at some facelifts I performed ten to twenty years ago and think that they don't look bad at all considering I did them before the new techniques. Some patients still look better than before their original procedures. However, have facelift procedures improved? You bet. So what has evolved? I have directed my personal efforts toward ways to reduce post-operative recovery time, shorten scars and make them less conspicuous, elevate the nasolabial fold better, correct the tear trough, and restore the cheek mass

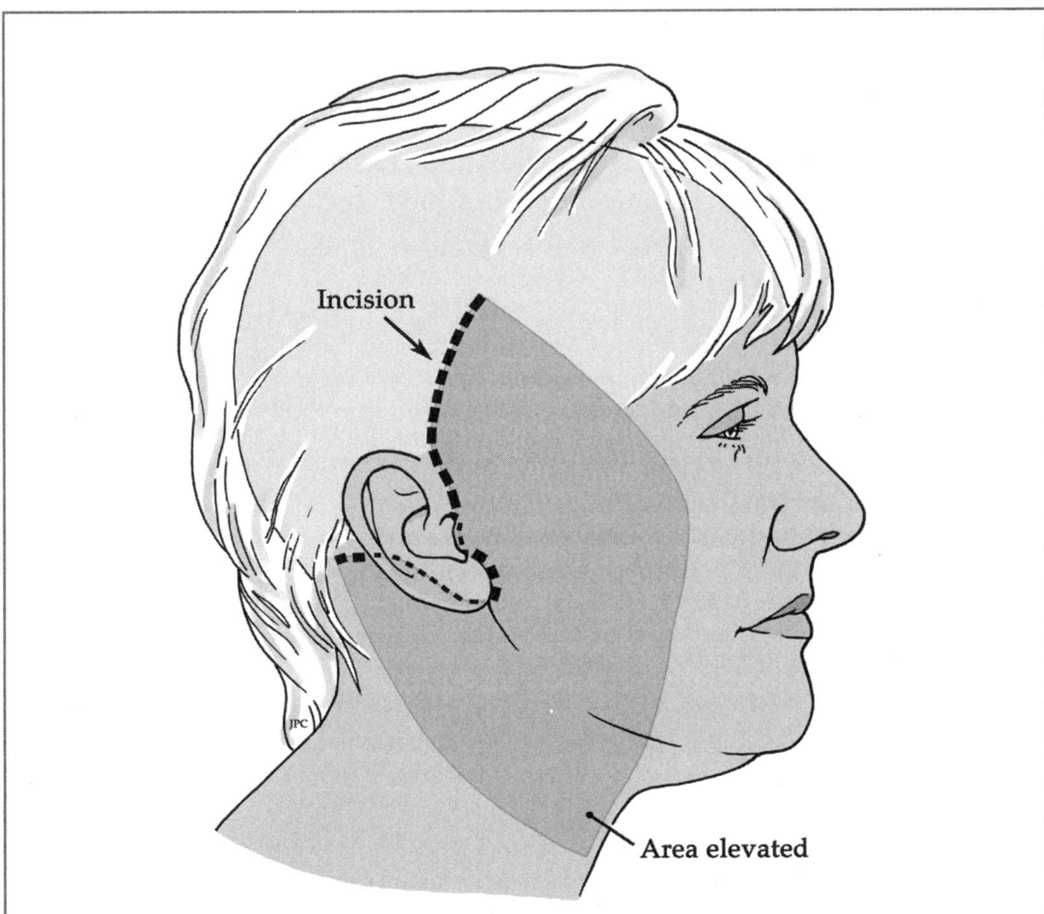

FIGURE 12-2. The surgeon lifts the skin in shaded areas to expose the underlying tissues where he/she performs suspension procedures.

(refer to Figure 10-6). These details make the patients look younger and more natural—basically better ways to move the aforementioned tissue volumes back to their youthful positions. And, as you might guess, actual volumizing is often necessary for this with fat injections or the mentioned injectable substances.

Loss of elasticity is not the only cause of sagging skin. The shape of the entire face changes with age, which involves volume changes and shifts. Loss of fat in the subcutaneous tissue causes the face to actually deflate. No one, neither patient nor plastic surgeon, can expect that tightening the skin and inserting a few muscle sutures will return these tissue volumes to their more youthful locations, shapes, and volumes. These problems must be addressed as we want to avoid the tight, pulled skin appearance. With facelifts without re-volumizing, tissue volumes may be relocated, but their sizes stay the same, except the jowl and fat in the neck, which we usually remove.

A surgeon can change locations of these volumes with various types of suspension sutures, with or without an endoscope (a scope to view the anatomy through a small incision). For instance, the periosteum is the lining on all bones and is what muscles attach to. A subperiosteal dissection means dissecting under the lining of the bones. I have found subperiosteal techniques to be a good way to elevate the foundation of the soft tissues of the face, which in turn elevates the muscles and skin. Doing this procedure through the lower eyelid may leave irreversible deformities of the lower lid if not done exactly right. However, excellent results depend more on the surgeon than the technique. Attention to details is key. Good surgeons can use any number of good techniques and do them well because they strive for a younger, natural look and have the artistic ability and dexterity to achieve these goals.

Details to look for indicating less than the best surgical technique:

- Earlobes pulled down abnormally.
- Very visible scars in front of the ear.
- Very visible scars in the scalp behind the ear (they're likely too low and not near the top of the ear).
- "Chipmunk" pouches just outside the mouth.
- A draped look in the lower cheek (like a curtain draped between the mouth and earlobe. (I hate this one.)
- Depressed, scooped-out looking area in the neck and under the chin.
- Visible suture marks, a feature I find inexcusable.
- A lift that is hardly noticeable—more common in the smoker and with severe sun damage.

A relatively new addition to facelifting procedures is the already mentioned fat grafting technique or other injectables which can replace lost fat, which occurs because of facial animation (constant smiling, frowning, squinting, and other animation that squeezes fat until it diminishes) or from trauma (Often I have seen patients who had a dent in their legs from bumping into something, such as the corner of a table. Such traumatic fat loss is usually permanent.) This fat loss causes deflation. Fat grafting alone may be done in some patients, or it can occur simultaneous to a facelift. If the patient is not having surgery already, I prefer to use injectables such as Sculptra for re-inflation, as it only takes a few minutes and requires no anesthesia. Fat for grafting can be taken from virtually anywhere, such as the abdomen or thighs. An additional point to consider—if the fat for grafting is taken from the abdomen and the patient gains weight, the fat grafts will act as they did in the abdomen, and the patient may get a very fat face!

Limitations

Limitations of facelift could also be titled unrealistic expectations. A facelift can remove only about ten years or possibly fifteen years from the appearance of your face. Think back to how you looked at that time. Even then you may have had some loose skin and wrinkles. Can you get more even results? Absolutely! But this may take a follow-up laser or deep peel, Sculptra or other injectables, or even another facelift in a few years. The second facelift is often more effective than the first, providing that the first was done properly. I must emphasize proper diet and skin care at this time. These continue to be of critical importance, and occasionally patients have canceled facelifts after healthful dieting, consistent skin care with products such as New Youth Skin Treatment System, and injectables because the patients felt they looked too good for surgery. I agreed.

Postoperative Course

For the first several days after surgery, you will hate yourself and may despise your plastic surgeon. The problem is the swelling and bruising. The peak for swelling is the second day, so use ice until then and keep your head elevated. And don't look in a mirror! But I know that curiosity will keep you from listening to that advice. If you anticipate these results beforehand, you won't be surprised. My patients stay overnight in our facility for one night and return on the second day to have their surgical drains removed, which sounds worse than it is. Some sutures are removed on the fifth day and final sutures at about one week. At this time you will start feeling like an actual human being and not an alien from another planet. You may not even detest your surgeon anymore! I allow my patients to wash their hair with warm water and baby shampoo on the third day, which usually provides an emotional boost. You begin to look reasonably good about two to three weeks postoperatively and great at two months. However, you'll still have some swelling, usually minor, which decreases over a period of four to six months. Your surgeon will direct you to someone who will give you ideas about how to use makeup for the first month or so, and you may want to wear dark glasses if you also had your eyes done.

13 Forehead Lift (Brow Lift)

Age

If you look at youthful brows in magazines or photos, you will most likely find an arch between the middle two-thirds and the lateral (outer) one-third of the brow. Generally, as we get older the lateral part of the forehead sags. Other aging characteristics are deep frown lines and deep furrows across the forehead, all of which are undesirable. In some people these problems (particularly the forehead furrows) appear early in life. In fact, some develop in people in their early twenties. When examining patients with this problem carefully, we often see congenital hooding of the eyelids or at least very full upper eyelids. As a result, these people must continually and subconsciously elevate their brows to lift the weight of this extra skin from their upper eyelids—a repeated movement that causes forehead furrows. For this reason, an upper eyelid lift offers the additional benefit of reducing these forehead furrows, which can be seen completely eliminated in many cases.

Frown lines usually occur in the thirties and, like most aging problems, just get worse with age. Patients feel that these lines make them look angry, and they often say, "I am a happy person, but I look angry all the time." This problem can be corrected, but the corrugator muscles (causing the frown), which go from the top of the nose to the middle of the brow, must be removed.

Botox injections are very effective, but last only three to five months. The muscle does get weaker after several injections, however. There are several methods to surgically remove the corrugator muscles: through an incision in the frown crease itself (also excising the frown lines) via a forehead incision while having a forehead lift, or with a brow lift using an endoscope.

Once again, lots of sun damage, cigarette smoking, and other bad health habits cause the skin, forehead, and brow (and everything else) to sag much faster.

Physical Problems of Aging

To summarize:

- Sagging brow: This usually occurs more on the outside rather than the middle section of the brow, and it is usually worse in men.
- Deep furrows of the forehead: A common aging characteristic due to constant elevation of the brow. This is often due to excess upper eyelid skin, which may even rest on the eyelashes. This problem would require you to elevate the brow for a full field of vision, thereby creating furrows.
- Deep frown lines: Due to squinting of the eyes as well as frowning itself. These lines occur singly or as more than one line.
- Heaviness of skin on the upper eyelid: A sagging brow itself can cause some extra skin on the upper lid, and we have discussed how heavy upper lids can cause deep furrows of the forehead. This is a clear example of how interrelated different physical characteristics are.
- Crow's feet: These are the wrinkles at the outside corner of the eyelids, which increase with a sagging brow. Botox is an effective temporary treatment.

Expectations

With proper surgery, you can expect the brow to be elevated to a normal height, but not excessively. Too much elevation results in a surprised appearance—definitely not desirable unless we are surprised. Often the brow doesn't stay up as much as we would like, but it remains improved. Expect improved, but not completely removed, frown lines and deep furrows. The corrugator muscle is stubborn, and just a few remaining muscle fibers can cause some continued frowning. If you have no need to elevate the brow continuously, the forehead furrows relax and diminish. The upper eyelids always improve after a brow lift, though often an upper eyelid lift should still be performed—not always, but often. It is important that each patient be evaluated individually, as there is no successful cookbook approach to facial rejuvenation.

Treatment Techniques

Historically, brow lifts made their appearance long after facelifts and eyelid lifts. They were, however, a wonderful addition to the rejuvenation of the face. The first type of brow lift was the coronal lift. During a coronal lift, the surgeon makes an incision from one ear to the other across the top of the head (Figure 13–1).

During this procedure, which many excellent surgeons still use today, the surgeon lifts tissues off the bone from the point of the incision down to the brow.

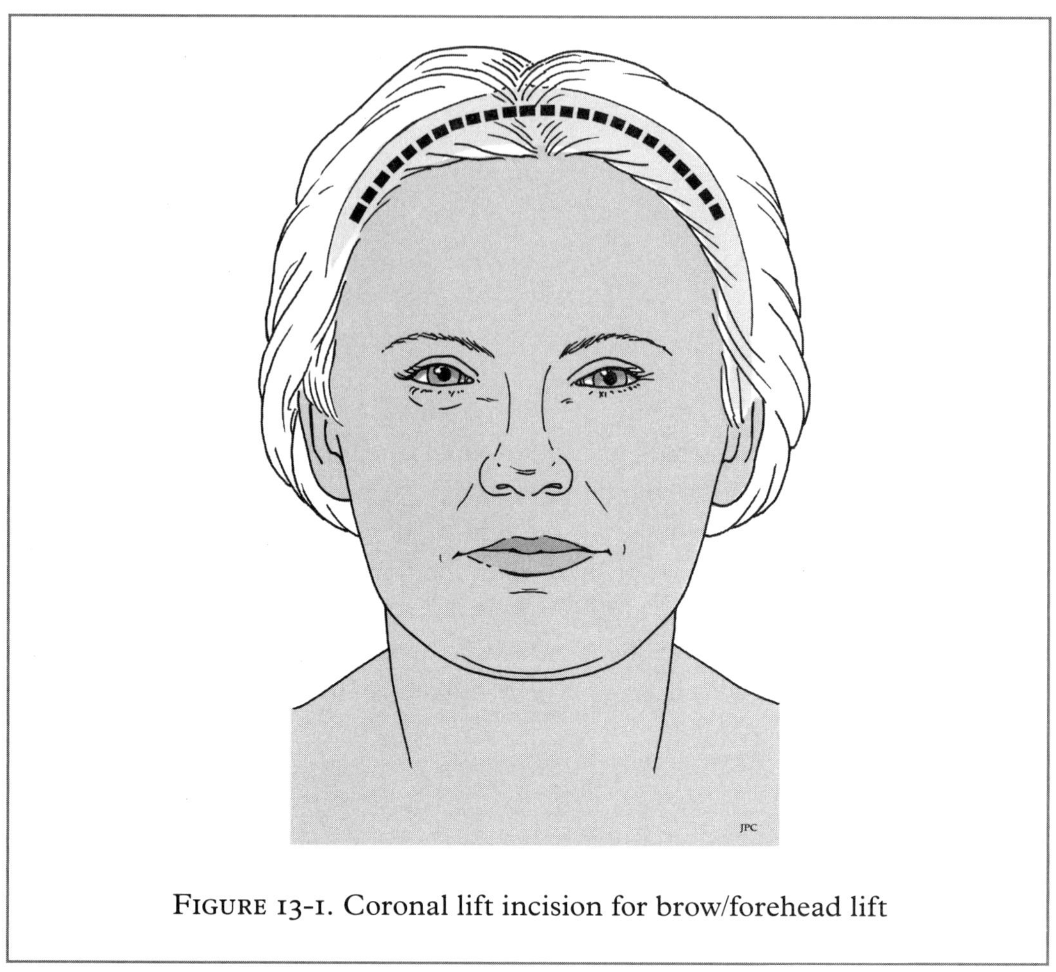

FIGURE 13-1. Coronal lift incision for brow/forehead lift

Then the surgeon exerts tension upward and removes excess skin. This approach can be effective, but it elevates the hairline, which is particularly undesirable in someone with a tall forehead. The coronal lift is excellent for a bald man with a sagging brow, as the scar is hardly noticeable.

Some surgeons prefer to make the incision at the hairline so that the hairline itself is not elevated. This approach may leave a visible scar, however. But if the incision is angled correctly, hair can be made to grow through the scar, minimizing its appearance. Also, when men and women comb their hair forward, they hide the scar. Another problem with the coronal forehead incision is that numbness of the scalp occurs behind the scar. People seem to forget this problem after a year or so, however, and coronal lifts offer excellent results for most patients.

The newest technique is the endoscopic brow lift, which is often my personal preference, though each of the techniques in use offers benefits. Basically, endoscopic surgery involves short incisions, allowing an endoscope (about the size of a fat pen) to be inserted to visualize the anatomy beneath the skin. The resulting image is viewed on a television-like monitor. During the brow lift, the surgeon makes four or five small incisions behind the hairline (Figure 13-2) and lifts the tissues from the underlying bone with special instruments. The surgeon removes muscles, such as the corrugators, to reduce or eliminate frown lines, and elevates tissues and attaches them to underlying bone with the device of the surgeon's choice.

Advantages of the endoscopic approach are minimal postsurgical numbness and no subsequent elevation of the hairline. I always insert a drain for about two days to minimize swelling. No bandages are necessary after the procedure, but ice soaks or an icepack are recommended.

Limitations

In some patients, elevation of the lateral brow is difficult, though it must always be elevated higher than the inner brow. In some the brow doesn't stay up as long as we would like, though the brow lift gives very satisfactory results in most cases. A few words of wisdom about facial rejuvenation: Don't be surprised if no one notices the difference in your appearance. In fact, I've been impressed by how seldom people notice even major changes. Sometimes patients have dramatic results

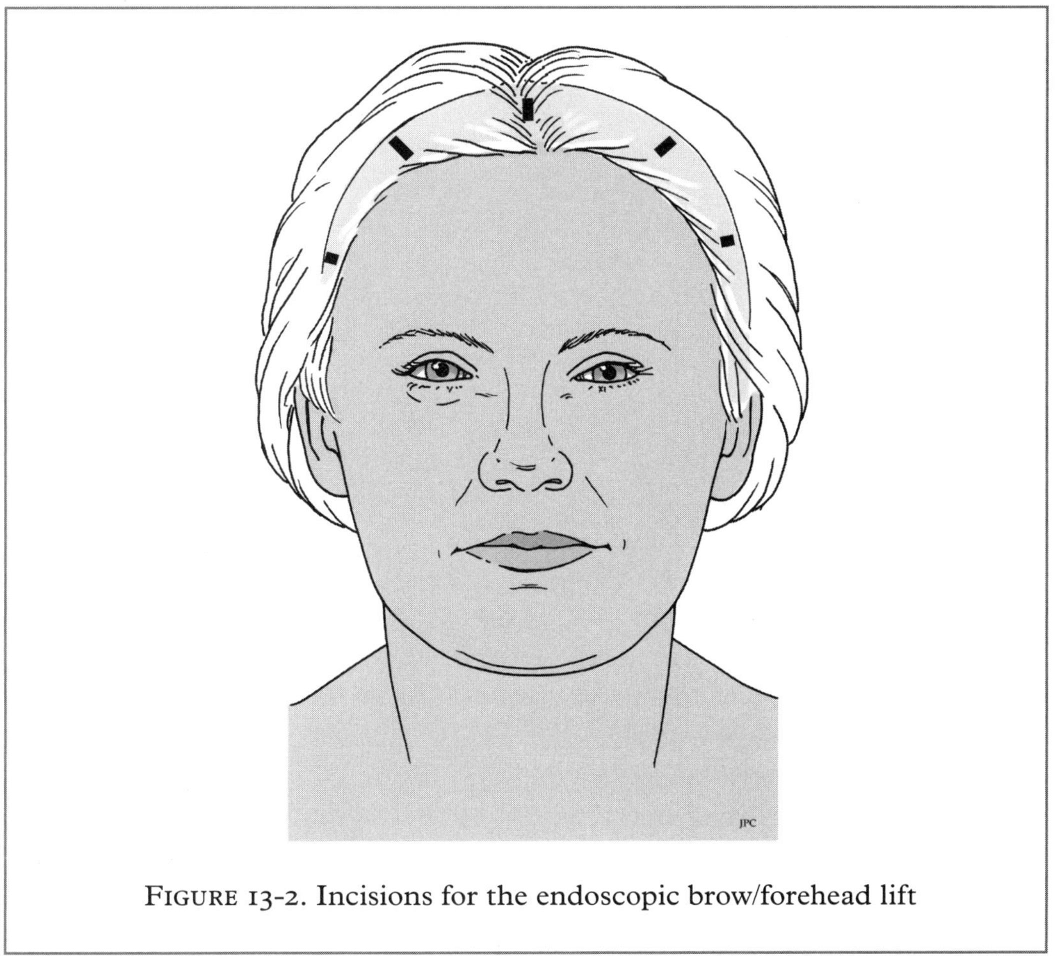

FIGURE 13-2. Incisions for the endoscopic brow/forehead lift

and friends say something like, "You look good. What did you do to your hair?" This reaction is actually typical, though sometimes people made no comment at all. I once made a dramatic change in a lady's nose and her own father did not notice the change. Try not to be upset by the possible lack of reaction. It's helpful if you can understand and expect these responses beforehand. Most people notice changes only when looking at themselves in a mirror.

Postoperative Course

The sutures or staples are generally removed at about seven days. If a drain is used, we remove this in two days. Swelling can be expected for a week or two with some minor swelling for several months. You may have bruising around the eyes for a week or so as well.

14 Nose (Rhinoplasty)

Age

A rhinoplasty can be performed at almost any age. The youngest patients are typically around sixteen years old, but I have done a rhinoplasty on a twelve-year-old girl who has now matured into a lovely lady. Patients with cleft lip deformities have specialized nose reconstructions sometimes even before they are one year old. Some plastic surgeons believe that we should wait until the nose is fully grown, at about age sixteen, before doing a rhinoplasty. I do not agree with this premise in every case. I do, however, believe that patients should be emotionally mature enough for such a procedure because it does change their appearance, and this change can be significant, especially when the nose is very large. The twelve-year-old girl I mentioned above actually had emotional problems because of her nose, which was enormous for her size. So each patient's care must be individualized emotionally as well as physically.

Most rhinoplasties are done in the late teens or twenties. The oldest patients that ask for these procedures are probably in the sixties. Why in the sixties, after having lived that long with their nose shape and size? This is a fair question. Here is the bad news: our noses continue to grow. Cartilage such as in the nose, ear, and ribs never stops growing. So a characteristic of an aging face is a larger nose, often with a bulbous tip. In fact, a rhinoplasty often accompanies a facelift as a complete facial rejuvenation procedure.

Rhinoplasties can also accompany septoplasty. The septum is the partition that separates one nostril from the other. With a break (called a fracture), the septum becomes bent or buckled, and breathing becomes difficult. This problem is what is referred to as a deviated septum. Rhinoplasty plus a septoplasty (surgery on the nasal septum) is called a septorhinoplasty.

Physical Problems of Aging

It's amazing the assortment that we see in various shapes of noses (see Figure 14-1).

The corrective surgery for each of these (and other) variations requires a very different approach.

To help you better understand, the nose has been divided into three areas: Tip—the lower one-third of the nose, which is made up of cartilage. The upper two-thirds—this contains mostly bone, with some cartilage in its lower part. Septum—the partition between the two sides of the nose.

The tip of the nose is entirely cartilage, containing two main cartilages, one on each side. The tip can be droopy, too large, bulbous, or with either too much or not enough projection. Some have what is called a "boxy tip," which is, well, like a box.

The upper two-thirds is mostly bone and can be deviated from a previous fracture, may have a hump of various sizes, or may be too wide. It may even sink

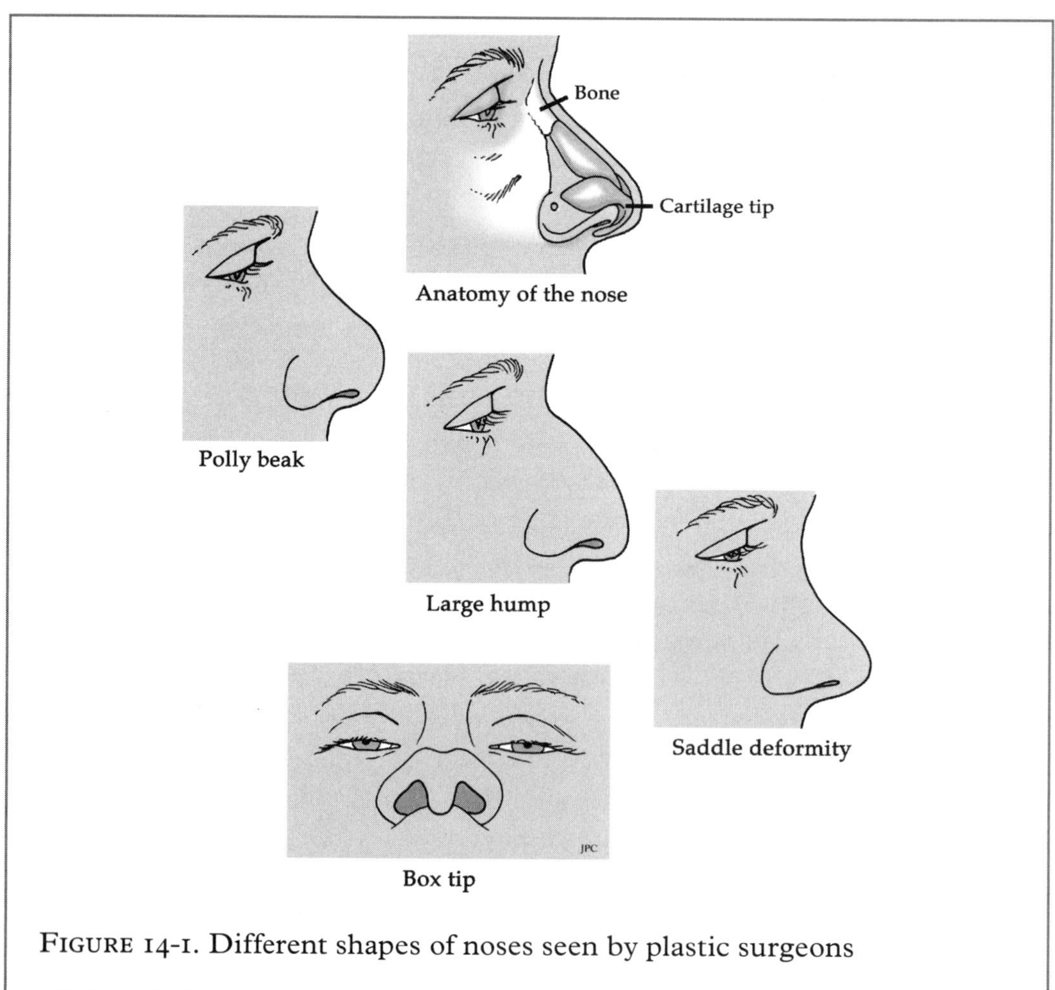

FIGURE 14-1. Different shapes of noses seen by plastic surgeons

in, called a saddle deformity, usually from a fracture or previous surgical over-removal of the septum.

Finally, the septum is the partition between the two sides of the nose. The septum may be deviated to one side or buckled, or it may even protrude out of one nostril.

Some plastic surgeons consider a rhinoplasty as the most difficult type of surgery because of its unpredictability. There are surgeons who specialize only in rhinoplasties. (See Photo 14-1.)

Treatment Techniques

Rhinoplasties can be open or closed. Open procedures involve a cut across the partition between the nostrils, called the columella. Some surgeons use this approach for better visualization of the area they are operating on. In closed procedures all of the surgery occurs through the nostrils, with no external incisions. The closed method is my preference, though beautiful work is also possible with the open technique, and the scar is most often hardly visible. Swelling may be slightly prolonged with the open technique.

Typically, the first thing to address in a rhinoplasty is the nasal tip. To correct a bulbous tip, the surgeon removes some of the cartilage (when required) and often sutures it to create a more desirable shape. Patients with thick skin may not ever have the refined nose they desire, however, because thick skin may not mold to the underlying changes made in the cartilage. A nasal tip may have a multitude of unattractive problems, and these are addressed on an individual basis. A tip with too much projection can be corrected. A tip with not enough projection, which is a more common problem, may necessitate a cartilage graft to increase projection. This graft comes from the cartilage of the septum or the ear. Do not worry. You won't miss or notice it.

Next on the agenda is the upper two-thirds of the nose. If it is too wide, the surgeon cuts bones (he/she does not break them, as many people believe) with a small chisel through the nostrils. If there is a hump, the surgeon lowers it with either a chisel or rasp, or both. It is always amazing how a small amount of removal can make a big difference, and this is why this procedure is challenging.

Once the surgeon does all the above, he/she scrutinizes the nose from every angle and corrects small imperfections.

Limitations

If you are realistic, rhinoplasty can be a very satisfying procedure. We cannot pick out a nose for ourselves, however. We have to work with what is there. For example, a huge nose will never be a small delicate nose. One that droops significantly will probably not be a turned-up nose, which I find unattractive and unnatural anyway. As mentioned, thick skin will not change shape as much as normal or thin skin.

A crooked nose may never be completely straight or symmetrical. It is usually improved with surgery and sometimes quite straight, but rarely perfectly straight. Crooked noses can be very challenging, often requiring multiple cartilage grafts.

My least favorite rhinoplasty surgery result is a nose that looks unnatural, pinched at the tip, turned up too much or like a polly beak (see Figure 14-1). Always ask to see photos and if you see these problems as a trend in a surgeon's work, get a second opinion, unless that is what you want.

Features of an unnatural-looking rhinoplasty are:

- Scooped out like a ski slope
- A "pinched" or pointed nose

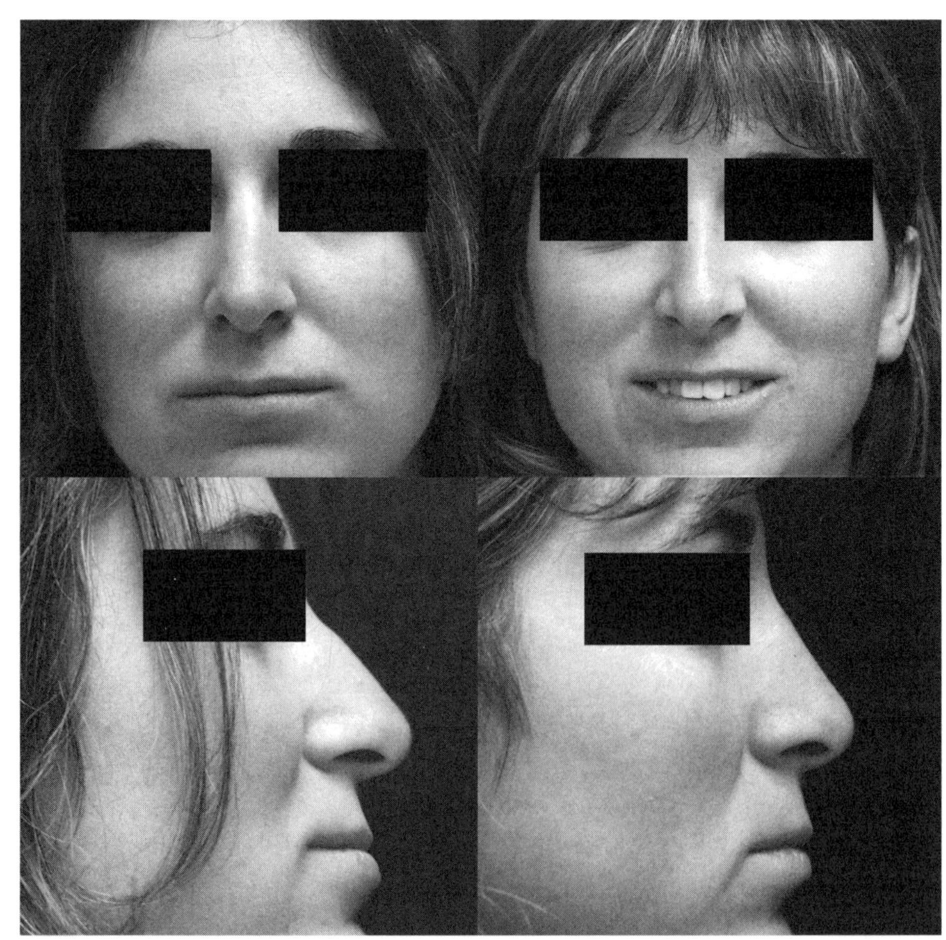

PHOTO 14-1. Before and after photos of a patient who had a closed rhinoplasty

- The nose turned up too much
- The famous "polly beak" with the most projection just above the tip instead of at the tip itself (Figure 14-1)
- A nose that "looks like a nose job." This is one that you yourself must decide upon.

Any procedure that looks "operated upon" is very distasteful to me (as surely you have concluded by now), including breast surgery, facelifts and, as is too often the subject, the nose. A nose that is over-operated on is often very difficult to correct because too much cartilage and/or bone has been removed. To correct this problem, the surgeon must graft cartilage from other places, such as the aforementioned ear, septum of the nose, or even in rare cases, a rib.

Postoperative Course

After a rhinoplasty, you will likely have a splint made of metal or of some other material. I leave splints on for one week. The nose is "packed" with gauze, but this is a misnomer—it is not actually packed. Only a small amount of cotton gauze is inserted in each side and usually removed after two days. As with other procedures, the greatest swelling is on the second day, and for this reason use ice soaks for a minimum of two days. Most noses look better as soon as the splint is removed at one week, but they still have a long way to go. There is literally some swelling for one full year, but practically speaking most is gone in three to four months. The amount of swelling depends on how much surgery was done. Noses continue to "shrink" or get smaller and more refined for a year or longer.

Rhinoplasties also cause black eyes, sometimes a lot, but often hardly any at all. This bruising also depends on the extent of correction as well as the patient's willingness to stay off the list of medications, foods, and nutrients that increase bleeding, such as aspirin, Advil, Aleve, vitamin E, and Omega-3 supplements. Also, younger patients bruise less and heal faster. Most bruising is usually gone by ten to fourteen days.

15 Other Facial Rejuvenation Procedures

Facial Implants

Malar (cheek) implants are used to enlarge the malar process (the cheek bone) and/or the tear trough (Figure 15-1 below). A smaller cheek bone area and presence of a tear trough are signs of the aging face, though some people are born with these appearances. Malar implants are made of rubber-like silicone and are very helpful for such deficiencies. They may be used alone or with face and eyelid lifts. I have inserted many in younger ladies with deficient infraorbital bones (the rim under the eye) with spectacular results. This procedure reduces the dark circles and the hollowness under the eyes. The incision is usually just under the lashes of the lower eyelid, but can be made inside the upper lip where it connects to the gum.

These implants come in different sizes and shapes and must be tailored to the patient. Postsurgical swelling decreases enough for normal activity in two to three weeks, but all the swelling takes six months or so to completely disappear. Even so, after two weeks the patient usually looks better than before surgery. Anesthesia can be light sedation or a general anesthetic with local injections to help reduce bleeding and postoperative pain.

The infraorbital depression (hollowness under the eyes) can also be treated with injectables, such as Sculptra, Restylane, Perlane, Juvederm, or fat grafts. My current preference is Sculptra, Restylane, or Perlane for most patients. Submalar implants are also used, though they are just another variety of malar implants. Your surgeon can discuss them with you.

Chin implants (Figure 15-1) are for deficient or small chins and are very effective. A person with a severe overbite may need chin or jaw advancement, which requires actually sawing through the mandible (the jaw bone) and would typically be performed by an oral surgeon. Otherwise a chin implant is an option. The implant is positioned to bring the chin straight out, as opposed to below or under the chin. Implants come in different sizes and shapes. Your plastic surgeon will help you decide which implant or procedure is right for you.

The incision for a chin implant is below the chin and usually difficult to see. It can also be made inside the lip near the gums, though proper placement is a little more difficult. The only postsurgical infection that ever occurred among my patients happened after this type of incision. Technically, I believe the implant should be on top of the periosteum (the covering on the bone), with the ends of the implant under the periosteum. Otherwise, it may erode into the bone. Postoperatively, some swelling occurs below the chin, so be patient. It will look much better when the swelling has subsided.

An alternative to the chin implant is fat grafting or injections of one of the fillers, such as Sculptra, Restylane, Perlane, or Juvederm, which are not permanent but do not require surgery.

This minor procedure can dramatically improve a person's appearance and profile because of the neck-jaw ratio. In an older person a small chin accentu-

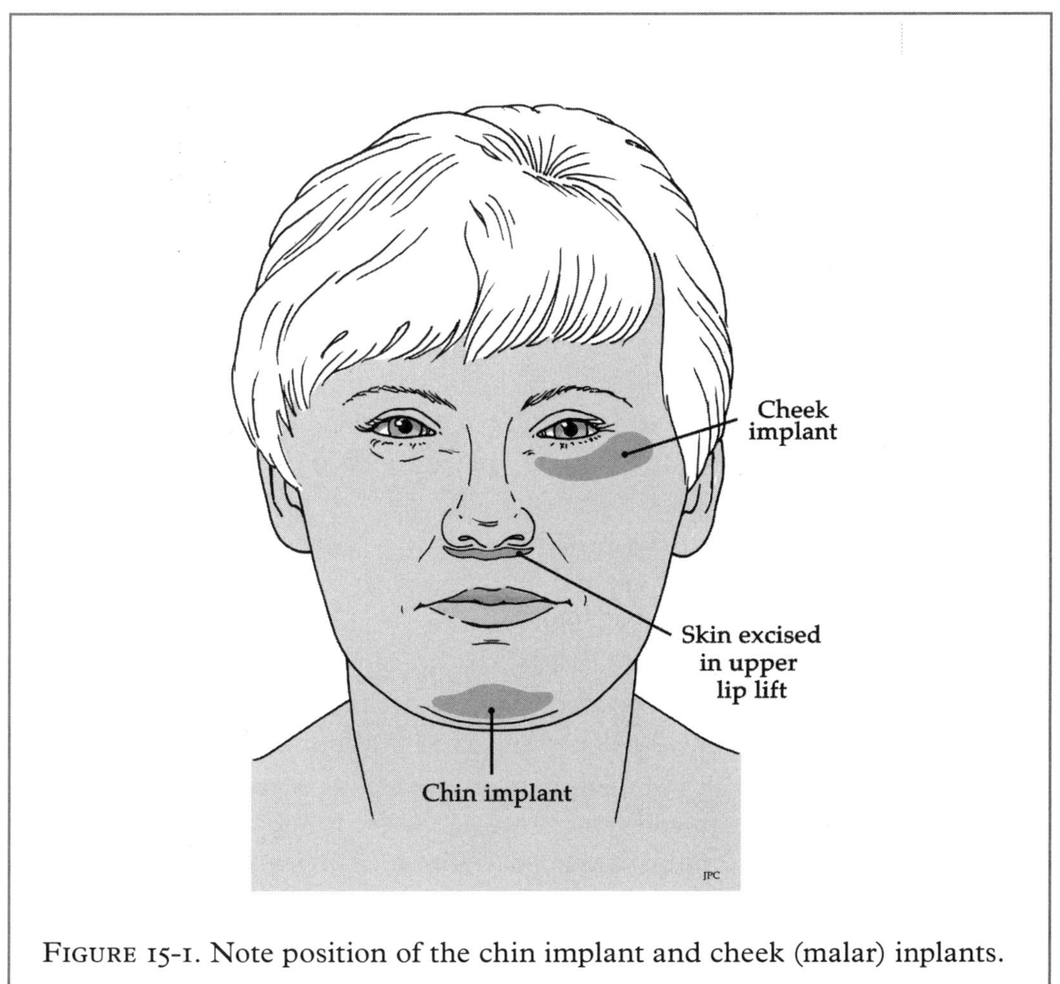

Figure 15-1. Note position of the chin implant and cheek (malar) inplants.

ates both jowls and "turkey gobbler" problems. So, when needed, a chin implant significantly enhances a facelift. It also often accompanies nose reductions, as a small chin magnifies the appearance of a large nose.

I once gave a lecture to a group of advanced high school science students who were shown a photo of a person with a large nose and deficient chin. I asked them for some suggestions as to how to correct the person's appearance. One student said that we should remove some of the patient's nose and put it on his chin. I told the student that if he decided to become a plastic surgeon, he would be welcomed as an associate.

Lip Surgery

Age is tough on lips. They get longer from the nose to the red part of the upper lip (called the vermillion). They also get thinner; the corners turn down, and we get multiple "whistle" wrinkles. We use up the fat separating the skin from the underlying muscle, and the skin ultimately lies directly on the muscle. Then with each motion of the mouth, the skin contracts like the muscle causing the wrinkles. A facelift cannot improve these wrinkles, but the best facelift in the world can usually be improved with proper attention to problems and details such as the upper lip.

An overly long lip can be improved with a lip lift, a relatively minor procedure done under local anesthesia. The surgeon makes an incision just below the nose from one side to the other, and removes a very small strip of skin. Of course, the skin must be measured and removed very accurately, but the procedure is a very effective procedure shortening the upper lip. The scar is virtually imperceptible (Figure 15-1).

The surgery for the droopy corners of the mouth is not quite as easy. It can be done, but leaves faintly visible scars going out from the corner of the mouth for a quarter of an inch or so. Still, I like the procedure because is gives the appearance of a happier face. Of course, the drooping must be bad enough to warrant the surgery. This problem sometimes improves with a facelift with the midface lift extension, which is actually the standard facelift at our office.

Perioral wrinkles ("whistle" wrinkles) can be improved but not eliminated. Injectable substances always help. With the exception of Sculptra, these substances are like gels and come in syringes with very small needles. The substance is injected directly into the depression of the wrinkle. This approach sounds wonderful, but it has its problems. Mainly it improves but does not eliminate the wrinkle, and it lasts only for a few months to a year according to the product (and the claim of the parent company). Years ago I used collagen, but it lasts only for four to five months at best. It must be refrigerated, and it requires a patch test because of the possibility of allergic reactions. In my opinion, these wrinkle fillers do not address the basic problem, which is loss of the subcutaneous padding between the skin and the muscle. Thus, I find myself using Sculptra more and more for this area of the upper lip, sometimes in combination with a wrinkle filler and even a Fraxel Laser for the severe cases.

The new injectables I use are either Restylane, Perlane, Juvederm, Radiesse, or Sculptra. The first three are hyaluronic acid products and will last six months to a year. The Radiesse will last a year (the company claims). Radiesse is more expensive. In non-active areas like a depression in the cheek, these products last longer than in highly mobile areas like the lips. New injectable gels and solutions seem to be introduced into the market every month or so. All of these products cause some swelling for one or two days, so use ice packs after the injections when possible.

Sculptra is my favorite for reshaping the face. As described, the face deflates with age. The fat under our eyes diminishes causing dark circles, the cheek bones get smaller, and mid-cheek depressions and tear troughs appear (See Figure 10-1 through 10-6). Also the areas around the mouth and lateral chin lose tissue. Sculptra is designed to fill these areas specifically. It re-inflates the face in areas of lost subcutaneous fat, which is one of the main causes of sagging. Correcting these problems may take three treatment sessions, each separated by about six weeks for optimal results. Typically patients return in two years for touch-up injections. The injections take about thirty minutes, and there is no downtime for recovery.

Fat injections from one's abdomen also reduce the appearance of wrinkles or various depressions in the face or body. The procedure also augments the chin (instead of an implant), cheeks, tear troughs, or any other body part. Some very fine facelift surgeons perform fat injections with virtually every facelift or, in some cases, instead of facelifts. In this surgical procedure, the surgeon removes fat with a syringe, separates it from any excess serum with a centrifuge or other method, and injects it into the deficient area. Some well-respected plastic surgeons are impressed with the results, even in lips, a highly mobile area. The fat usually comes from the abdomen, but it can be removed and used from almost any area with an adequate volume. Fat injections, however, usually take place under general anesthesia and in my experience are unreliable.

Combinations such as fat or Sculptra injections in conjunction with Botox effectively reduce the appearance of aging and delay the onset of the aging face. The Botox prevents excessive animation, which causes various wrinkles and folds in certain areas, and both fat, Sculptra, and other fillers fill the above mentioned depressed areas, such as the mid-cheek depression, atrophic cheek bone area, chin, lips, marionette lines, and nasolabial depressions (Figure 10-6). For the fine whistle wrinkles around the mouth, the surgeon may combine fat with small amounts of a filler such as Restylane.

My favorite combination for whistle wrinkles is a Fraxel or CO2 laser procedure performed in addition to Sculptra or one of the wrinkle fillers. Occasionally I use small amounts of Botox as well.

Fraxel Laser

The Fraxel is another nonsurgical and laser treatment for skin rejuvenation that has minimal recovery time. And it is the only laser that has truly made scientific sense to me. My experience is with the Fraxels Re:store and the Re:pair. The difference is in the heat produced, the depth of the penetration, the recovery time, and the degree of improvement, which are greater in the more powerful Re:pair. However, it usually requires one treatment instead of three or four for the Re:store. Unlike other such lasers which apply heat to make collagen tighten, the Fraxel actually coagulates microscopic holes, called microthermal treatment columns, into the epidermis and well into dermis to a depth of 1.4 to 1.7 millimeters. The laser actually vaporizes the microholes, meaning it eliminates the tissue. About 20% of the surface is treated leaving 80% untouched. Think of this as 20% of the surface being essentially removed. The body removes the debris from these micro-holes, which results in tighter skin in everyone treated. The Fraxel requires no anesthesia other than a topical cream. At the patient's request, the surgeon may use mild oral sedation and local anesthesia for the deeper treatments. The Fraxel laser causes no post-treatment drainage, and no dressings are required. As for recovery, patients will usually have slight swelling for a few days and be pink for three to ten days according to the Fraxel used. The skin may be dry for a week or two, requiring a moisturizer and sunscreen.

The Fraxel laser can treat the neck, hands, arms, chest, knees, and virtually any part of the body, including the eyelids. Virtually any skin type can be treated with the Fraxel laser.

Fraxel laser treatments typically yield the following results:

- Reduction of pigmentation spots, such as melasma (pregnancy mask)
- Reduction of age spots
- Smoother skin
- Tighter skin
- Significant reduction in fine wrinkles
- Reduction of scars, including those from acne

For more information, check the Fraxel web site: www.fraxel.com.

Thin Lips

How do we correct the thin lip? Injecting fat or any of the products mentioned above can be effective for a few months. If enough fat is injected, some seems to stay put in most patients. Postoperatively, however, patients may look like ducks for a while, though no one seems to complain. In addition, there are surgical procedures that roll the inner lip mucosa outward, which helps. It is usually pref-

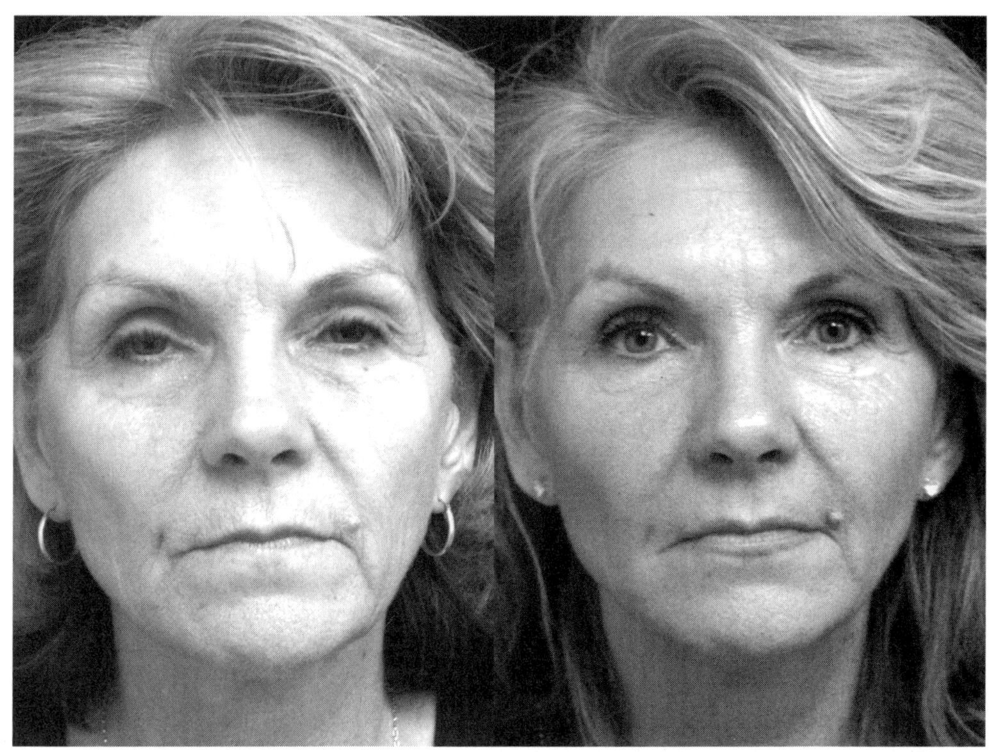

Photo 15-1. This patient had Sculptra injections to re-volumize her face and the Fraxel Re:pair (CO2) laser to tighten and resurface her skin. She is also using New Youth Skin Care. She has had no surgery.

erable to take a combination of measures to achieve the best and most lasting results. Artefill can also be used in the lips, but due to its permanence the procedure should only be performed by highly trained specialists.

Injecting any of the filler products is painful, so your surgeon will probably use ice on the area first and may use a local anesthetic as well. I also treat patients with a topical anesthetic cream for thirty minutes prior to the injections. This is very helpful and well worth the wait. Fat injections require some additional sedation.

Skin Resurfacing

The purpose of resurfacing is to:

- Reduce fine wrinkles
- "Shrink" the skin to make it tighter
- Reduce abnormal pigmentation and age spots
- Reduce large pores
- Increase collagen production

Skin resurfacing is done with lasers or chemical peels. (See photo 15-2). Depending upon the expertise of your surgeon, both techniques can be very effective and about equally so. We are, however, looking for a procedure with the lowest possibility for error and the fewest possible complications. Complications can occur with any technique, and, of course, we never want them. But they can occur even in the best hands, though rarely. Complications include herpes infections (not uncommon in someone who carries the virus), so we treat every patient with proper antiviral antibiotics starting the day before the procedure. Another complication would be depigmentation or scarring, usually as a result of going too deep with the laser or chemical peel or not matching the power and depth of the laser with the patient's skin type.

The peel agent, phenol, appears to have a much higher risk of depigmentation. It's best to be a little conservative, although some may want to come back at a later date for a repeat treatments. Trying to correct every wrinkle is the usual problem. This elusive goal is usually unreachable (without at least some depigmentation) even when going very deep, so it's best to be safe.

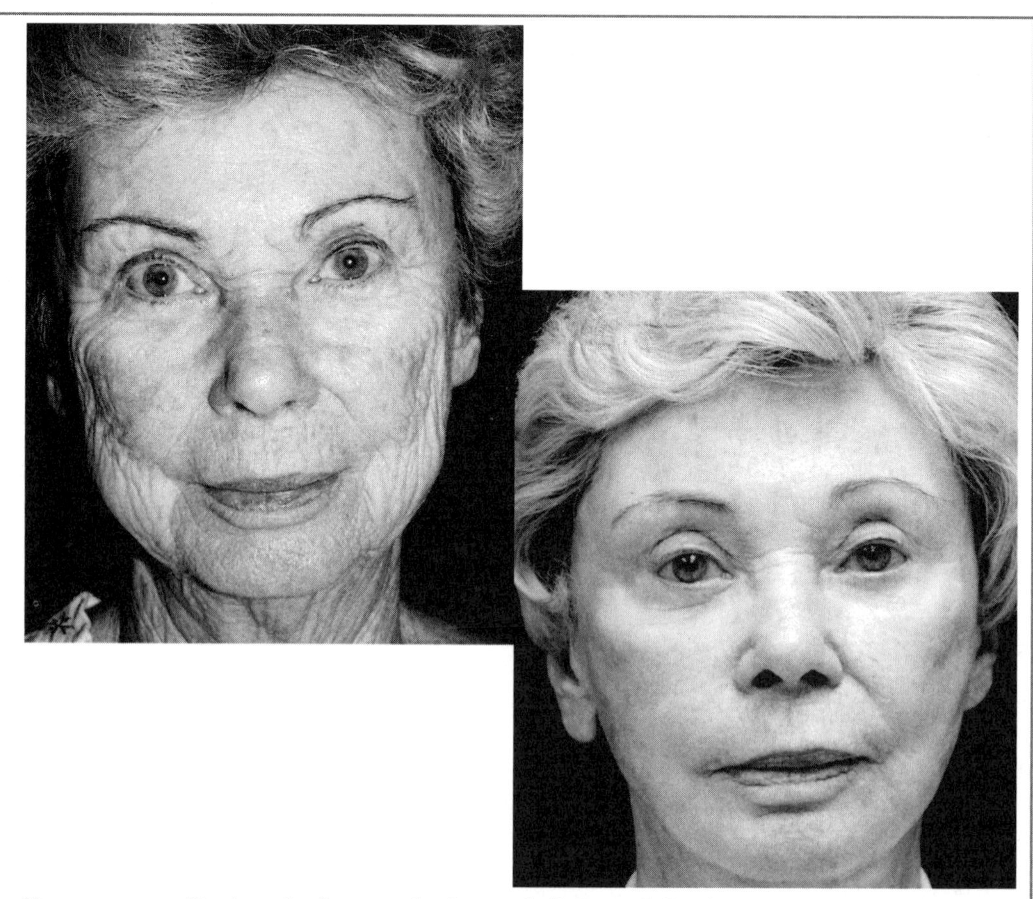

Photo 15-2. Patient before and after a full face CO2 laser

These primary types of resurfacing lasers are available:

- The CO2 (carbon dioxide) laser can yield dramatic results, requires general anesthesia, and has potential for depigmentation. This laser may cause significant drainage from the skin requiring dressings or ointment for a week or so. Skin pinkness may last four to six months, according to the depth of the laser treatment. Photo 15-1 represents a patient following a CO2 laser.
- The Erbium laser is much the same as the CO2, but it produces less heat and heals about 50% faster than the CO2 with less posttreatment care. Results are less dramatic.
- Finally, the Fraxel lasers are types of erbium (Re:store) or CO2 (Re:pair) lasers, but rather than taking a uniform layer from the face, they resurface with micro-holes, as mentioned earlier. Recovery time is less than the others.

In all, very impressive results have resulted from laser resurfacing. In my opinion, the Fraxel laser usually yields tighter, clearer, more youthful skin with a lower risk of pigmentation problems than other lasers.

Many other fine lasers are not mentioned here. New lasers seem to be coming on the market faster than we can keep up with them.

Potential complications of laser and chemical peel resurfacing include:

- Scarring: I have seen photos of post-resurfacing scars ranging from mild to severe.
- Hypo-pigmentation (reduced pigmentation): Little can be done about this problem, and it is permanent.
- Hyper-pigmentation (increased pigmentation): This result can cause a color difference between the neck and face. This problem is usually temporary and more easily controlled than hypo-pigmentation.

16 Breast Enlargement (Augmentation Mammoplasty)

Breast augmentation began in the first half of the last century using various kinds of sponges, and fortunately I had to remove only very few of these, as they were like shrunken bricks. In 1962, Dr. Thomas Cronin in Houston, a wonderful plastic surgeon with whom I almost joined in practice, began using the silicone implant. Initially, silicone implants contained adhesive patches for the body to grow into to help immobilize the implant. The first type of silicone used was stiff and eventually replaced with an almost liquid gel-like substance that proved problematic because if the implant leaked, the silicone oozed into the tissues causing lumps called granulomas. Now implants use a cohesive, much more natural gel. At one time in the late 1970s and early 1980s I performed breast augmentations with silicone implants on about 200 women a year for several years and, with the exception of a very few cases, my patients said the implants were very satisfactory in spite of what some of the news media and certain plaintiff lawyers claimed.

Since that time, from about 1990 until about 2004, the Food and Drug Administration ruled against silicone implants. Many independent studies have detected no increased incidence of lupus, collagen diseases of any type, or other diseases claimed during lawsuits to be caused by silicone implants. Some considered the evidence presented against their use as junk science, as it was based on emotion and motivated by monetary gain in opposition to scientific fact.

Interestingly, the incidence of breast cancer is actually decreased among patients with silicone implants when compared to the normal population.

Silicone implants are once again available and are by far the most common implants that we use. The newer implants have been greatly improved with cohesive gel—more like Jello and less likely to leak. The positive side to the FDA's earlier ruling is better silicone implants and more rigorous control over implantable devices.

Saline implants still have a silicone shell, but are filled with saltwater instead of silicone gel. They are durable, and the incidence of leakage was about 2% during the first five years based upon my experience using a smooth implant instead of a textured surface implant. If they do leak, only saltwater leaks into the tissues because the implant contains no silicone gel, and the body rapidly absorbs the saltwater without problems. Overall, opinions vary about which kind of implant is best for breast augmentation. Exact statistics are difficult to determine regarding medical procedure outcomes because some patients do not return to see their doctors for many years, and some may move from the area or in other ways be unavailable for long-term follow-up.

Age

Women requesting augmentation mammoplasty usually range in age from about twenty to fifty years old. I have, however, performed a breast augmentation procedure on a sixteen-year-old girl with the approval of both parents. Now, decades later, this young woman remains satisfied with the results. I have also performed the procedure on women over sixty years old. In most older patients (and some in their mid-thirties as well), sagging of the breasts occurs. This problem is exacerbated with multiple pregnancies, great variations of weight, excess sun exposure, and poor health habits such as smoking and inappropriate diet.

Sagging breasts sometimes necessitate a breast implant plus a breast uplift (mastopexy) for correction, which will be discussed later. Many young ladies had ample breasts at one time, but after having children, breast volume decreases—a very common occurrence. Other women have simply had very small breasts since puberty. Because of these variations, each patient's care must be individualized. Patients also have individual goals and desires that must be addressed.

Physical Aspects to Be Considered

The assortment of breast sizes and shapes and the technical differences in breast surgery are surprisingly varied, as are patients' goals for the surgery. Open and thorough communication must exist between doctor and patient to achieve these goals, if this is possible. If communication with the doctor is difficult, the patient should consult another surgeon.

Physical Problems of Aging

Very small breasts: If a woman has too little breast tissue to cover the implant, it must be placed beneath the pectoralis muscle that lies behind the breast. If it is placed above the muscle, only skin and maybe a small amount of breast tissue will cover the implant, and the patient may see and feel unattractive wrinkles in the implant itself.

Moderate, but not large breasts: The implant may be placed beneath or above the muscle in this case, based on the patient's and the doctor's preference. If the patient has adequate breast tissue, I prefer placement above the muscle in most cases because the recovery time is shorter, there is less postoperative pain, the implants can be placed a little closer to the midline, and the implants don't move when the pectoralis muscles flex. Natural outcomes seem a little more frequent in my hands when implants are placed in front of the pectoralis muscle, but this decision is based mostly on the surgeon's preference. I have seen happy results with both approaches.

Moderately large, but sagging breasts: My preference in this case is to place the implant in front of the pectoralis muscle, often in combination with a breast uplift procedure. However, if sagging is already a problem and a woman wants a large implant, she can expect to see repeated sagging. I use the adage of "sand in a sock"—that is, more sand results in more sagging. The patient's tissue simply may not have enough elasticity to hold up a heavy implant. Additionally, if the implant is placed behind the pectoralis muscle in this case, the breast often sags over the implant. In other words, the implant stays up, but the breast tissue sags, hanging off the front of the implant—a very unattractive outcome and a risk I don't want my patients to take.

Unusual breast shapes: Visually, the breast is a mound with a nipple on it. How many shapes can there be? The range and variety of breast shapes are actually quite large. Different aspects of the breast shape that may technically affect the procedure include:

- The size of the areola (the dark area around the nipple) and/or nipple. The areola may be huge—even as large as the breast, creating the impression that the breast is herniating into the areola. This deformity is repairable with an implant and a type of breast uplift.
- The position of the breast on the chest wall (some are high, some low).
- The shape of the rib cage. On a round chest the nipple and breast will point more to the side (laterally), while on a flatter rib cage the nipple and breast will point toward the front of the body. The degree of cleavage is also related to the shape of the rib cage as well as the size of the breast.
- The position of the inframammary fold (the fold below the breast). Sometimes this fold is very high with a short space between the nipple and the fold. This measurement will necessarily limit the size of the implant; otherwise the nipple will point down, or the fold may cut across the bottom of the implant, creating an indention. Sometimes the fold can be lowered to avoid creating an indention.

So, in augmentation mammoplasty as in everything else, we must have balance and moderation. We must think in advance about all aspects of the surgery to get as close to the patient's goals as possible. Regarding size, a good question to ask yourself is, if the size isn't exactly what you have in mind, would you be more unhappy if your breasts were too large or too small? The answer to this question is important, and you should relate it to your plastic surgeon.

Treatment Techniques

Implant insertions require various incisions:

- Inframammary incision usually in or just above the crease below the breast.
- Periareolar incision: a short incision at the junction of the areola and normal skin, usually in the lower one third at the edge of the areola.
- Transaxillary incision: the scar is placed in a crease just below the center of the axilla (armpit). This one is more difficult to perform well, but it leaves virtually no scar. It was my preference for about twenty years, but with the advent of the saline implants, the other incisional approaches offered some advantages. I still offer it occasionally to someone in the twenty to thirty-year-old range with at least a B cup breast. It is difficult to use for the submuscular position unless done endoscopically by a surgeon with lots of experience in this technique.

None of the incisions leaves bad or conspicuous scars, and if these procedures are done properly, suture marks should never be visible, either right after surgery or after the healing process is complete.

Implant locations (position)

As mentioned, the breast implant can be placed either in front of or behind the pectoralis muscle. Placement in front of the pectoralis muscle is called the "pre-pectoral" or "sub-glandular" position, while placement beneath the muscle is called the "sub-pectoral" or "sub-muscular" position (see Figure 16-1).

An important point to realize is that no implant is placed within the breast tissue itself. All are placed behind the breast, whether in the sub-pectoral or pre-pectoral position. Therefore, they do not affect breast function, and most women have breastfed successfully after breast augmentation.

My preference is always to tailor breast augmentation techniques to the patient's needs and anatomy as well as her personal goals. If a patient has enough breast tissue, the implant may be placed in the pre-pectoral location. For patients who want as much cleavage as possible, and providing they have enough breast tissue, they will get more cleavage with a pre-pectoral implant, as implants can be placed a little closer together in the pre-pectoral position. However, thin women with minimal breast tissue may never have much cleavage. Saggy breasts look better, in my opinion, with a pre-pectoral implant, because after a year or so follow-

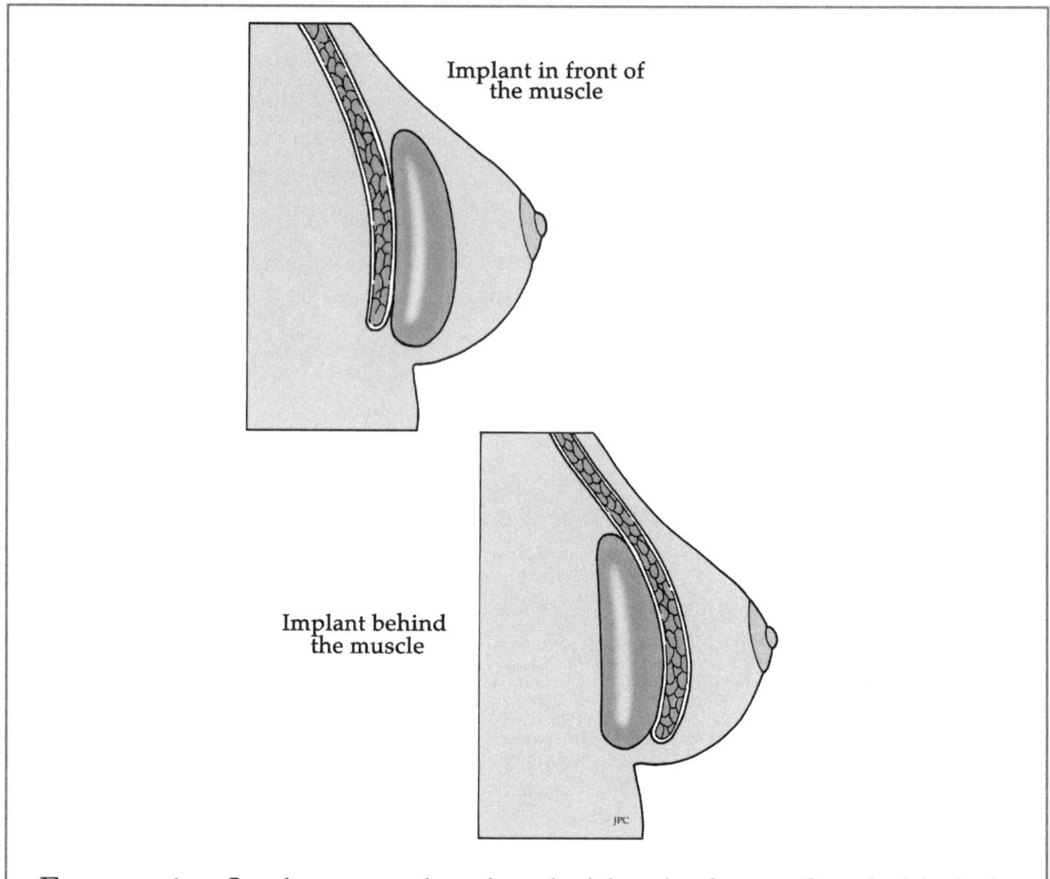

FIGURE 16-1. Implants can be placed either in front of or behind the muscle.

ing a sub-pectoral implant, the breast may sag over the implant. Many patients will also need an uplift to help with this problem.

An encapsulation occurs when scar tissue around the implant shrinks, causing the implant to become firm. Encapsulations can actually cause the breast to become very firm and shaped like a ball—not a pretty sight. According to nationwide studies, the encapsulation rate is slightly higher when implants are placed in a pre-pectoral position, but in my experience this difference is not clinically significant.

Although both the pre- and sub-pectoral implantation techniques can create normal-appearing breasts, implants in the pre-pectoral position result more often in natural-looking breasts in a higher percentage of cases in my experience. Overall, we must remember that if one of these techniques were perfect, there would be only one technique.

Most surgeons try to use the technique that will give a patient the best chance of a great result. When deciding which technique to use, we must consider the small percentage of patients who will not get their desired results no matter which technique is used as well as those who will achieve excellent results regardless of the technique. Still, a high percentage of excellent results is what all surgeons strive for. However, some surgeons consistently get better results than others.

Implant types

Only saline and silicone implants are currently available. Since the time of the aforementioned silicone implant legal problems, the saline implant was (except in very special situations) the only implant available for breast augmentation for the past fifteen years, until December 2002. Saline implants are associated with a lower encapsulation rate, but incur a higher risk of surface wrinkles, which is one reason many surgeons use the sub-pectoral position for these implants. If surgery goes perfectly, the silicone implants look and feel more natural. Remember, however, that if a patient has enough breast tissue to cover the implant, surface wrinkles are not an issue.

In summary

Silicone implants, now FDA approved for breast enhancement, often feel softer than saline implants if they do not encapsulate, and if the result is technically perfect, and if the patient follows the postoperative instructions. Some silicone implants are actually undetectable, if they don't encapsulate. Unfortunately, however, a slightly higher percentage of silicone implants do encapsulate. I remember several instances of patients with silicone implants being examined by physicians who later commented to me that they did not know the patient had breast implants until the patients themselves told them. However, when either silicone or saline implants do encapsulate, they can be round like a ball and quite firm—not a pleasant outcome for either the patient or the plastic surgeon.

At one time Dow Corning introduced a textured silicone implant that I liked. The textured shell was unlike anything else available and had very small closely adjacent silicone pins (protrusions) designed to prevent scar tissue from becoming organized into a tight capsule around the implant. That design made perfect sense to me. I inserted them into about twenty patients and never saw encapsulation in any of them. Unfortunately, the news media had their story about the evil of silicone implants about that time. These implants are now history, as is the Dow Corning Corporation.

In addition to increased potential for encapsulation, silicone implants also undergo a phenomenon called "silicone bleed," which is when the silicone gel inside the silicone shell actually bleeds through the shell over a period of years. An easy way to demonstrate this problem was to place the implant on a sheet of paper for a period of time. When the implant was removed, there would be a silicone stickiness or stain on the paper. At one time silicone bleed was a severe problem, but fortunately with additional scientific developments this tendency to bleed is much reduced. In the human body this phenomenon may cause breast lumps called silicone granulomas, which necessitate replacement of the implant and removal of the granulomas—a very challenging task in some patients. We always attempt to remove all granulomas and encapsulation scar capsules in every patient, and believe most plastic surgeons do as well. This approach is not the simplest way, just the best way to solve the problem. Practically speaking, it is impossible to remove all of the silicone, but that should be the goal. Unfortunately, it is difficult to differentiate a cancer mass from a granulomatous mass, so granuloma presence might in fact delay detection of breast cancer. Obviously, silicone granulomas also appear when silicone implants rupture. As mentioned, one positive aspect of the FDA ban on silicone implants is that the implants have been greatly improved.

Saline implants, when the results are perfect with no encapsulation, still do not feel as soft and natural as silicone implants. Ideally they should be placed behind the pectoral muscle in patients with minimal breast tissue, as saline implants sometimes have a more wrinkled appearance than silicone implants, and these wrinkles can sometimes be felt and even seen. If the patient has enough breast tissue to cover the implant, wrinkles pose no problem.

A significant advantage of saline implants is that there is no possibility of silicone gel bleed and thus no risk of silicone granuloma formation, as saline is just plain saltwater. So, if saline implants rupture or leak, they go flat and the body absorbs the saline. Going flat does not sound good, but it is better than the formation of silicone granulomas. Also, a woman can easily tell when a saline implant is leaking, but a silicone implant leak may take months or years to appear. With the better quality of today's silicone implants, leaks should no longer be a problem.

What exactly causes the encapsulation phenomenon? Encapsulation happens when fibroblast cells around the implant form collagen and scar tissue to try to wall off the implant, forming a scar shell (capsule) around it. After all, the implant is a foreign body, so the body will work to isolate it from the body tissues. The fibroblasts, once organized, may shrink around the implant making it tight and firm. Why does encapsulation happen in some patients and not in others? The short answer is we don't know, even after hundreds of studies over several decades. However, we've made some important findings about encapsulation over the years. For example, the breast is not a sterile organ, just as skin is not sterile, and a common breast and skin bacteria called Staphylococcus epidermidis is known to cause encapsulation. Accordingly, placing of an antibacterial agent around the implant reduces the encapsulation percentage rate dramatically. While encapsulation occurs with both saline and silicone implants, it can also result from bleeding around the implant. Notice that I said "can," and herein lies one of the mysteries of encapsulation. Some patients bleed a little more on one side than the other, with encapsulation occurring on the side with no bleeding, though it is usually the other way around. Nature plays strange tricks on us sometimes.

Breast implants come in different shapes and textures, and you will find plastic surgeons who use only one type while others exclusively use another. So what does this difference tell us? No single implant is infallible, just as no single implant technique is perfect. Implants can be contoured or rounded and can have height/width ratios to better tailor shapes to the patient. Overall, I prefer to use smooth implants because wrinkles are less obvious and the deflation rate is lower, but I will occasionally use a textured implant in women with sagging breasts, as the texture seems to help hold the breasts up. The point of the textured surface on an implant is for the body to adhere to the implant and (theoretically, at least) reduce the encapsulation rate. The encapsulation rate is, however, about the same with textured and smooth implants in my experience.

Nothing lasts forever, and all implants will deflate or leak sooner or later. However, many implants last for twenty-five years or more.

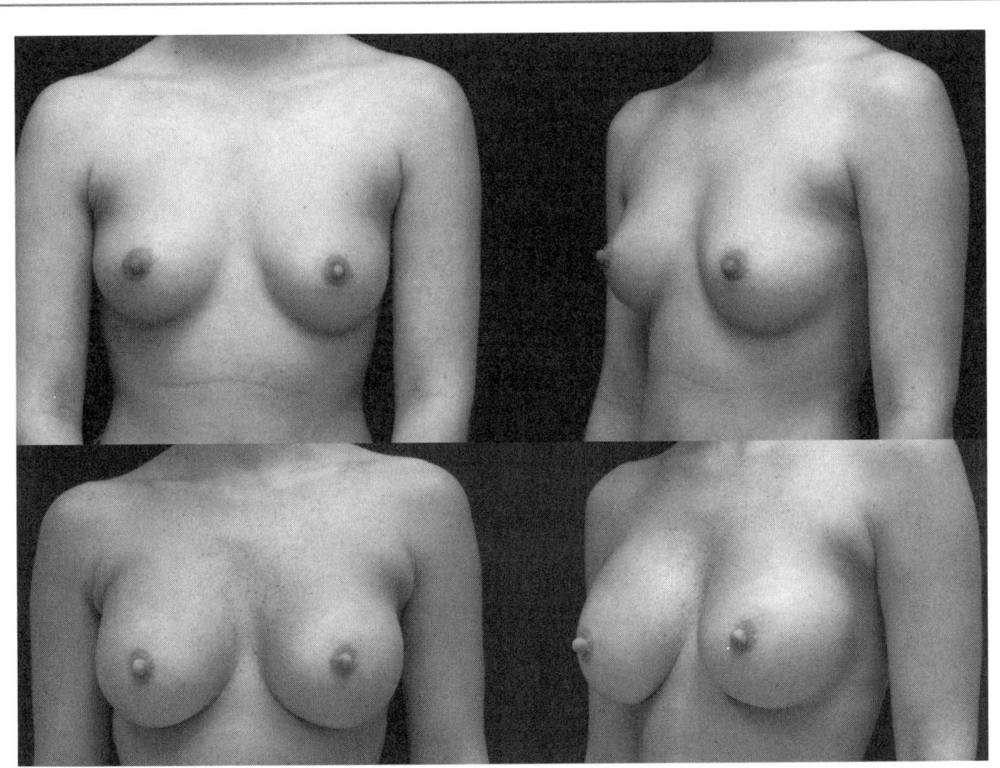

Photo 16-1. This patient has 350 ml. silicone gel implants placed in the pre-pectoral (above the muscle) space. The goal is a natural-looking breast, which was achieved.

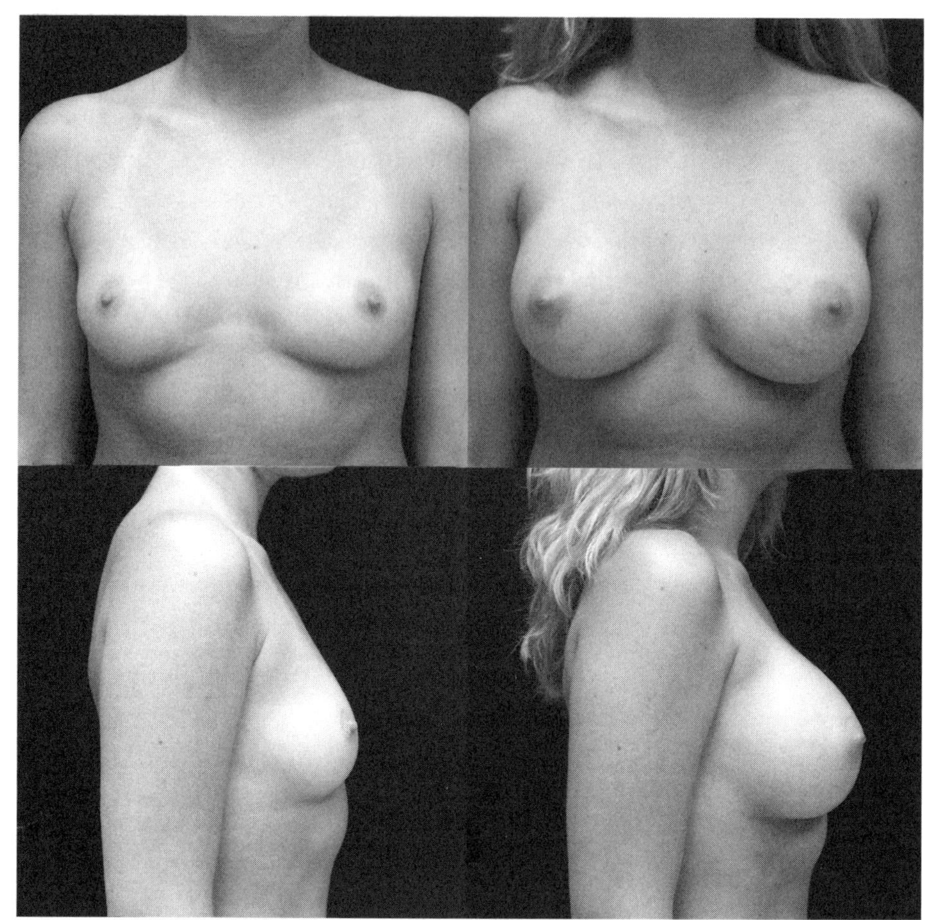

PHOTO 16-2. This patient has 400 ml. silicone gel implants placed in the pre-pectoral space. Typically, the patient relates to us her desired size, and we choose the implant size to achieve her goal, but always trying to create a natural appearing, soft breast.

Limitations

If the patient is reasonable, she will experience no significant limitations with breast augmentation mammoplasty. An example of unreasonable expectations is someone petite in stature wanting huge implants. Yes, she can have them, but they may not look as natural and will have a higher risk of encapsulation, deformation, and even numbness. Sometimes a patient with significant sagging wants an implant, but not an uplift. Again, this procedure can be done, but it may look like the aforementioned "sand in a sock," and the nipples may point down toward her feet. Not a pretty sight. Generally, if the nipple is as low as the inframammary crease below the breast, I recommend an uplift procedure.

If a patient has a round chest which is not very flat in the front, the breasts and nipple will point outward. These people will never have much, if any, cleavage. Some surgeons try to correct this problem by putting the implants closer together, but this strategy makes the nipples point outward even more. The implant must be placed directly behind the nipple, so if the implant is placed too high, the nipple will point downward and so forth.

Therefore, the principal limitation is that a patient must be reasonable if she wants a natural-looking breast. The "moundy" appearance we see in some movie stars, models, and even on some magazine covers is not the look of natural-looking breasts by any stretch of the imagination. However, this look is occasionally what patients ask for and want.

An additional limitation pertains to exercise. I recommend no strenuous pectoralis muscle (chest) exercises basically forever (as I explain later).

Postoperative Course

Patients will receive pain medicine postoperatively because any time tissues are stretched, they can be quite sore. For this reason, the sub-pectoral approach tends to be more painful, but only for a day or so more than pre-pectoral placement. The pain medication prescribed after surgery should be sufficient to manage typical postoperative pain, so if the flares of pain occur in spite of the pain medication (breakthrough pain), the patient should notify the surgeon.

We, and certain other plastic surgeons, perform the rapid recovery breast augmentation, which is relatively painless. This procedure involves meticulous dissection and early massaging exercises. Ask your plastic surgeon about this technique.

I recommend that patients limit activity for the first three days or so after breast augmentation. Heavy exercising should be postponed for a few weeks and not be done to the point of feeling "the burn." In my practice, some patients with perfect breast augmentation results began doing pectoralis exercises ten to fifteen years after their operations and subsequently developed encapsulations. Even without doing pectoralis muscle exercises, a woman still has the rest of the body to exercise, which is plenty to keep her busy.

Patients learn mobility exercises to do at about the first postsurgical day, except in the case of textured implants. Patients with textured implants should avoid breast exercises entirely to allow the tissues to grow to the implants, which supposedly helps keep the implant pocket from encapsulating and closing around the implant. A good general guideline is that if an activity hurts, don't do it—your body is telling you "no." Also, as after any surgery, heat encourages increased swelling for the first month. This pertains to any kind of heat—external or internal (internal heat refers to any activity that makes one perspire).

17 Breast Uplift (Mastopexy)

The breast is unique in that it is made up of a combination of glandular tissue plus fat and is loosely covered with skin. Breasts sag with time, as does everything else, from legs and buttocks to the brow. However, breasts seem to sag more, and no exercise or trick can change that as there is no muscle in the breast. You may have seen extreme sagging of the breasts combined with dark brown, multi-pigmented, wrinkled skin between the breasts caused by excess sun exposure. A system of collagen and elastin fibers hold breast tissues in place for a while, but excess sun exposure plus habits such as smoking, poor diet, obesity, going braless, and even jogging without proper support destroy the integrity of these fibers causing premature sagging. Other factors also increase sagging, such as the increased weight in a larger breast, pregnancy, breastfeeding, and large fluctuations in body weight. Sagging breasts may be small or large. Some breasts have a high inframammary crease, which tilts the breast downward, making them sag more. Large breasts may require reduction mammoplasty, which will be discussed later in this chapter. With the exception of large breasts, most mastopexies also require small implants. However, in patients with moderate-sized breasts, their own breast tissue may be used for their augmentation, called an "auto-augmentation." The patient's tissue is folded upon itself beneath the skin along with a mastopexy instead of using an implant. Some ladies use the term "perky" to describe their breasts after a breast uplift, and this term seems appropriate.

With every plastic surgery procedure there is a trade-off of some kind (as with most things in life) and mastopexy is no different. The trade-off in this case is some unavoidable scarring on the breasts. I cannot, however, recall many patients who objected to these scars as the breasts have a much more youthful shape after surgery. Some people do scar more extensively than others, though bathing suits or bras easily conceal the scars. A bit of advice, however: ask your plastic surgeon if you will have visible stitch marks. A properly performed procedure should reveal none as sutures should be hidden beneath the skin. If any skin sutures are necessary, the surgeon should take them out four to five days after the surgery, leaving no visible suture scars.

Age

People living healthy lives usually feel energized and want to look their best at any age. As with breast augmentation, the age range of women seeking breast uplift procedures is quite diverse, varying from the early thirties on up. Most women are in their thirties or forties, though I have had patients from their twenties to their sixties request the procedure.

Physical Aspects to Be Considered

The usual requirement for eligibility for a mastopexy is that the nipple be below the inframammary crease. If the nipple lies at or very slightly below the inframammary crease, an implant alone may provide adequate lift. Sometimes, however, the patient and/or doctor are tempted to insert an implant without an uplift procedure even when the nipple is well below the crease, but they both should be very careful with this approach. An implant should not be considered a treatment to elevate the breast, although initially there is some slight lift. Eventually, however, the weight of the implant will increase sagging. There are, of course, exceptions to any rule, so you must talk to your plastic surgeon and listen very carefully to his or her advice.

For the most part, the main differences between patients pertain to the size and degree of sagging of the breasts. Always remember that a heavier breast sags sooner and more than a smaller breast. Because a mastopexy does not change the size of the breast itself, women with smaller breasts usually opt for implants along with a minimal uplift. With larger breasts, depending upon the patient's desired final breast size, implants may or may not be necessary.

Another area requiring careful decision-making is when the breast size is ample and the patient doesn't want to be larger, just uplifted. This goal can be achieved, but the area above the nipple may appear somewhat flat after a year or so if an uplift is performed alone. An implant, even if small, will help correct this problem (or ask your plastic surgeon about the auto-augmentation procedure). My choice of implants in this situation is often a textured implant, as the texture sticks to the breast and maintains the lift for a longer period of time. Although everything continues to sag with time, whether one has a breast uplift, a facelift, or no surgery at all, a patient will always be better off having a properly indicated, well-performed procedure. You simply want to look good for many years to come, and it may be many years before additional sagging is as bothersome to you as the original sagging was before plastic surgery.

Expectations

After surgery and recovery, the nipple will point straight ahead and not down toward your feet. The breast will be lifted, but it will not appear as it did when you were a teenager. The actual mound of the breast is difficult to lift as much as is desired sometimes, which may leave less fullness in the upper versus the lower part of the breast. A small implant may correct this problem. Either way you'll see significant improvement, and patients are usually pleased with the results. Extreme sagging, of course, is more difficult to elevate as much as we might like, but surgeons should tell this to patients in advance to avoid surprises. Still, improvement following an uplift procedure can be quite significant.

Treatment Techniques

Generally I use two techniques for breast uplifts. For the mildly sagging breast the resulting scar is shaped like a lollipop, and in the more extensive case the scar has an anchor-like shape (Figure 17-1).

The "lollipop" approach can also be used in any breast with a genetically short space between the nipple and inframammary crease. The difference between

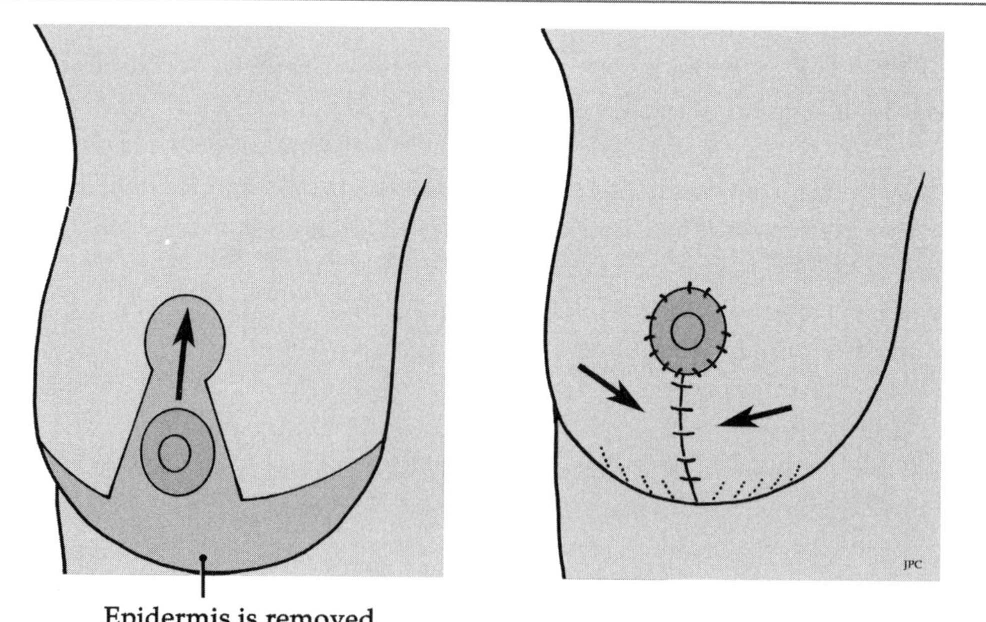

Figure 17-1. The resulting scar is shaped like an anchor. The lollipop incision lacks the lower horizontal scar in the inframammary crease, and thus has the shape of a lollipop.

these two approaches is the absence or presence of an incision within the inframammary crease, which is fairly inconspicuous. In the lollipop mastopexy, such an inframammary incision is not necessary. After making the incision, the surgeon reduces the skin area, folds over the breast tissue beneath the skin, and sutures the tissue to itself to create a mounded shape. Then, if needed, the surgeon adds a breast implant as explained in Chapter 16.

Limitations

Patients with reasonable expectations have high satisfaction rates even with the inevitable scarring caused by uplift procedures. The main limitation regarding breast uplifts is how youthful the breast can be made to look, which depends upon its size, the patient's desires, and how much initial sagging exists. If a patient has large breasts with moderate-to-severe sagging and still wants to be a D cup, she can achieve her goal, but in a short time the breast will regain the appearance of "sand in a sock," especially if an implant is used. Breasts with stretched tissues cannot support a heavy breast. With plastic surgery, as with life, there are some things people simply cannot have, not for long, anyway.

Postoperative Course

Initially the breasts look bruised, distorted, and swollen. Count on this happening, because if you expect this, it won't be a shock to you. Within a couple of weeks, much of the swelling subsides, and the breasts begin to take their final shape. The scars will look their best after about one year, but they usually look good after three months. Be very careful about pulling on the incision lines or doing anything that makes the breast bounce for three months or so. The longer you wait the better, as you want the breast to scar firmly in its new elevated position. Also, expect to wear a bra in the daytime forever, except with certain attire in which one cannot be worn, like a bathing suit. When jogging or exercising, you may want to wear two sports bras.

18 Breast Reduction (Reduction Mammoplasty)

This procedure is more common than you might think. Large, heavy breasts can cause pain in the shoulders, neck, upper back, and even in the breasts themselves. For this reason, insurance may cover breast reduction, depending upon how much breast tissue is removed. Usually around one pound of tissue removal per breast is required for insurance coverage. Each year, however, the amount of removal required seems to increase even as payments to patients, doctors, and hospitals decrease. I doubt if these changes come as a surprise to anyone.

Reduction mammoplasty is uniformly one of the most satisfying procedures that we perform for our patients, as women get absolutely sick of carrying around overly large, heavy breasts. Sometimes husbands rebel at the idea of a breast reduction, but in this case I suggest that they hang a belt around their necks with a pound or two at each end for a few days and then give their opinions. They usually get the idea at this point.

Age

You may be shocked to learn that the youngest patient I have performed this procedure on was twelve years old. This young lady weighed eighty-five pounds and had breasts that were huge and seemingly growing by the day. Her breasts would have ultimately outgrown their own blood supply, resulting in a necrotic breast (something like gangrene), which would have been a disaster. The procedure went well and, amazingly, she was so outgoing that all her friends visited her in the hospital after the surgery. This young lady was healthy mentally because of the support and love from her family. Though interesting, the above case is unusual. The usual age range for breast reduction procedures is from the late teens to the sixties.

Physical Aspects to Consider

Breast size and body weight are important factors regarding surgical planning and insurance coverage of a breast reduction. If the patient is significantly overweight, the insurance company may require her to lose weight before providing coverage. Another significant consideration is whether the breast is made up primarily of glandular tissue or fat. Though this information doesn't alter the type of mammoplasty performed, it does affect the results, as glandular breasts can be made to appear more youthful-looking and perky. Other factors such as breast size after surgery depend primarily on patient preference. Final breast size is determined by patient height as much as anything, as large breasts can make a short person look overweight.

Expectations

In addition to reducing breast size, reduction mammoplasty creates an effective lift of the breasts. The nipples will be higher, and the breast will be smaller and more elevated. The postsurgical scars will be anchor-shaped as in mastopexy. Some techniques leave a scar around the areola and straight down as in the previously mentioned lollipop mastopexy. In others, the lollipop "stick" goes off to the side, though I prefer not to use this approach because it often distorts the breast shape. Other surgeons may not share this opinion, however. When choosing a surgeon, always ask to see photos of his or her work taken at least one year after surgery so that you can make your decisions based on long-term results. Also, I encourage second opinions, but ask these surgeons for photos as well.

Patients with pain in their shoulders and neck due to overly large breasts can expect to be almost entirely relieved of these symptoms. This outcome has been fairly consistent. Breast numbness, usually in the nipple area, can be a significant problem after reduction mammoplasty. Some patients state that sensation is normal, but I find that difficult to believe, as this procedure's extensive incisions around the areola and nipple affect many nerve fibers. So the incidence and extent of post-reduction numbness is unpredictable, though most sensation usually remains, and patients infrequently complain about this problem. Sensation may continue to improve for a year or so, as the nerve fibers affected by the procedure slowly heal and regenerate.

Treatment Techniques

A reduction mammoplasty is performed under general anesthesia and can take anywhere from two to four hours, depending upon the breast size and the surgeon. A local anesthetic is also injected during surgery to reduce postoperative pain, though my patients say this procedure is not very painful. The surgeon makes incisions and moves the nipple and areola upward to a predetermined location. The nipple is not removed from the body like a graft. Instead, it remains attached to a flap of breast tissue and never loses its blood supply as would a graft. The surgeon then removes tissue not involved in the nipple-areola flap as desired, and sutures together the remaining flaps in a layered fashion (Figure 17-1). Suture marks should not be visible.

Limitations

Limitations regarding reduction mammoplasty pertain to the extremes of patient desires and circumstances. If a woman with large, sagging breasts wants exceptionally large breasts after surgery, then pain symptoms related to breast size and weight will not subside, and her breasts will still sag. If the patient wants very small breasts, it may be difficult to make them round without flat spots somewhere. Also, if a patient is quite overweight, the breast will also be mostly fat, and the uplift part of the reduction probably will not last. This is because fat does not hold sutures very securely, so the breast will sag again. Still, patients seem to be elated with the procedure.

If the patient is a smoker, flap survival is at increased risk. A patient could lose a nipple or part of her areola after reduction mammoplasty because the blood supply to the area may not be sufficient to sustain the flap tissue, in which case all or part of the flap may die. Typically in this case that part of the areola or nipple would turn blue, then turn black and eventually become ulcerated. This problem may take several months to heal, with scar tissue replacing the tissue that did not survive. And all this trouble is a consequence of smoking! The problem is that cigarettes cause small blood vessels in the tissue to constrict, reducing the amount of blood and oxygen reaching the tissues. In any type of flap surgery, such as a reduction mammoplasty, facelift, or tummy tuck, many blood vessels are cut, so it is imperative that the remaining ones maintain full blood flow. Nicotine of any form, even in chewing gum, reduces this blood flow.

Postoperative Course

Surgical drains are usually necessary after breast reduction surgery because of the extensive incisions, flaps, and tissue removal. I usually remove these drains on the second postoperative day, and this removal is not painful. As mentioned, there are no sutures to remove, as they are hidden under the skin. Patients usually go home on the day of or the day after surgery. After the drains are removed, patients change their dressings twice daily and return for follow-up examination on about the fifth postsurgical day.

The breasts will be black and blue, distorted, and swollen for a couple of weeks, and the swelling will remain for several months, going away a little each day. The scars, as with any scar, will take a year to look their best. Keloids (large, red scars) may occur in some patients. If you develop them, your doctor will treat them, usually with cortisone injections and topical silicone dressings. In such cases the scar appearance is compromised.

19 Body-Contouring Surgery

By Michael Rae Huntly, M.D., F.A.C.S.
Board Certified Plastic Surgeon
Finger and Associates, Plastic Surgery Center, PC
Savannah, Georgia

Body-contouring surgery employs surgical techniques to modify body shape in an attempt to approach more closely a patient's ideal body image. Body-contouring involves the following three types of surgery:

- liposuction
- excisional surgery
- fat-grafting (a recently added category)

These techniques can be performed separately or together, depending on the patient's individual needs. It should be understood, however, that liposuction essentially removes subcutaneous fat alone through small incisions utilizing hollow tubes or cannulas connected to a suction apparatus. Excisional (skin-removing) surgery, on the other hand, removes both skin and fat if both are judged to be in excess.

Candidates for Surgery

Patients requesting body-contouring surgery are usually women desiring slimmer, more sculpted figures. Today's media is obsessed with diet, fitness, youth, and extreme slimness, and as we all know, they portray these attributes as the norm for which we should all strive thereby creating a stereotype which can in reality only an extremely small minority of people can attain. Professional models are carefully selected for genetically determined characteristics such as height, slimness, bone structure, and skin quality. In addition, many models undergo plastic surgery and/or spend countless hours each day in the gym honing their figures to perfection. This is their occupation. Also, many are on extremely strict diets, and some are anorexic.

Often, media images reaching the public eye have been digitally enhanced to air-brush imperfections and slim or stretch proportions. So these media images, which are the "ideal" many people strive for, are unachievable for most women and men despite any amount of dieting, exercise, or surgery. We can, however, make efforts with these ideal body images in mind. These efforts should start with a diet and exercise program to optimize shape and fitness, with surgery reserved for final modification of contour after diet and exercise have provided their maximum benefits. Body-contouring surgery is possible for people aged from the teenage years to over seventy. Breast modification is the body-contouring procedure most frequently sought by teenagers of both genders. Surgical correction of breast development in teenaged boys may require liposuction or excisional surgery, or a combination of both. Correction of excessive breast development in teenaged women may require breast reduction surgery, which is discussed in Chapter 18.

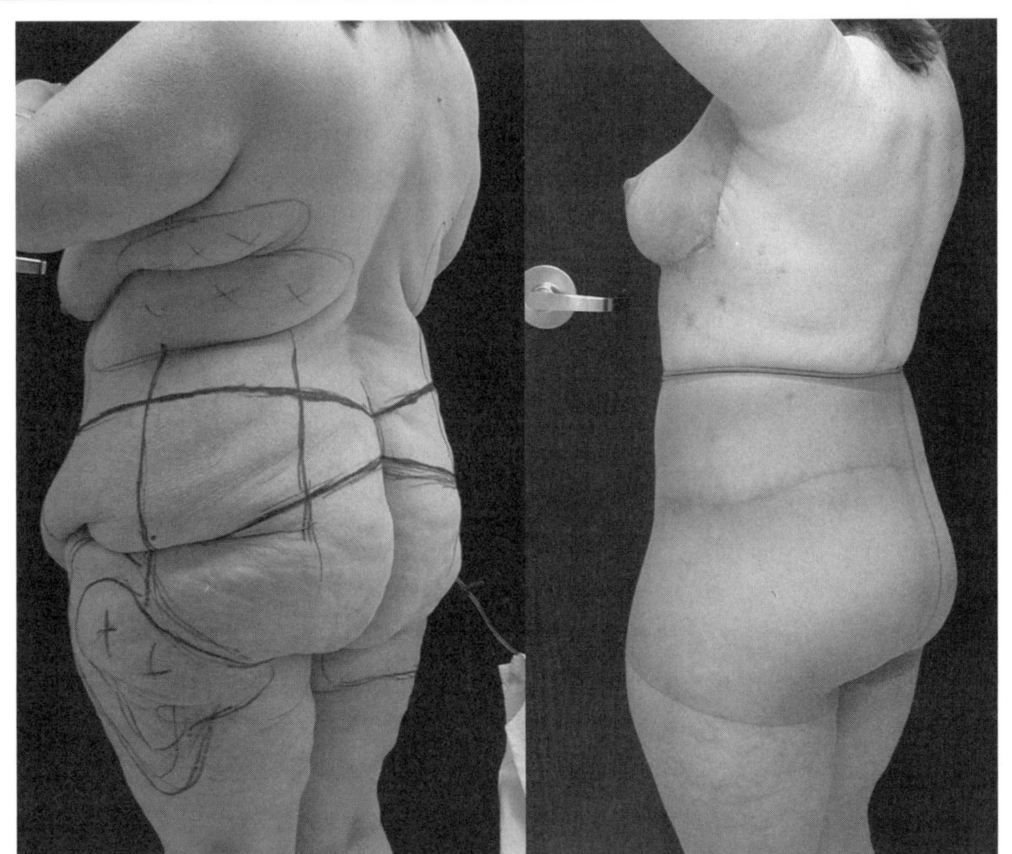

PHOTO 19-1. Following gastric bypass surgery, this patient had a total body lift, reduction mammoplasty, and liposuction. In the postoperative photo, she is still wearing her postoperative pressure garment to help reduce swelling.

Most patients seeking body-contouring surgery fall into two main categories. More than half of these patients are twenty to forty years old and are typically not significantly overweight but very body-conscious and dissatisfied with perceived figure flaws that fall short of their ideals. A smaller group of patients forty to seventy years old typically expresses the same concerns as these younger patients, with additional concerns related to changes brought on by aging, weight gain, hormonal changes, and a less active life-style, often due to the rigors of work and raising a family. Inevitably, women and men undergo an age-related widening or thickening of the midsection. Under the relentless force of gravity, structures of the torso, breasts, hips, buttocks, thighs, and arms sag as the support structures and skin quality deteriorate. Younger patients generally have better skin and tissue quality with better elastic properties and often respond well to liposuction alone. In such situations, we rely on the skin's natural elastic recoil to remodel and recontour the treated areas. Older patients exhibit more skin looseness, as well as stretch marks and sagging that will respond better to excisional techniques which remove excess skin and fat and restore sagging tissues to their previous, more desirable locations. Even with these excisional techniques, some amount of liposuction is usually necessary for older patients (see Photo 19-1).

Patients having lost large amounts of weight through diet and exercise or gastric bypass generally have enormous flaps of extra skin remaining after reduction of the skin "envelope," which contains large quantities of excess fat. This skin has been stretched beyond its elastic limits, as evidenced by stretch marks, which are internal tears of the deeper elements of the skin. In this case, the skin has lost its elastic recoil and is incapable of contracting to take up slack areas caused by weight loss. In these situations, liposuction often makes skin folds more pronounced, so excisional techniques are usually necessary to remove extra skin and fat.

Pregnancy and Childbirth

Not surprisingly, pregnancy and childbirth take a toll on women's bodies. In particular, large or multiple babies may stretch the abdominal wall dramatically, especially in small women. Pregnancy stretches all layers of the abdominal wall, including muscle, fascia (the strong fibrous layer that wraps around the muscles), skin, and fat. Generalized weight gain with pregnancy and breast-feeding stretches the skin of the hips, thighs, buttocks, breasts, and arms and can create stretch marks in these locations. Stretch marks are permanent scars that cannot be erased. Well-known remedies such as massaging the abdomen and breasts with cocoa butter throughout pregnancy may help to minimize stretch marks, but keeping weight within the obstetrician's recommended range is the most strongly advised preventive intervention. It's tempting during pregnancy to completely abandon your previous dietary habits, accepting weight gain as inevitable. Maintaining an obstetrician-approved diet and exercise regimen during pregnancy can, however, minimize weight gain and the resulting looseness, sagging, and stretch marks after pregnancy. When these problems do happen, excisional techniques such as abdominoplasty (also known as the tummy tuck) can restore muscle and fascial tightness after pregnancy and help restore abdominal contour. These techniques reduce stretch marks by direct removal as well.

Cellulite

The word "cellulite" has no precise medical meaning, but it is used to describe the dimpling and surface irregularities seen on the skin, most commonly on the thighs and lower torso. It is associated with loosening of the skin and relaxation of the collagen matrix supporting the skin and the subcutaneous fat. The skin and fat layer adhere to the deeper structures, the muscle and fascia, by multiple collagen strands or ligaments, and these strands or ligaments create a compartmentalization of the fat layer. As the skin and the support ligaments loosen and a person gains weight, the contained fat bulges between the support ligaments, creating the quilted effect that we see and recognize as cellulite. These dimples are much like the depressions that we see around the buttons on a sofa cushion.

Liposuction will not cure cellulite, but it may be helpful in milder cases. Severe cases require skin tightening and re-suspension in the form of an abdominoplasty, or thigh- or body-lifting procedures.

Expectations

Generally, patients considering body-contour surgery seek slimmer, more shapely figures wrapped in tight youthful skin, devoid of surface irregularities and imperfections. Some patients mistakenly perceive liposuction as a method of weight reduction and an easy substitute for a healthful life-style. They believe they can abuse their bodies with dietary indiscretions and sedentary habits and simply have the fat deposits sucked out, often on an annual basis. Nothing, however, could be further from the truth.

Ideally, patients should optimize their shape, weight, and physical fitness before proceeding with contouring surgery. A surgeon can then address residual problem areas with better outcomes. Often problem areas are localized fat collections in the lateral thighs, inner thighs, hips, flanks, bra-line, or tummy areas. These areas respond well to liposuction if skin quality is good and major areas of excess skin are not evident. Liposuction is most effective on the localized fat deposits due to a patient's genetic body type. Despite being very weight-conscious, many women may have saddlebags that resist diet and exercise. Upper arms, abdomens, "love handles," and the neck can be similarly problematic as well.

People are born with a certain number of fat cells. During childhood these numbers may increase slightly, but by mid-teen years it is generally considered that the number of fat cells in the body is fixed. People put on weight by storing more fat in individual fat cells. In other words, existing fat cells get fatter as the body increases in weight. Liposuction removes some of the existing fat cells, and if more fat cells exist in particular problematic areas, liposuction permanently removes some cells, which will not regenerate. Overeating, however, will continue to add fat to existing fat cells throughout the body. A more generalized accumulation of fat would result, though preferential deposition of fat in the problem areas will no longer be as pronounced.

Why shouldn't obese people have liposuction alone? Severely overweight people exhibit a diffuse thickening of the fat layer throughout the body. In this situation, even extensive tissue removal via liposuction will make little discernible difference in these patients' appearances. Furthermore, in these people, body-contouring surgery by liposuction alone can be fraught with complications such as wrinkling and hanging skin, fluid collections under the skin and, sometimes, excessive blood loss. Obese patients are not generally considered good candidates for liposuction. The best plan prior to liposuction is proper pre-surgical weight loss, followed by the best procedure for each situation.

Liposuction can be a most gratifying procedure in the properly indicated patient; however, without a plan and without discipline, liposuction is often a waste of money and time. I know of one patient who has undergone liposuction almost every year for the past four years, but continues to gain weight. Though the liposuctioned areas are less likely to accumulate fat, the excess weight from overeating must go somewhere. In her case it goes preferentially to her arms, neck, face, and legs. In sharp contrast to this patient's situation, I have also seen patients who use liposuction or even excisional surgery as an incentive to become more careful and diligent about their overall health.

20 Liposuction

By Michael Rae Huntly, M.D., F.A.C.S.

Liposuction, or lipoplasty, was first developed in France during the 1970s. The technique rapidly gained popularity and is now the most commonly performed cosmetic procedure. In principle, liposuction involves suctioning subcutaneous fat from the body through small incisions strategically placed to allow access with minimal scarring. This procedure requires hollow tubes of various lengths and diameters with various tip designs. These tubes are hand-held by the surgeon and attached to a vacuum pump producing approximately one atmosphere of negative pressure. The surgeon manipulates the tube (or cannula) back and forth through the treated area, vacuuming out fat globules. After treatment, the appearance of the fat layer is similar to Swiss cheese, with a honeycomb effect where the fat has been removed. Early cannulas were large, some as large as one centimeter (about one-half inch) in diameter. These tubes removed fat quickly and effectively, but made it difficult to achieve a smooth result. With today's smaller diameter cannulas and different tip designs, fat can still be removed effectively with contour irregularities less likely to occur. Some surgeons also leave an undisturbed layer of fat over the treated area, which helps achieve a smoother surface contour. Surgeons treat most areas from more than one direction, a strategy creating a crisscross pattern of tunnels through the treated segment, allowing a smoother result.

A key addition to treatment is the use of pressure garments to compress the treated area after the liposuction procedure. Compression controls postoperative swelling and helps remodel the fat layer during the six- to twelve-week healing phase following surgery. I prefer that patients use compression garments around the clock the first two to three weeks after liposuction, according to the area, and then twelve hours per day for the next three weeks. Six to twelve weeks after surgery, body-formers or slimming garments, available at department stores and sized to fit individual patients, can be substituted for the compression garment and are often more user-friendly, especially in hotter climates.

The following major changes in liposuction techniques have evolved over the past two decades:

- Tumescent liposuction
- Ultrasound-assisted liposuction
- Mechanically assisted liposuction

Tumescent Liposuction

Tumescent liposuction is arguably the most important of these procedures. Prior to the invention of tumescent liposuction, 40% of fluid suctioned from the body was blood, so blood loss was a significant limitation of the procedure. More than two liters of tissue removal could result in significant blood loss requiring transfusion.

Tumescent liposuction involves pre-treating the area to be suctioned by injecting a salt solution containing local anesthetic and adrenalin, a drug that constricts small blood vessels in the fat layer, reducing the blood loss. Typically, surgeons inject or pump a fairly large volume of this solution into the fat layer and allow several minutes for the medications to take effect, usually evident by blanching of the skin overlying the "tumesced" tissues. Liposuction then proceeds, which removes a comparable amount of fat-containing fluid. The fluid removed after tumescent liposuction contains much less blood than when prior techniques were used. Typically, with this technique, 50% to 80% of the fluid removed will consist of fat. Essentially, a volume exchange occurs during which a volume of clear fat-free fluid is injected into the body and a similar quantity of fat-containing fluid is removed. So, overall tumescent liposuction allows more fat removal without significant blood loss, which in turn allows more fat to be removed. Furthermore, the local anesthetic in the injected fluid dramatically diminishes pain when the patient awakens from general anesthesia.

Initially, the patient will not see a dramatic change in shape because the fluid exchange that has occurred is approximately equal—that is, the injected volume is similar to the volume of fluid removed during surgery. It is important to realize that, as in any surgery, liposuction creates an injury and swelling is the body's natural response to injury of any sort. Of course, the injured areas take time to fully recover. The new body contour will emerge in six to twelve weeks, as swelling decreases with the help of compression garments. Patients can resume normal exercise three to four weeks after the procedure. Importantly, patients must guard against overeating during the recovery phase, as they are less active and so may be likely to gain weight. Also, tissues retain fluid during the healing phase, much like sponges retain fluid. Lymphatic massage and ultrasound treatments can help to free and remove this retained fluid. I also recommend a low-salt diet with plenty of water intake to help reduce swelling, and let's not forget the importance of the "binder" garment. Patients should avoid hot baths and sunbathing during the healing phase because these activities encourage additional swelling.

Ultrasound-Assisted Liposuction

Ultrasound-assisted liposuction evolved in the 1990s. During this procedure, the surgeon injects tumescent fluid as in a standard liposuction, then with an ultrasonic energy source delivers sound waves into the tissues from the tip of the cannula basically melting the fat during suction. This ultrasonic energy mechanically breaks up the fat cells to optimize fat removal. This approach is helpful in high-volume procedures required in some people who have larger problem areas, as well as during liposuction revisions and liposuction of areas such as the back, where fat is typically harder to remove. The technique, however, is less forgiving and surgeons must use great care to avoid excessive fat removal and burning internal skin caused with the tip of the cannula. In slimmer patients, the margin for error is very small and I believe more control is possible with either traditional liposuction or mechanically assisted liposuction. Some plastic surgeons, however, believe that more skin shrinkage can be achieved with ultrasound-assisted procedures. In addition, areas that have already been treated, scarred areas, and the "love handles" are areas that ultrasonic liposuction is particularly effective in treating. Ultrasonic liposuction is particularly technique-oriented (and some feel, more difficult), so I recommend that patients consult a plastic surgeon with lots of experience.

A newer technique is the laser-assisted liposuction, which is energized with a laser, rather than ultrasound. This too is supposed to tighten the skin more than traditional liposuction. The light (laser) wave apparently is emitted through the entire length of the cannula rather than the tip alone. Time and experience will yield the advantages and disadvantages.

Mechanically Assisted Liposuction

This technique is another recent arrival on the liposuction scene. The cannula, or tube, used to remove the fat tissue is driven by an electric or air-driven motor in the hand-piece that creates movement of the cannula's tip. The range of this movement is only a few millimeters to centimeters (approximately 1 inch) depending on the design of the instrument. However, it more efficiently removes fat and greatly reduces surgeon fatigue. The surgeon can then concentrate on guiding the tip of the suction cannula through the target areas without providing all the mechanical effort required for tissue removal himself or herself. Personally, I have found this technique extremely useful for patients requiring a larger volume of fat removal. (See Photo 20-1.)

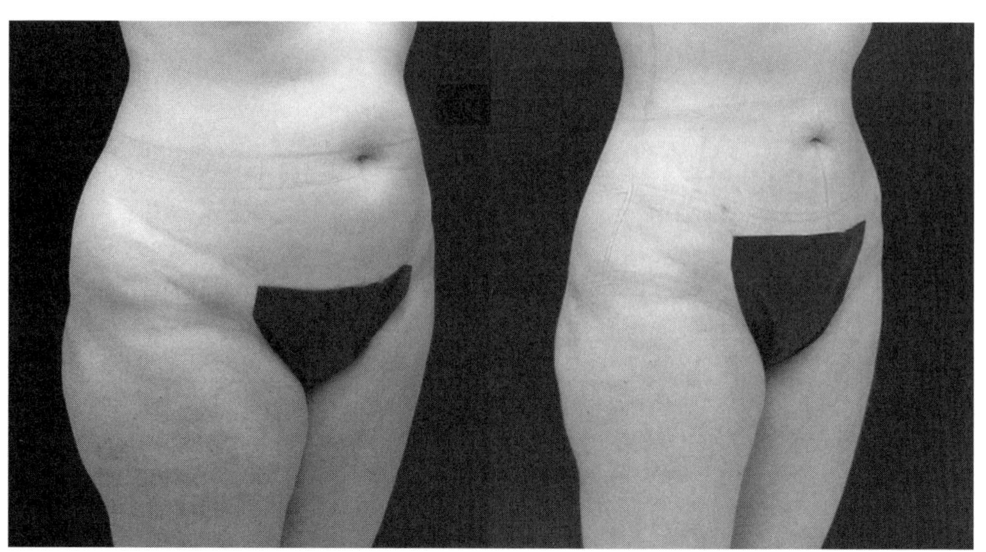

PHOTO 20-1. Before and after photos of a patient following liposuction of the abdomen, sides, and inner and outer thighs.

21 Abdominoplasty ("Tummy-Tuck") and Other Body Lifts

By Michael Rae Huntly, M.D., F.A.C.S.

Several well-recognized excisional procedures are available to improve body contour:

- Abdominoplasty (or "tummy-tuck"), circumferential body lift, and Fleur-de-Lys
- Medial (or inner) thigh lift
- Brachioplasty (or arm lift)

Abdominoplasty or Tummy-Tuck

Abdominoplasty (also known as the "tummy-tuck") consists of excising (cutting out) extra folds of skin and fat from the lower abdomen and using the patient's remaining skin and fat to resurface the area. For this procedure, the surgeon makes a lower incision just above the pubic area, extending upward and outward parallel to (but approximately one inch above) the groin crease and extending over the hip bone area. The extent of this horizontal and vertical excision depends upon the amount of tissue to be removed. The surgeon separates skin and underlying fat layers from the muscle layer extending along the hip and pubic area to the breast bone, taking care to preserve the blood vessels running between the muscle and the fat layer on either side of this central muscle layer. The surgeon uses a spreading technique along the direction of the blood vessels in order to elevate and move the abdominal tissues while preserving blood supply to abdominal fat and skin. This approach helps improve wound healing and decreases problems related to fluid collection under the skin after surgery.

In most abdominoplasty candidates, this central abdominal muscle layer is overstretched and loose, resulting in protrusion of the lower abdomen. This protrusion is particularly common among women in whom all layers of the abdominal wall have been stretched due to pregnancy. During the surgery, the anesthesiologist administers medication to relax these central muscles so the surgeon can assess the degree of looseness. The surgeon places permanent sutures along the midline of the abdomen from the breast bone to the pubic bone, cinching the muscle and fascia together, tightening the muscle layer and flattening the lower abdomen. The surgeon also makes an incision around the rim of the umbilicus (the belly button) to allow the apron of skin and underlying fat to be brought down and removed, leaving the belly button attached by its stalk to the muscle and fascia. To position the belly button "in" rather than "out," the surgeon secures it tightly to the underlying muscle layer using permanent buried sutures. Then he or she stretches skin and fat layers with the hips flexed to assess the extra folds of tissue that must be removed. Often, all extra tissue from the pubic bone to the umbilicus can be removed from the front of the abdomen, though this techinque may not be possible in patients with a high umbilicus. In these situations the surgeon will close the old belly button opening vertically in the midline of the abdomen between the old umbilicus position and the pubis, leaving a small scar. Then the surgeon brings the umbilicus through a new hole created by excising an ellipse of skin at the new chosen location above the old location. (The old location, now only a hole, will be much lower due to the tension on the skin and subcutaneous flap that is brought downward.) The surgeon trims excess tissue symmetrically on both sides, closes the wound in layers with internal sutures, and reinforces them with paper tape. To explain further, a small ellipse of skin is excised in the overlying skin at the site of the umbilicus, which is still attached to the underlying muscles and the umbilicus, on its preserved stalk, is brought through this new opening. Permanent sutures securing the umbilicus to the underlying muscle layer help pull the incision downward, hiding the incision in the umbilical depression and creating an "inny" belly button. (See Figures 21-1 and 21-2.)

Two drainage tubes are usually left under the skin and fat layers, exiting below the incision. These remove any fluid collecting under the skin and generally remain in place for four to seven days, sliding out easily during the follow-up office visit.

Recovery

Patients should walk as soon as possible after surgery. Walking with the knees slightly bent for the first week takes some of the tension off the healing wound incision, though an upright posture can be resumed approximately seven days after surgery. Patients should avoid vigorous exercise for a few weeks. Afterward, they can make a gradual return to their pre-surgical exercise routines, avoiding abdominal crunches or sit-ups for eight weeks. Swelling subsides gradually, but is often near completion after twelve weeks. Overall, however, as with all wounds, it takes a full year for swelling to disappear completely. Sensation below the umbilicus will be diminished after surgery. It gradually returns over several months as

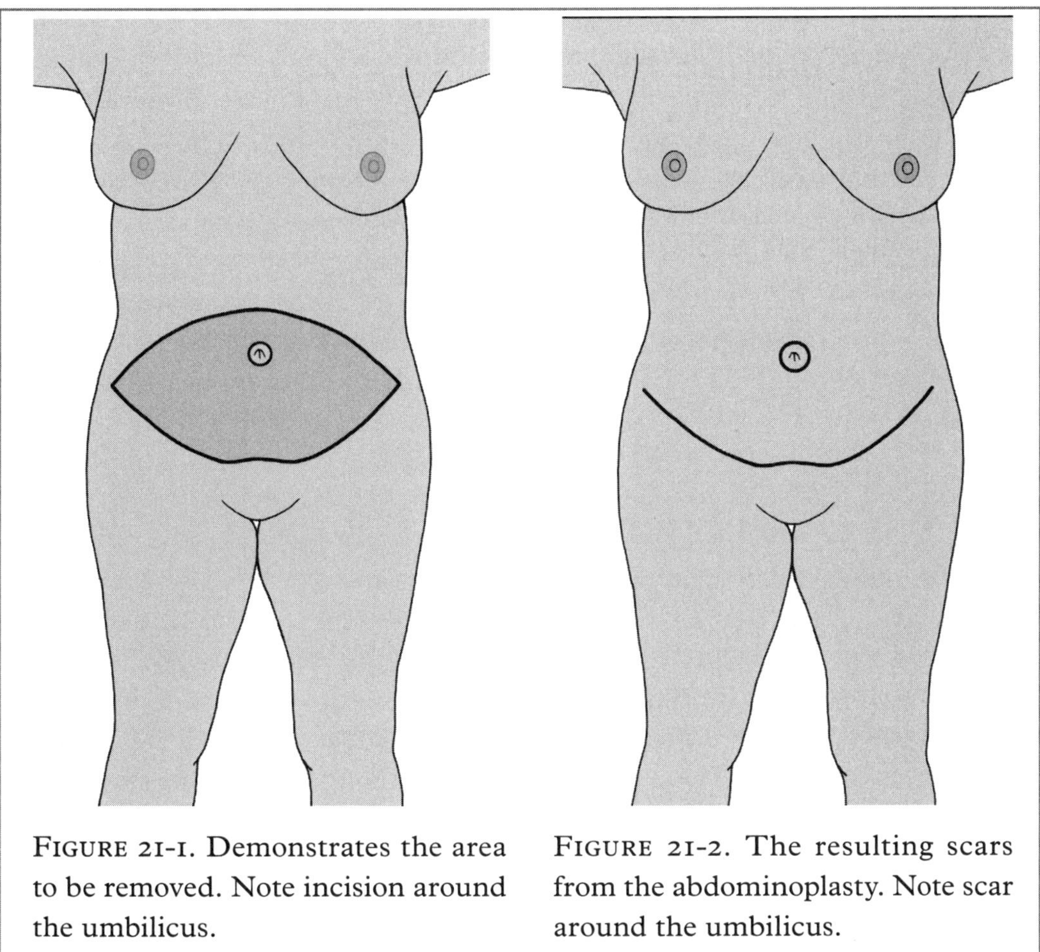

Figure 21-1. Demonstrates the area to be removed. Note incision around the umbilicus.

Figure 21-2. The resulting scars from the abdominoplasty. Note scar around the umbilicus.

the nerves in this area regenerate. Avoid smoking for at least three weeks before and after surgery to avoid problems related to poor healing of the surgical flap. In addition, avoid tight clothing and belts for the first eight weeks following surgery. Also, patients should not soak in hot baths or sunbathe for prolonged periods for a few weeks after surgery, as these activities prolong swelling and therefore delay full recovery.

Benefits

An abdominoplasty creates a tighter, flatter, more youthful abdominal appearance, while also possibly achieving some lifting and rejuvenation of a sagging pubic and groin area. Old Cesarean section scars, appendix scars, and stretch marks below the umbilicus can be partially or completely removed, depending on individual circumstances. Patients often lose several dress sizes.

Limitations

Abdominoplasty essentially removes a horizontal ellipse-shaped piece of skin and fat from the lower abdomen. Closure of this incision tightens tissue most effectively in the midline, with tightening diminishing toward either end of the ellipse. Most patients need tightening centrally, though some also have looseness in the flanks and hip areas. Traditional abdominoplasty will not effectively correct looseness in these areas, though patients with these problems may benefit from a circumferential-belt skin lipectomy (or body lift). The fat layer in these areas may require additional thinning by diet and exercise, lipodissolve, or liposuction.

Mini-Abdominoplasty

A mini-abdominoplasty may be appropriate for patients carrying the majority of their extra skin and fat below the umbilicus and in whom the area above the umbilicus is snug and tight. This procedure requires no repositioning of the belly button. The surgeon removes a smaller ellipse of lower abdominal tissue to tighten the lower abdominal skin and lifts the pubic and groin areas, incorporating muscle tightening if necessary. A high belly button can be lowered with this technique though; conversely, a patient with a low belly button is not a candidate for a mini-abdominoplasty because it will lower the belly button excessively.

Fleur-de-Lys Body Lift

Patients who have lost considerable weight may have circumferential folds of excess skin around the body. These patients can benefit from a triangular vertical excision of skin and fat in addition to the lower abdominal elliptical excision. This approach creates a "fleur-de-lys" pattern, which is sutured together in an inverted T shape. This procedure tightens the waistline significantly in selected patients, but also leaves a vertical scar. Many patients already have a scar in the abdominal midline from gastric bypass surgery, and in these cases this new scar is often an improvement. (See Figures 21-3, 21-4, and Photo 19-1 on page 187.)

Extended High Lateral Tension Abdominoplasty

This modification is helpful for patients with laxity of the flanks and is an intermediate technique between standard abdominoplasty and circumferential belt-lipectomy. This technique extends the abdominoplasty incision around the sides of the body for additional tightening in the flank area.

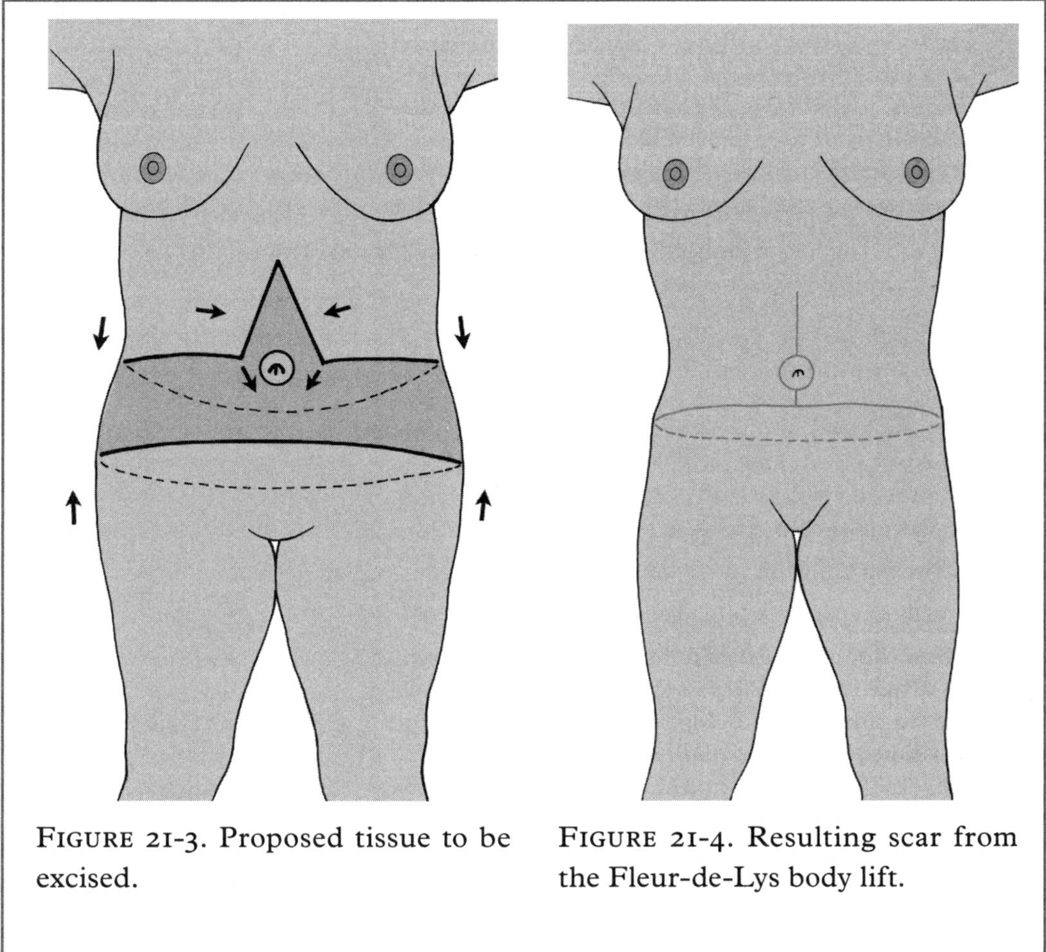

FIGURE 21-3. Proposed tissue to be excised.

FIGURE 21-4. Resulting scar from the Fleur-de-Lys body lift.

Circumferential Belt Lipectomy (Body Lift)

Patients who have gained and lost significant amounts of weight on one or more occasions will often have stretched skin and fat layers over the trunk, buttocks, and thighs. This excess of skin and subcutaneous fat sags in circumferential rolls around the trunk, which resembles a sleeve of skin and fat from the bra line to the knees, with correction requiring reduction of the vertical length of the sleeve. As already described, abdominoplasty reduces the sleeve length on the front of the torso, which is where most of the vertical excess is usually located. Body lifts require assessment of the vertical excess around the body at the level of the bikini line. The surgeon identifies the optimal position for the final closure line (scar), and evaluates the amount of skin and fat above and below this line at various parts around the trunk, extending to the back's midline. Removing tissue and bringing the resulting skin edges together creates equal and opposite forces at the line of closure that lift the sagging buttocks and thighs and pull downward on the flank rolls above. The balance of these forces determines the final scar position.

Generally, the procedure removes more tissue below the planned closure line, as extra folds of skin and fat are most pronounced in this area. The body lift frees the fat layer from underlying tissues in the "zone of adherence," an area over the hips where the fat layer is tethered securely to the deep fascia and muscle. Freeing the fat layer improves mobility of the lateral thighs and buttocks and enhances the lifting effect. The surgeon then uses permanent sutures to achieve a secure closure in several layers. He or she then repeats the procedure on the opposite side, creating a symmetrical lifting effect that reduces flank rolls and lifts the lateral thighs and buttocks.

Results of the belt lipectomy are most dramatic in patients with massive weight loss, though significant improvement can also be achieved in slimmer patients who have looseness and sagging of the lateral thighs and buttocks. The procedure often improves cellulite in these areas by the tightening effect achieved in the outer thighs. Surgery time is lengthy when belt lipectomy is combined with abdominoplasty, so it may be performed later as a separate procedure in some cases.

Recovery

Recovery is similar to that of abdominoplasty in terms of swelling, postoperative activities, and time necessary for resolution of postoperative changes. In addition, patients should have a caregiver at home for the first week after surgery to help with recovery, as it is often difficult for patients to walk after belt lipectomy without a helping hand. This caregiver is very important, as it is always best to get up and start moving as soon as possible after surgery.

Benefits

In addition to a tighter, more youthful abdomen, if done in addition to abdominoplasty, this procedure helps tighten and reduce flank and hip rolls. It also lifts and smooths the buttocks and outer thighs. Results can be quite dramatic.

Limitations

Looseness around the knees will not be significantly improved by belt lipectomy, as the effect of the lift diminishes with increasing distance from the line of closure. Likewise, the procedure will improve inner thighs to some degree, but not as much as can be achieved with an inner thigh lift. Some flatness of the buttocks can occur, especially in patients with massive weight loss, as they may also exhibit atrophy of the buttock muscles. Specific gluteal or buttock exercises or buttock implants can help restore contour in this area.

Medial (Inner) Thigh Lift

The medial thigh lift addresses excessive looseness of the inner thigh skin and fat layers. Typically, patients who are candidates for this procedure have rolls of excess skin and fat that may rub together, causing irritation. A lift procedure is more appropriate than liposuction to repair this problem when excess skin is the predominant problem. The procedure can, however, take place with or without liposuction, depending on the patient's needs. In the medial thigh lift, the surgeon makes an elliptical incision around the skin and fat of the upper inner thigh, tapering into the groin crease in the front of the body and into the buttock crease on the back side of the leg. He or she must consider carefully the amount of tissue removal, taking into account the laxity of the groin tissues. The surgeon then secures the inner thigh tissue to the tough tissue along the pelvic bone with permanent internal buried sutures. Without this secure anchor (or if there is excessive tissue removal) the scar line can migrate downward, becoming visible in a bathing suit.

Occasionally, patients who have undergone massive weight loss may have a circumferential as well as vertical excess of inner thigh tissues. In these patients, a vertical excision along the front of the inner thigh extending down to the knee may be required for an optimal result. Obviously, this approach leaves a permanent scar on the inner side of the thigh, extending vertically from the groin crease to the inner knee, though this scar may be acceptable to the patient with an extreme degree of circumferential thigh laxity. The trade-off in this case is loose, saggy skin on the inner thigh for tight skin with a scar. Most patients feel this is a worthwhile trade.

Brachioplasty (Tightening Skin of the Upper Arm)

Patients who have gained and lost a lot of weight can be left with loose, flabby skin on the upper arms. These patients are candidates for brachioplasty, which involves direct excision of skin and fat along the inner side of the upper arm, extending upward to the underarm and downward below the elbow. The surgeon creates an elliptical incision in the crease of the underarm to tighten the skin along the length of the arm and around the arm itself. Usually, he or she uses a slightly S-shaped closure to prevent contracture (shrinkage of the scar) across the elbow and underarm creases. The scar created by this procedure is well hidden on the inner side of the arm, but it commonly widens during healing because of tension on the suture line. Because of this widening, the scar may need to be revised after tension from the initial procedure has resolved. In addition, many will need additional liposuction.

Extended Brachioplasty

Extended brachioplasty extends the excision across the underarm area, along the border of the pectoral muscle and into the fold under the breast. This technique helps tighten the upper chest and back after extreme weight loss and is performed after a gastric bypass procedure.

Fat Grafting (Fat Transfer)

In recent years, fat grafting has evolved as a "filler" procedure for many areas and is now used commonly to augment soft tissue deficiencies. This procedure is useful in areas of the body and is particularly helpful in restoring the contour of the face to a more youthful configuration (see Chapter 10). With age, our lips lose volume and become thin, and our cheeks can hollow out so that we lose the youthful "apple cheeks" we once had. In addition, lower eyelids may become indented where they meet the nose, extending down obliquely across the cheek, called the "tear troughs" (Figure 10-6), leaving a sunken, dark appearance. Fat grafting can restore both these types of deficiencies. During fat grafting, the surgeon harvests the patient's own fat with a syringe and a blunt specialized needle usually from the abdomen through a small incision within the umbilicus. The surgeon then spins collected fat lightly in a centrifuge to separate viable fat cells from tissue fluid. The doctor then transfers the fat into 1 cc syringes and injects it into the chosen areas. To do so, the surgeon creates several tunnels, injecting the fat evenly as the specialized needle passes repeatedly through the target area. This approach ensures that healthy tissue surrounds the injected fat strands, providing the best possible chance of survival. Gentle handling of the harvested fat is essential to preserving viability of the fat cells and achieving a good "take" of the grafted fat. If the fat cells die, the body will reabsorb them, and volume added by the procedure will diminish. In practice, surgeons anticipate some resorption after this procedure, so they usually perform some degree of over-correction during fat injection to ensure long-term correction of the deficiency. This technique is useful in areas where fat has been lost due to a bruising or overzealous liposuction.

22 Lipodissolve (Injection Lipolysis)

You are now familiar with the routine methods of surgically removing excess fat, the most common of which is liposuction. The most common areas for liposuction are the abdomen, thighs, sides, back, arms, and neck. If excess skin is also present, the necessary surgical procedure is dermatolipectomy: surgically removing skin and underlying fat. The most common excision of skin plus fat is the abdomen, as in the tummy tuck. These procedures usually require general anesthesia and some recovery time.

Lipodissolve, a new technique, has entered the arena for fat removal. It is not indicated for overweight people or for those with excessive loose skin or people simply wanting to lose weight. However, for those people with small areas of fat that they wish reduced, lipodissolve may be ideal. Simply melting superfluous fat away with injections is a practical idea that has thus far been effective in most cases. So far lipodissolve is mostly performed by European plastic surgeons; their experience is with tens of thousands of patients. Also called Injection Lipolysis, lipodissolve is injecting a soybean-based product called phosphatidylcholine (PPC) into the fat just under the skin to dissolve the fat. We expect to see some minimal skin shrinkage also. PPC is not indicated for patients allergic to soybeans.

Technically, a treatment takes about thirty minutes, requiring numerous injections of PPC with very small needles every one-half inch or so into the area of the unwanted fat. In spite of the number of injections, no anesthesia is needed, except a topical anesthetic cream. Rarely, a patient will request a mild tranquilizer.

Following the injections the patient can expect swelling for a week or more. The area will be sore, tender, and pink. Immediately after the injections, we treat the area with a very powerful ultrasound to aid in product distribution. Most people who undergo lipodissolve go right back to work, although they may be somewhat uncomfortable. For optimum results, two to four sessions spaced at intervals of six to eight weeks may be required. Basically, each injection removes a certain amount of fat, and if more reduction is desired another lipodissolve treatment session is needed. My impression is that it can be effective if not too much fat is present. Although it is not for generalized weight loss, some weight loss may occur in addition to reduction of the area injected. The best areas to inject are the abdomen, sides (such as love-handles), back, arms, knees, neck, and jowls. However, lipodissolve can also be effective in the saddlebags and other fatty bulges such as inner thighs.

The FDA has not approved the use of PPC for injection, and this restriction may be regarded as a general risk. Studies have been ongoing for several years for the lipodissolve treatment, and it is rapidly becoming commonly used because it's nonsurgical and requires no downtime.

For many years PPC has been used for liver protection and to reduce fat embolism in the blood. This information can be found on the Internet under lecithin, phosphatidylcholine, or Lipodissolve. NETWORK-Lipolysis and others are doing many studies, which are available on the Internet to anyone interested in the procedure. After thousands of treatments across the world, no serious side effects have been reported to date. However, I feel strongly that lipodissolve should be performed by a physician with knowledge of sterile technique, such as a plastic surgeon, or at least under his or her direct supervision. This stipulation will also ensure treatment by one with experience in aesthetic surgery and with an aesthetic sense.

Surgical procedures such as liposuction have very few complications, but with the development of so many nonsurgical procedures, we will see much more use of lipodissolve in the near future.

23 Nonsurgical Treatments for Facial Rejuvenation

First we must understand what happens when faces age. The problems causing facial sagging are:

- Loss of elasticity
- Deflation

Deflation is the problem most people don't realize is happening. Although everywhere else in the body muscles go from bone to bone for joint motion, the face muscles originate on bone and insert in the skin for facial expression. The constant expressions such as smiling, squinting, and frowning burn off and traumatize the fat, and our faces deflate. We lose much subcutaneous tissue, including in the upper lip. Look at someone with minimal facial expressions and you will notice fewer wrinkles and depressions, for example Russia's Prime Minister Putin. See Figure 10-6 for names of depressions from fat loss in the face. It is also noteworthy to know that bones lose volume and muscles elongate and change as well, but the losses mentioned above are the primary problems. Fortunately, deflation and loss of elasticity can be improved.

Nonsurgical methods of tightening the skin of the face are with lasers or peels. Peels mostly reduce sun damage and pigmentation problems; however, some lasers can reduce sun damage and age spots as well as tighten the skin.

Laser Treatments With Minimal Recovery

Fraxel Lasers (Re:store and Re:pair)

The Re:pair is a more aggressive laser for more damaged skin. The Re:pair usually requires one treatment and the Re:store three to four treatments.

The Fraxel lasers resurface and tighten the skin and are also effective in reducing acne scars. The Fraxel differs from other lasers in that it coagulates microcolumns into the epidermis and dermis, and the penetration is deeper than with other lasers. Our white blood cells and mast cells take away the coagulated cells in these columns. Think of it as removing up to 20% of the surface, thus tightening the skin. Because the micro-columns leave normal skin between each column, healing is very rapid. Generally, residual pinkness and swelling last for five to ten days according to the treatment depth. Also the skin may feel dry and scaly for a few weeks. A moisturizing sun block is recommended following treatment.

A Fraxel laser treatment takes thirty to forty-five minutes depending on the size of the area treated. Optimum results are with three to four treatments spaced at least one month apart for the Re:store. What results can you expect from Fraxel treatments?

- Reduced or eliminated pigment abnormalities such as age spots or pregnancy mask (melasma)
- Tighter skin
- Fewer wrinkles such as crow's feet wrinkles around the mouth and virtually anywhere
- Reduced pore size
- Improved acne scars, other scars, and stretch marks

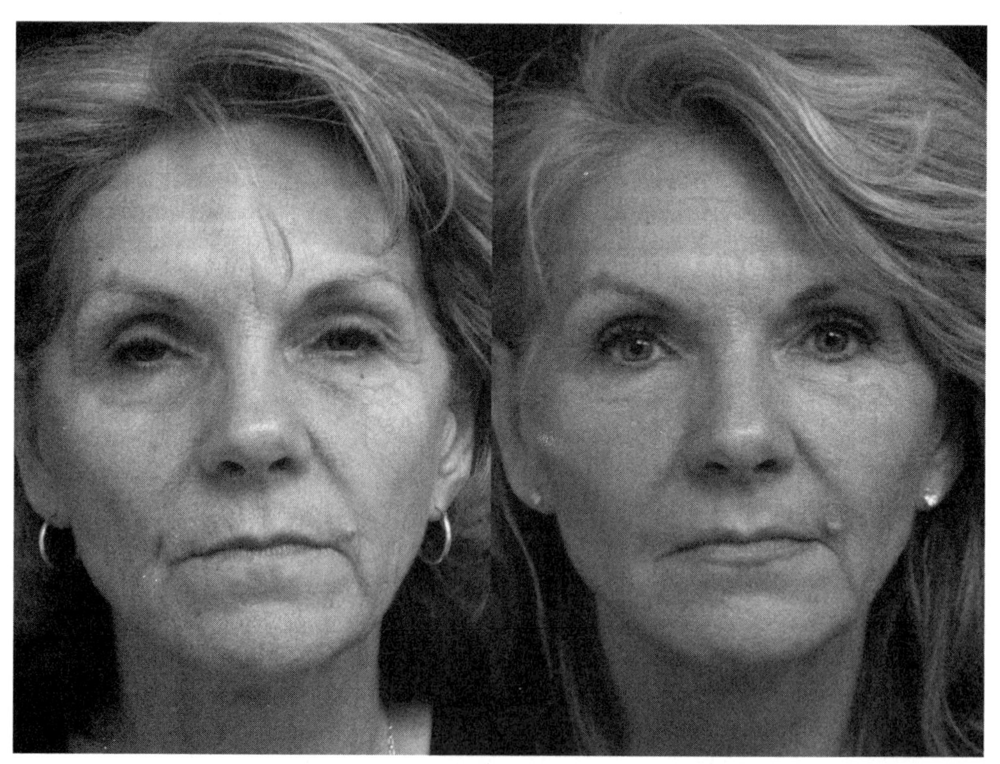

Photo 23-1. Before and after photos following Sculptra injections to revolumize the face and Fraxel Re:pair (CO2) laser to resurface and tighten the skin. Sculptra was injected into the hollows under the eyes, the tear trough, cheeks, nasolabial creases, and lateral to the chin (marionette lines).

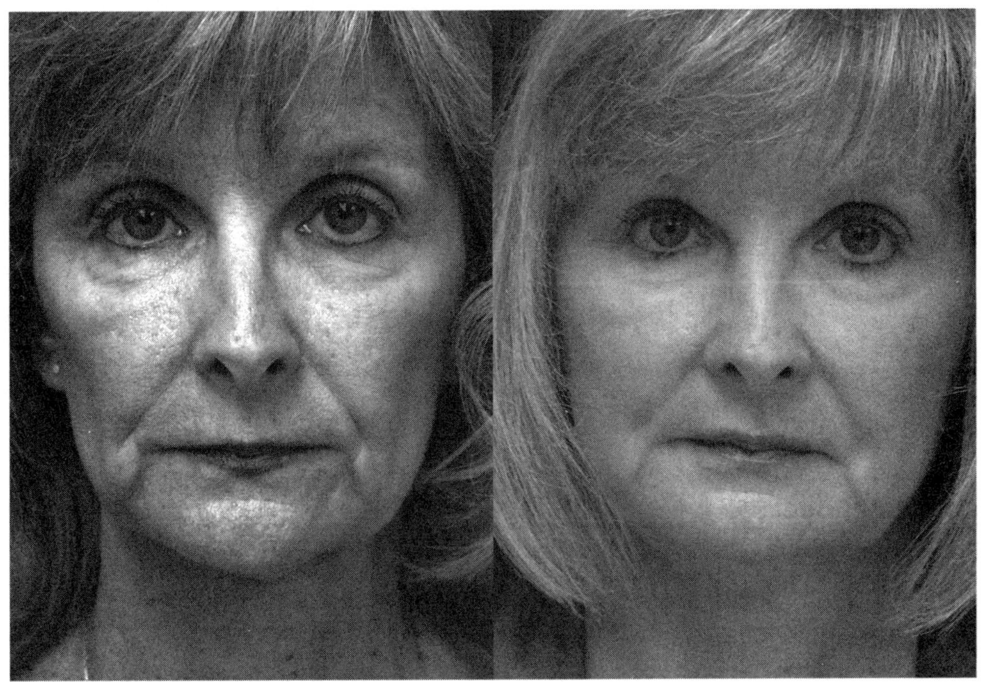

Photo 23-2. This patient has Sculptra injections to re-volumize her face and the Fraxel Re:store (erbium) laser to tighten and resurface her face. She also had a small amount of Perlane injected in her lips.

The Fraxel treats the face, neck, chest, hands, and arms. Any type skin can be treated. Using the Fraxel with an injectable filler, such as Sculptra (to inflate the face), can dramatically rejuvenate the face as well as the hands.

The risks of the Fraxel are hyperpigmentation (too much pigmentation), usually rare and temporary, and/or fever blisters. Discomfort and scaly skin may occur for a longer period of time also.

There are additional minimal-recovery lasers such as the Titan, Thermage, and others, which heat the collagen causing it to shrink. In my opinion, they are less consistent and do not reduce the sun damage as well, but no recovery is required in most cases. They can, however, tighten the skin in different areas of the face and body.

Injectable Fillers

Many injectable fillers are available to treat wrinkles in addition to those discussed here. However, I have had the most personal experience using the following with my patients:

Restylane: has been considered the gold standard up to now. A hyaluronic acid product, Restylane is a wrinkle filler in that when injected into the dermis of the skin, it actually elevates and reduces the wrinkle or scar. It is mostly used around the mouth, in the nasolabial creases, marionette lines below the corners of the mouth, and actually any depression of the skin. Generally it lasts about six to eight months.

Another hyaluronic acid filler recently approaching the forefront is *Juvederm.* I expect it to be much like Restylane in its performance. When injected properly, both are effective for short-term wrinkle fillers with virtually no complications. The company's latest product at this point is Juvederm Ultra Plus, which is advertised as lasting one year. It is excellent for injection into the lips.

Perlane is another hyaluronic acid product, but with a larger molecule than Restylane for deeper filling and longer duration, possibly one year as well. I find it an excellent product and use it often with Restylane. Actually, I like the results of all of the hyaluronic acid products for filling wrinkles. The Internet offers a more detailed description of each of the products.

Radiesse (calcium hydroxylapatite microspheres) is another filler for wrinkles or scars, but it is generally injected just below the dermis or into the deep dermis rather than in the superficial skin, and it lasts for about a year. However, injecting Radiesse into the lips has the possibility of creating white lumps, which may have to be surgically removed. Great care must be exercised when injecting Radiesse for this purpose. When properly injected, Radiesse is an excellent product. All of these fillers thus far mentioned are often used to plump up the lips, when desired. Your plastic surgeon will decide which is best for you.

Sculptra (poly-L-lactic acid) is not exactly a skin or wrinkle filler, as it is injected below the skin into the subcutaneous tissue adjacent to the dermis as well as close to the facial bones. Sculptra is a true "inflator." Although it's not exactly an injectable filler for wrinkles, it does improve wrinkles because it elevates tissues in a deflated face. Deflated faces sag, and re-inflating them elevates them back to a more youthful shape, sometimes dramatically. Sculptra is thus used for reducing the deflation that occurs with aging. Sculptra is now approved by the FDA for cosmetic use.

Think of this product as different from those mentioned above. Sculptra is a powder suspended in water. When injected in the various depressions of the face, such as the hollow beneath the eyes, tear trough, and mid-cheek depression, it looks great for a few days. Then the body absorbs the water, and the wonderful inflation that you saw immediately after the injections disappears. The Sculptra powder then stimulates formation of collagen and thickening of the skin, and injected tissues, or re-inflation, over a period of months. You can see a difference in about a month, and it lasts for one and a half to three years. Typically a patient will then come in for a touch-up injection in one and a half to two years even though they may still have substantial correction. Sculptra often requires three treatments, one every six weeks. I like this product and have seen it reverse the appearance of many years of aging. Sculptra can be used in combination with other products. (See Photo 23-1.)

All of the injection treatments discussed require only topical anesthesia for thirty minutes, and the procedure takes twenty to thirty minutes. To help prevent bruising with any of these mentioned products, stay off aspirin, Advil, vitamin E, fish oil, or other herbs for a week (two weeks is better) as they inhibit blood clotting.

What are combinations of nonsurgical treatments for rejuvenation?

A commonly used nonsurgical technique for rejuvenating the neck would be lipodissolve to reduce the fat and the Fraxel laser to tighten the skin. Rejuvenation of the hands may require Sculptra or Radiesse and the Fraxel laser. The face responds well to the Fraxel plus injectables such as Sculptra, Restylane, Radiesse, Juvederm, Perlane, and/or Botox. Each person must be assessed individually and artfully by a physician. Nonsurgical rejuvenation seems to be the latest trend, but even with the best results some people still need eyelid lifts (blepharoplasy) or other surgical treatments as well. Also, many facelifts need inflation with fat grafts or Sculptra and/or laser treatment in certain areas, such as the upper lip or lower eyelids.

Let's Wrap It Up

Even though this book has been written for the lay person, some of its content is fairly complex. Lots of information has been covered in this book, and in the three appendices is more information by Peter Brodhead, Certified Nutritionist. Peter's appendices explain nutritional supplements and how to get the most out of your local grocery store. These appendices will be invaluable in your search for optimal health and will answer any additional questions about nutritional supplementation and even how to shop for groceries.

If you've read all the way through the book to this point, you are serious about your health and are on the road to a healthier life. If you skipped around to different parts of the book, that isn't so bad either. Everyone wants to feel good, energetic, and healthy, and that always involves a healthy dose of positive self-esteem. *Why Grow Old?* offers a plan for healthier, happier, more energetic living. With the exception of the sections on hormonal therapy and supplements, following the plan mostly involves common sense. Once you implement some suggestions offered in *Why Grow Old*? you will be on the road toward a habit of healthier living that I hope will become your life-style. We all know it takes time to change old habits.

I can remember first arriving in Savannah and loading sugar in my tea and consuming a big piece of pie after lunch and dinner. I now find that behavior totally disgusting! Now, anything sweet actually tastes bad, besides making me salivate like I have rabies and then crash about an hour later, unless I get another sugar "fix." Over time I changed to a much healthier life-style that took work and commitment. That conversion has paid off many, many times over in more energy, less fat, but more muscle mass and simply better health.

We come from millions of years of evolution based on a hunter-and-gatherer life-style. Try to imagine the diet and habits of these ancient people, whose average male height was about five feet ten inches tall before the agricultural revolution 10,000 years ago, when their height fell to about five feet six inches. They ate unprocessed vegetables, fruits, roots and other plant sources. Meats were lean, lean, lean. They had no feed-lot animals back then. Overall, for millions of years man and his ancestors ate this unprocessed diet, in contrast to the few thousand years of eating a diet high in simple carbohydrates, transfats, and saturated fats that have led, in combination with an unhealthy life-style, to most of our chronic diseases and obesity. In addition, our ancestors' only mode of transportation was walking and running, so they in effect exercised constantly. I understand that no one wants to live like a caveman, but we can think of their wholesome diets and activity as a guide for our own diet, exercise, and life-style habits.

How and where do we start?

1. Lean protein sources (seafood, lean meats, beans, soy, low fat dairy products, cottage cheese), unprocessed and organic if possible, should take up one-third of your plate.
2. Vegetables—unprocessed and organic when possible with a fruit should take up the remaining two-thirds of your plate. Remember to eat all the bright colors that you can. Many phytonutrients are the pigments themselves.
3. Generally stay away from candy, desserts, and white foods such as white bread, pasta, potato (except the skin), and white rice. Be aware of "enriched" foods also. They may also cause the vitamin deficiencies they are supposed to correct. Read the labels.
4. Eat foods with soluble and insoluble fiber, such as whole grain bread, and pasta, brown rice, vegetables, and fruit.
5. Forget the low-fat diets. Fats such as the polyunsaturated (especially Omega-3) and monosaturated fats (olive oil) are necessary and good for you. Stay completely away from transfats!
6. Start a good organic whole-food nutrition supplement program and stick with it.
7. Give your skin the extra care and nutrition that it needs with the products such as those described in Chapter 8.

8. Exercise at least three times a week, even if it is only brisk walking. Use stairs instead of an elevator when possible. Take an exercise class or get a partner to exercise with.
9. Relax and enjoy the first day of the rest of your life. And don't forget the breathing exercises!

Regarding your diet, I strongly endorse *The South Beach Diet* by Arthur Agatston, M.D., and/or *A Week in the Zone* by Barry Sears, Ph.D., who both offer reasonable, healthy plans. (See the Reference List for details on other excellent books on diet and nutrition.)

If you have a desire or need for plastic surgery, educate yourself as much as possible about the procedure you are considering. Go to a plastic surgeon certified by the American Board of Plastic Surgery who will listen to your needs and will tailor the procedure to you and your goals. Remember that the surgery is for you, and you are the one who has to live with the results. Plastic surgery can vary from simple injections to complex procedures. In general, I advocate doing the smallest amount of surgery to achieve patients' goals, though sometimes more advanced or extensive procedures are necessary.

Make sure you have realistic expectations for any potential surgery. Remember that virtually everything (including plastic surgery) is a trade-off of some sort. Even being a good athlete or student is a trade-off, as it takes much work and effort. Being healthy is similarly a trade-off—though well worth all the time and work you put into it. Make sure plastic surgery is a good trade-off for you by considering whether the potential scars, expense, and recovery time are worth your desired and expected results.

If you feel you are a candidate for any of the plastic surgery procedures we have discussed, this book will help you understand what is available and how you can decide whether the different options for surgery may fit your needs. Be an informed consumer, especially when it involves a possibly permanent surgical procedure performed on your body. Do your homework. Know your desired procedure and your alternatives, and inquire about your surgeon. Use the Internet when possible, but take any Internet advertisements (and all advertisements for that matter) with a grain of salt. To learn more about plastic surgery, I suggest the following web sites:

- American Society of Plastic Surgeons at www.plasticsurgery.org
- American Society of Aesthetic Plastic Surgeons at www.surgery.org

Why Grow Old? and its information-dense appendices offer much useful information for your journey toward better health. I wish you all the best with your endeavor toward a long and healthy life. Go for the gusto when it regards your health. Health is your most treasured gift, so take care of it with unwavering vigor and determination.

To a long, youthful life!

APPENDIX 1
CHOOSING EFFECTIVE NUTRIENT SUPPLEMENTS

By E. Ronald Finger, M.D., F.A.C.S:

Introduction

Again, this appendix is information-dense, so depending upon the amount of information you are interested in, you may choose to read through the entire appendix or simply use it as a reference. Nutritional supplements do not need to be approved by the FDA, so they can vary widely in quality. So it's essential to buy reputable brands of supplements to ensure your money is well-spent on high quality products that are effective toward better health. My personal choice is to use whole food supplement extracts rather than synthetics or those that are isolated fractions from vitamin complexes. The products discussed here are not intended to treat, diagnose, or cure patient illnesses or diseases of any kind. The recommended dosages and nutrient combinations may differ from person to person, and there are no guarantees made or suggested in this publication.

Choosing Effective Nutrition Supplements
By Peter Brodhead, Certified Nutritionist
Savannah, Georgia

Throughout my over twenty-five-year career, some nutritional supplement formulations have become my favorites. The following is a list of supplement manufacturers that consistently deliver high-quality products. In each case I have listed the manufacturer's name, followed in most instances by the name of the specific product I like.

Whole Food Grown Multiple Vitamins:

New Chapter (Every Woman and Every Man)

Offering nutrients in one-per-day and three-per-day formulations, New Chapter makes its products with a unique process that makes these formulas expensive, but with a very high nutrient absorption rate and concentration. These supplements are excellent for people who cannot tolerate regular vitamins.

In New Chapter's whole food grown supplements, the nutrients are put into organic soy milk and cultured with a food yeast which incorporates the nutrients into the yeast cell just like a plant. Then the company adds digestive enzymes to break down the cell walls of the yeast, making the nutrients super bio-available. Culturing this mixture with pro-biotic bacteria (the beneficial bacteria that lives in the small and large intestines) further enhances the bio-availability. These formulas cause no stomach upset and can be taken on an empty stomach as well as with food.

Standard Process

This company has been in the business of whole food nutrients for over seventy-five years and is one of the most reputable companies in the business. The company may have been the founders of whole food vitamins, and it fully understands the need for complete foods instead of synthetics or isolates. To order from Standard Process, you must contact the company and find a health care provider in your area that sells its products. There are very few nutrients that Standard Process does not supply. Contact them at: www.standardprocess.com or find other vendors through www.google.com.

High Quality Non-Whole Food Vitamins:

Source Naturals (Life Force Multiple)

Life Force Multiple is a convenient formula that can be taken twice-daily for regular use, or four times daily for an extra antioxidant effect. It is a comprehensive product and is available with or without iron.

Source Naturals (Elan Vital)

Elan Vital contains higher amounts of antioxidants than does Life Force Multiple and is what I consider the ultimate antioxidant product. It can be taken as a six-per-day or three-per-day regimen.

Country Life (Superior Multiple)

This is another excellent antioxidant formulation with additional ingredients that strengthen the immune system and help the body withstand stress. The six-per-day formulation is easy on the stomach because it contains plant enzymes that promote absorption of the product.

Country Life (Maxine and Max)

These are two of the best formulations I've seen and are designed specifically for women or men. Both formulations are two-per-day regimens and include digestive enzymes to enhance their bio-availability.

Kosher Vitamins

Solgar Vitamins has one of the most complete selections of certified kosher vitamins and minerals.

Antioxidant Formulas

Antioxidant formulas have gone well beyond basic formulas containing beta-carotene, vitamin C, vitamin E, and selenium. Look for new formulations containing alpha lipoic acid and plant extracts of curcumin, green tea, grape seed extract, rosemary, astexanthin, and resveratrol.

Jarrow Formulas (Antioxidant Optimizer)

Jarrow Formulas recently reformulated this product to include the antioxidants gamma tocopherol vitamin E, lutein, lycopene, milk thistle extract, green tea, curcumin, and olive fruit polyphenols.

Natural Factors (The Ultimate Antioxidant)

Formulated by Dr. Michael Murray, N.D., this product includes N-Acetyl-L-Cysteine (N-A-C), alpha lipoic acid, curcumin, rosemary, lutein, lycopene and extracts of grape seed, green tea, and broccoli.

Anti-Inflammatory Formulas

Source Naturals (Inflama-Rest)

This product is formulated to promote the body's production of superoxide dismutase (SOD), an antioxidant and anti-inflammatory enzyme. This outstanding combination of anti-inflammatory botanical agents reduces arthritis inflammation or any inflammation in the body, according to the manufacturer. The manufacturer also states that ingredients in this formulation act as natural Cox–2 inhibitors and reduce treatment side effects of chemotherapy and radiation (please use only with your doctor's permission).

New Chapter (Zyflamend and Zyflamend PM)

These botanical formulas should be taken during the day (Zyflamend) or before bedtime to aid restful sleep (Zyflamend PM). With a carbon dioxide extraction method New Chapter concentrates both fat-soluble and water-soluble components.

Jarrow Formulas (Resveratrol Synergy)

Resveratrol, a botanical compound with antioxidant and anticancer activity, has been found in more than seventy species of plants, but is present in large amounts in grape skin. Resveratrol Synergy combines resveratrol with grape seed and green tea extracts for an additional anti-inflammatory effect.

Fish Oil Supplements

Omega-3 is what we want to increase, especially in relationship to Omega-6. Fish oil, a great source of Omega-3 oils, can help lower blood triglyceride levels. It may also have anti-inflammatory and immune enhancing properties and may reduce excessive blood clotting, which contributes to coronary occlusion, strokes, and deep vein thromboses. Look carefully on the label to ensure the manufacturer uses pharmaceutical grade, molecularly distilled oil with antioxidants added to the oil such as vitamin E or rosemary extract to preserve the freshness of the product. The more unsaturated an oil the easier it can go rancid. Therefore, it needs antioxidants with the product.

Nordic Naturals makes excellent, high-quality fish oil supplements, including Omega-3 fish oil formulations and cod liver oil supplements, for children and adults as well as formulas specially made for women. The company offers fish oil formulas containing borage oil, a good source of the polyunsaturated fatty acid gamma-linolenic acid (GLA), which is believed to enhance anti-inflammatory activity. All Nordic Naturals fish oil products are rigorously tested for purity and freshness and guaranteed to be free of pesticides, PCBs, and mercury.

Natural Factors (Dr. Michael Murray's Fish Oil)

This fish oil product is the best value I've come across. It is a high quality product and offers twice the potency of many other products, so you can conveniently attain therapeutic blood levels of fish oils.

Sears Labs: Omega-3 products

Barry Sears, Ph.D., developed this product and wrote the various *Zone* books, including *Omega Rx*, which I highly recommend. This high-quality product has more actual Omega-3 and less Omega-6 than most products. Purchase this product at www.searslabs.com.

Other fish oil products that deserve honorable mention are Coromega Carlson Brand Cod Liver Oils and Fish Oils, Nature's Way Fisol, Country Life Fish Oils, and Health from the Sun. Fish oils become rancid very easily and can cause repeated burping, though you can reduce these problems or solve them entirely by choosing a high-quality fish oil product.

Green Tea Supplements

Catechins, the active ingredient in green tea, are effective antioxidants. They may in addition have anticancer, anti-inflammatory, and antimicrobial properties and may help people with venous insufficiency.

Jarrow Formulas (Green Tea 500 milligrams)

This water extract of green tea contains 40% polyphenols and 30% catechins. Two capsules contain caffeine equivalent to that in one cup of green tea.

Natural Factors (Green Tea Phytosome)

This decaffeinated product promotes greater retention and efficiency of the flavonoids and polyphenols in green tea.

Horse Chestnut Extracts

Extract of horse chestnut has proven helpful in treating problems such as varicose veins due to poor venous blood flow.

Solaray (Horse Chestnut Extract 400 milligrams)

This high-quality product is one of the best values in horse chestnut supplements, with each capsule containing 72 milligrams of aescin, the active constituent in horse chestnut.

Natural Factors (Horse Chestnut with Grape Seed Extract)

This formulation contains 300 milligrams of five to one horse chestnut extract and 50 milligrams of 100 to one grape seed extract. The company claims this supplement helps people with varicose veins, hemorrhoids, and those who bruise easily

Gotu Kola (Centella asiatica)

Clinical tests of gotu kola have suggested a number of beneficial properties, including the ability to reduce inflammation, combat certain tumors, discourage stomach ulcers, improve venous circulation, and speed the healing of skin wounds and burns. I highly recommend its use to promote healthy postsurgical healing.

WARNING: Much gotu kola comes from India and may be contaminated and of low quality. Both Herb Pharm and Gaia Herbs offer high quality liquid extracts of gotu kola made from fresh plants they grow themselves.

Solaray (Madagascar Gotu Kola)

Madagascar Gotu Kola is one of a few capsules standardized to guarantee potency. It is available in capsule form for those who don't want to use a liquid extract. A combination product called CentellaVein is available that combines gotu kola with butcher's broom and bilberry, which are also believed to improve venous circulation and speed wound healing.

Grape Seed Extract

Proanthocyanidins, the active ingredient in grape seed extract, are effective antioxidants. They also are anti-inflammatory and anti-carcinogenic. What's more, they fight plaque accumulation in arteries and are effective in the prevention of gastric ulcers.

Source Naturals.

This formulation is one of my favorites for grape seed extract because of its high quality, potency, and reasonable price. It is available in 100 milligram and 200 milligram strengths.

Natural Factors and Enzymatic Therapy

have created grape seed phytosome formulations in which grape seed extract is bound to phosphatidylcholine to enhance its bio-availability. The product is available in 50 milligram and 100 milligram strengths.

Silica

Silicon is an essential micro-mineral not found in nature in its pure form as it rapidly reacts with atmospheric oxygen and water. In its natural state silicon is therefore found almost exclusively in the form of silica. Silicon retards the onset of some aspects of the aging process. In the form of BioSil, it has been shown to reduce fine wrinkles 19% in twenty weeks. It is considered essential to the structural integrity and elasticity of blood vessels, including arteries, and so it may help reduce arteriosclerosis. Silicon (especially the colloidal silica form applied topically or administered orally) improves the condition of hair and nails. Hair loss can occur as a result of silicon deficiency, and silica supplementation may accelerate hair growth when the hair follicles are still alive.

BioSil—made by Natrol

This is the best silica product available and is produced in capsules to be taken twice a day. Made in Belgium, it has the best bio-availability. It offers great support for the skin, hair, connective tissue, joints, and capillaries.

Solaray—Bamboo

Bamboo has the highest concentration of silicon of any plant in the world. This product uses a standardized extract for high bio-availability.

General Skin and Hair Formulas

Source Natural Skin Eternal

This formula contains mostly hyaluronic acid, a natural component of skin and joints.

Country Life (Maxi-Hair)

My brother-in-law's mother, who is in her 80s, had an incredible response to this product. She was losing a lot of hair, especially on the top of her head, and after taking this supplement for three months, her beautician began selling it in her beauty parlor because of the large amount of hair she grew back.

Kal (Hair Force)

This is a formula I have recommended for years because of the high amount of cysteine in it. Cysteine is a sulphur-containing amino acid, and it's especially important for hair, skin, and nail growth. It was reformulated a few years ago with saw palmetto, which is helpful for removing DHT (dihydrotestosterone), a cause of hair loss in both women and men.

Zinc

Clinical studies suggest that zinc has immune-boosting and antioxidant properties. It may also have antiviral and fertility-enhancing actions and may protect the retina of the eye. Look for the words OptiZinc on the label of zinc supplements as this is a form of zinc bound to the amino acid methionine, which facilitates good absorption. Source Natural, Solaray, Now, and Jarrow are some companies that include OptiZinc in their supplements. Caution: excess zinc can interfere with absorption of magnesium, chromium, copper, and folic acid. We must always attempt to consume a balance of natural nutrients.

MSM

Methylsulfonylmethane (MSM) is a compound that occurs naturally in fruits, vegetables, grains, and animals, including humans, in at least trace amounts. It has also been found in such plants as Equisetem arvense, or horsetail. The biological role of MSM is not specifically understood yet, but MSM is a metabolite of dimethyl sulfoxide (DMSO) which has anti-inflammatory, antioxidant, and pain-relieving properties, so it is believed that some of the helpful effects of DMSO could be attributed to MSM.

The purest form of MSM you can purchase is from the raw material supplier Cardinal Nutrition, which makes Opti-MSM, so look carefully on the label for Opti-MSM. This product is made in the United States rather than China and is a distilled product. Some companies using Opti-MSM are Jarrow Formulas, Natural Factors, Solaray, Kal, Enzymatic Therapy, and Solgar.

L-Carnitine

L-carnitine is an antioxidant and mitochondrial stimulant. It may improve heart function, protect the heart, lower blood levels of triglycerides, and increase levels of HDL, the helpful cholesterol. L-carnitine may also have antioxidant properties. The Acetyl-L-carnitine form of carnitine has neuroprotective activity, so it may be helpful in the treatment of age-related neurological disorders such as Alzheimer's disease. The newest form of L-Carnitine is glysine proprionil L-Carnitine (GPLC), which is more easily absorbed and utilized.

Jarrow Formulas, Now, and Lonza from Italy produce high-quality L-carnitine and acetyl-L-carnitine products. Another excellent source for L-carnosine or any combination of amino acids is the company Montiff. Its owner, Don Tyson, is a true authority on all amino acids, and a conversation with him can be educational. Contact Tyson at 310-820-4883 or at Montiffinc@aol.com.

CoQ10

CoQ10 is a fat-soluble nutrient that must be taken with meals containing fat in order to be absorbed properly. Jarrow Formula's Q-absorb CoQ10 is one of my favorite CoQ10 formulations. The CoQ10 in this product has been emulsified with fat to promote its absorption. CoQ10 is available in 30 milligram and 100 milligram capsules. CoQ10 must be reduced by the body to be active. The most recent formula of CoQ10 is called Ubiquinol, which is the reduced form and more easily utilized. It is produced by Kaneka Nutrients.

Alpha Lipoic Acid

The Italian source for this supplement is superior to the Chinese. Jarrow makes high-quality alpha lipoic acid products.

APPENDIX 2
WHOLE-FOOD SOURCES FOR EACH NUTRIENT AND THE NUTRIENT'S FUNCTION

By Peter Brodhead, C.N., and E. Ronald Finger, M.D.

All sources mentioned in this section are nutrient-rich, though the richest sources of each nutrient are presented first, with others in descending order (except where otherwise stated). Generally, although the last source on the list contains the least amount of the nutrient, it's still a rich source. The source for much of this information is the Hyperhealth Pro CD-ROM from In-Tele-Health © 2002 at www.hyperhealth.com. Additionally, Worlds' Healthiest Foods can be found at www.whfoods.com, a most complete and helpful source. An additional excellent source is www.brighterday.com.

This section demonstrates the importance of eating eight to ten vegetables and fruits each day to get these marvelous nutrients in their proper ratios for the most effective quest for health. If you eat organically grown vegetables and free-range meats, you can hardly do better for your health. These whole foods will provide you with large numbers of nature's balanced nutrients, some of which have yet to be discovered but are necessary for effectiveness of each vitamin and nutrient.

Vitamins and Nutrients

Omega-3 Fatty Acids: This most important nutrient is first on our list. The best sources are cod, halibut, sardines, salmon (wild or Alaska), flax seed, tuna, and walnuts. Small amounts come from leafy green vegetables and cauliflower.

Vitamin E: Wheat germ oil, soybean oil, sunflower oil, sunflower seeds, peanut oil, kale, avocados, almonds, Swiss chard, turnip greens, and olives are rich in this nutrient.

Vitamin E has antioxidant activity. It may also have anti-atherogenic, antithrombotic, anticoagulant, neuroprotective, immune-enhancing, cell membrane-stabilizing, and antiviral actions. Although alpha-tocopherol is the most well absorbed and the most studied of the vitamin E components, you should take a vitamin E complex to include all other forms of vitamin E such as gamma tocopherol, as it has some specific benefits. Gamma tocopherol has been found to help prevent colon cancer and prostate cancer. Look for vitamin E from natural sources. That form is better absorbed by the body than is synthetic vitamin E.

Vitamin A (a retinoid): This nutrient comes in liver (organic is the safest), cod liver oil, butter, cheddar cheese, and egg yolk.

Carotenoids: Carotenoids comprise the complex of over 700 yellow, red, green, and orange pigments in vegetables and fruits, including alpha, beta, gamma, and delta carotenes. Carotenoids are found in bright orange, yellow, and dark green vegetables and fruits, which are excellent sources of the balanced, whole-food vitamin complex: carrots, sweet potatoes, all winter squash, dandelion greens, parsley, kale, collard greens, spinach, watercress, turnip greens, broccoli, Brussels sprouts, green beans, and lettuce (especially romaine, green, and red leaf–iceberg is the least), cantaloupe, persimmons, mangoes, apricots, peaches, nectarines, cherries, and plums. Algae supplements such as spirulina or chlorella are outstanding sources of carotenes. Beta-carotene is a precursor to vitamin A. It can be found in algae, such as chlorella and spirulina: Beta-Carotene is also in most fruit—papaya, melons, citrus, cantaloupe, apples, and bananas. Barley, wheat, alfalfa, spinach, squash, Brussels sprouts, lettuce, cabbage, corn, and broccoli also contain beta-carotene. Use caution, though: large doses of supplemental beta-carotene decrease the absorption of the other types of beneficial carotenoids. Also be aware that microwaving can destroy up to 60% of the carotenes in foods.

Carotene complexes are highly anti-carcinogenic, and alpha carotene is ten times more effective at protecting against skin cancer than is beta-carotene. Carotene complexes reduce numerous types of cancer, including lung, prostate, pancreas, breast, colon, larynx, stomach, and skin cancers. The complexes thwart heart attacks and strokes by 50%. Beta-carotene protects against candida (yeast) proliferation. Carotene complexes support kidney and pancreatic functions and help prevent cataracts in the eyes. They support immune function by promoting a healthy thymus gland and treat photosensitivity of the skin. Beta-carotene accelerates wound healing and protects the skin from damage caused by excessive exposure to sunlight. Hydrochloric acid is required for the absorption of beta-carotene, so if you take antacids or hydrochloric acid blockers, they could affect your absorption of the carotenes. Large amounts of isolated beta-carotene interfere with absorption of the other carotenes.

Alpha-Carotene: Carrots are its richest source, but pumpkin, all winter squash, sweet potatoes, red papaya, persimmons, apricots, mangoes, peaches, fresh corn, kale, brussels sprouts, avocado, and kiwi contain alpha carotene, plus those listed under carotene.

Alpha-carotene protects against many forms of cancer. It is ten times as potent as beta-carotene in reducing the risk of the forms of cancer listed in the section above.

Gamma-Carotene: Apricots, carrots, sweet potatoes, watermelon, corn, and tomatoes, plus those listed in the carotenoids section contain gamma-carotene. This nutrient is a potent antioxidant and deactivates singlet oxygen free radicals twice as effectively as beta-carotene.

Astaxanthin: This is a powerful carotenoid pigment from red marine algae. It is the pigment that gives the pink color to salmon, lobsters, shrimp, and pink flamingo. It protects against free radical damage from excess exposure to UV light, and is one of the most powerful antioxidants known, many times stronger than Vitamin C and beta-carotene. Astaxanthin is also an effective anti-inflammatory and booster of the immune system. The usual dose is four milligrams per day.

Lycopene ("The Red Carotene"): This nutrient can be found in ripe tomato products, tomato paste, and tomato sauce (organic has been shown to have higher levels). Red bell peppers, paprika, cayenne pepper, watermelon, red apples, pink grapefruit, guava, apricots, and rose hips also contain lycopene. Lycopene cannot be converted to vitamin A in the body like other carotenes. Currently it receives a huge amount of attention for its cancer-protecting effects and cardiovascular effects. It reduces inflammation associated with colitis, and it protects against numerous cancers, including cancer of the breast, uterus, mouth, esophagus, stomach, colon, bladder, and prostate. It is twice as effective as beta-carotene and is 100 times more effective than vitamin E in neutralizing the oxygen free radical, which may contribute to its anti-cancer activity. It protects against Alzheimer's disease and male infertility. Lycopene is destroyed at a greater rate in the skin when exposed to ultraviolet radiation. It also increases our tolerance to ultraviolet damage.

Lutein: One of the yellow carotenoids (xanthophylls), lutein exists in egg yolks (the most bioavailable source), spinach, kale, collards, mustard and turnip greens, calendula (marigold petals), butter beans, mangoes, papaya, honey dew melons, avocadoes, kiwi fruit, oranges, peaches, and prunes. Marigold petals can be used in salads and are what lutein supplements are made from.

Lutein is best known for protecting the eyes against all major aging problems, including macular degeneration, cataracts, and glaucoma. It concentrates in the lens, macula, and retina of the eye. It also helps prevent breast, colon, lung, and prostate cancers and protects against oxidation of LDL cholesterol.

B1 (Thiamin): Whole-food sources of thiamin are brown (unprocessed) rice, wheat germ, sunflower seeds, pecans, Brazil nuts, peanuts, pignolias, pistachios, oatmeal, tomatoes, cauliflower, and split peas. Thiamin helps prevent destructive cross-linking of collagen and elastin in the skin. Like all the B-complex vitamins it is important for the central nervous system's health, and it supports brain function, memory, and balanced moods. Deficiencies cause beriberi, an ailment of the nervous system.

B2 (Riboflavin): Riboflavin is found in nutritional (brewer's) yeast, unprocessed brown rice, wheat germ, spelt, egg yolk, sardines, mackerel, portabella mushrooms, liver (from organic sources only), almonds, cheddar and parmesan cheeses, broccoli, and brussels sprouts. Riboflavin enhances cell respiration, eye health, and energy and can help prevent migraine headaches. It is also involved in the production of collagen. Acne, eczema, rosacea, and susceptibility to sunburn can occur as a result of B2 deficiency. In addition to food sources, B2 is produced by beneficial bacteria within the body.

B3 (Niacin, Niacinamide): This nutrient comes from nutritional (brewer's) yeast, mackerel, beef, organic liver, turkey, brown rice, cod, almonds, sunflower seeds, peanuts, and portabella mushrooms. When choosing supplemental niacin look for formulations designed to avoid the red skin flush (niacin flush) that niacin causes in many people. (Remember, no-flush niacin is safe, but do not use timed-release niacin.)

Niacin helps with blood circulation and energy production and supports health of the brain and nervous system. It also lowers blood cholesterol and triglyceride levels and inhibits glycation cross-linking. It lowers fibrinogen levels in the blood, reducing excessive blood clotting. It also improves skin health and helps prevent sunburn. Finally, it helps the polyunsaturated fatty acids in primrose or borage oils convert into beneficial anti-inflammatory compounds.

B5 (Pantothenic Acid): Get this nutrient from nutritional (brewer's) yeast, organic liver, mushrooms, blue cheese, peanuts, pecans, split peas, sunflower seeds, lobster, salmon, hazelnuts (filberts), egg yolk, soy beans, lentils, cashews, broccoli, cauliflower, kale, sardines, and avocados. Pantothenic acid helps in the metabolism of acetylcholine in the brain and helps the adrenal gland produce stress hormones. It retards glycation in the skin and supports energy and stamina. It helps acne, dermatitis, dry skin, and wound healing.

B6 (Pydroxine): nutritional (brewer's) yeast, brown rice, beef, organic liver, salmon, hazelnuts (filberts), bananas, chicken, avocado, halibut, tuna, peanuts, broccoli, chestnuts, Brazil nuts, peanuts, garlic, spirulina, celery, and collards contain this nutrient. Pydroxine contributes to proper functioning of all the body's proteins, including collagen and brain neurotransmitters. It is important for the conversion of energy from foods and helps with skin problems such as dandruff, eczema, rosacea, and seborrhea.

B12: This vitamin comes in organic beef liver, organic chicken liver, clams, spirulina, kombu, sardines, mackerel, Swiss cheese, edam cheese, cheddar cheese, blue cheese, and flounder. Absorption of B12 declines with age, and insufficient B12 causes cardiovascular disease, dementia, anemia, and insomnia among many other disorders. To help lower homocysteine levels in the blood, use B12 with B6, and folic acid.

Folic Acid (Folate, a B complex vitamin): Nutritional yeast, organic beef liver, wheat germ, soy beans, wheat bran, kidney beans, mung beans, lima beans, navy beans, chick peas, lentils, walnuts, spinach, kale, peanuts, broccoli, split peas, brussels sprouts, almonds, cauliflower, romaine lettuce, beets, papaya, figs, avocados, oatmeal, green beans, and mushrooms all contain folic acid. This nutrient helps lower homocysteine, which reduces cardiovascular diseases such as stroke, heart disease, and generalized arteriosclerosis. Deficiencies lead to memory loss and dementia. Age-related hearing loss is related to folic acid deficiency as is macrocytic (large cell) anemia.

Choline (a B vitamin): Get this vitamin from lecithin granules, organic liver, egg yolk (300 mg per egg), coffee, all beans, soybean oil, peanuts, cauliflower, cabbage, and bee pollen. Choline in the form of acetylcholine is an abundant neurotransmitter on the brain and neuromuscular transmitter for muscles. As phosphatidylcholine it is considered a "smart" drug. Other "smart" drugs are galanthamine and DMAE, which prevent acetylcholine from being enzymatically broken down.

Inositol (from the vitamin B family and called anti-alopecia factor): Inositol comes in lecithin granules, wheat germ, navy beans, rice germ, whole wheat, barley, chick peas, black-eyed peas, nutritional yeast, soy beans, peanuts, green peas, split peas, lentils, grapefruit, raisins, oranges, molasses, cantaloupe, cabbage, cauliflower, peaches, onions, sweet potato, watermelon, and strawberries. Inositol is vital for hair growth and color. As an integral part of the cell membrane, it retards arteriosclerosis. It helps prevent both bladder and lung cancer, and it prevents cross-linking in the eye and thus cataracts. Inosotol alleviates depression, anxiety, panic disorder.

Biotin (Vitamin B7): Organic chicken liver, organic beef liver, soy beans, walnuts, peanuts, pecans, egg yolk, oatmeal, almonds, and cauliflower all contain biotin. It is also produced by our intestinal tract bacteria and thus is killed by some antibiotics. Biotin alleviates diabetes mellitus by decreasing insulin resistance. It reduces gray hair and delays hair loss on male pattern baldness. It's also used for dry skin. Deficiencies of this nutrient cause dementia, depression, nervousness, and fatigue.

Vitamin K: This nutrient comes in cauliflower, brussels sprouts, green beans, parsley, asparagus, strawberries, kale, green tea, turnip greens, spinach, cabbage, tomatoes, string beans, and dark green lettuces. It is important for utilizing calcium for strengthening bone and reducing arteriosclerosis, thus reducing heart disease and stroke. Vitamin K is necessary for proper blood clotting and is anti-carcinogenic (reduces formation of various types of cancer). This is a most underrated vitamin.

The remaining vitamins are discussed in the text and in Appendix I. Thus, we'll mention only the whole-food source (with some exceptions) here.

Vitamin C: This vitamin is found in acerola cherries, bell peppers, red chili peppers, guavas, black currants, kale, parsley, brussels sprouts, mustard greens, watercress, cauliflower, romaine lettuce, green beans, persimmons, carrots, kiwi, lemon, papaya, spinach (which contains thirteen different flavonoids), oranges, cabbage, grapefruit, elderberries, turnips, asparagus, cantaloupe, tangerines, mangoes, and celery.

Vitamin D: You can get this vitamin from sunshine as well as cod liver oil, kippers, and sardines. Fifty percent of Americans are deficient in Vitamin D. It is necessary for calcium utilization and reduces insulin resistance, autoimmune disorders, obesity, and certain cancers.

Oligomeric Proanthocyanidins (OPCs): Get this nutrient from grape seeds and grape skins (especially dark-colored ones), bilberry, blueberry, cranberry, rhubarb, dark chocolate, peanuts, sorghum, and barley.

Anthocyanidins: This nutrient is in red wine, blueberry, cranberry, kiwi, orange, persimmon, raspberry, black currant, cherry, elderberry, grape, mulberry, pomegranate, strawberry, red onion, red cabbage, eggplant, and blue corn.

OPCs and anthocyanidins—enhance connective tissue and blood vessels. They both have anti-inflammatory properties. Anthocyanidins support eye health.

Indole-3-carbinol: This nutrient comes from cruciform vegetables, such as cauliflower, broccoli, brussels sprouts, and cabbage. It is very anti-carcinogenic against cancers of breast, cervix, ovaries, prostate, colon, skin, and leukemia. It also may alleviate fibromyalgia and chronic fatigue syndrome.

Quercetin: The skins of red apples, red onions, and russet potatoes contain this nutrient. It is also in red wine, green tea, pears, kiwi, cauliflower, spinach, broccoli, cabbage, okra, and squash (not in order of concentration of quercetin). Quercetin has important anti-allergy activity. It prevents the release of leukotrienes, which cause inflammation and swelling during an allergic reaction. Quercetin also protects the eyes against cataract formation and has potent anti-cancer properties.

Resveratrol: Dark muscadine and scuppernong grapes contain resveratrol, as do red wine and red grapes, raisins, cranberries, mulberries, and peanuts.

Resveratrol may be one of the most potent anti-inflammatory substances found in nature. It protects against cardiovascular disease and cancer.

Rutin: Bee pollen, buckwheat, yerbamate, red wine, and garlic contain this nutrient, though here they are not listed in decreasing order of concentration. Rutin strengthens connective tissue and the capillaries. It reduces bruising, bleeding gums, hemorrhoids, and general health for blood vessels and capillaries. It is also an antioxidant, anti-inflammatory and antihistamine.

Minerals

Calcium: This nutrient comes in dolomite and sesame seeds (though it is not highly bioavailable from this source). It's also in kelp, swiss cheese, cheddar cheese, molasses, whey powder, chocolate, flax seeds, almonds, kale, figs, soy beans, brewer's yeast, parsley, watercress, hazelnuts, brazil nuts, beans, pistachios, egg yolk, onions, broccoli, tofu, sunflower seeds, yogurt, and goat's milk. Only 25% of calcium is absorbed from cow's milk. Ninety-eight percent of calcium is concentrated bone. It is necessary for bone healing and strength as well as clotting, regulating blood Ph, normalizing cardiac rhythm, alleviating gastric ulcers, for cell membrane function, maintaining muscle function, alleviating muscle cramps, and much more.

Chromium: Onions, romaine lettuce, and tomatoes contain chromium, which stabilizes the utilization of glucose.

Copper: This mineral comes in oysters, crab, brazil nuts, sunflower seeds, lobster, crimini mushrooms, cashews, blackstrap molasses, olives, almonds, walnuts, wheat bran, hazelnuts, pistachio nuts, pecans, liver, wheat germ, peanuts, chocolate, peaches, parsley, and apples. It stimulates elastin production and healthy collagen cross-linking. It's also involved in bone formation. Chromium deficiency causes gray hair and hair loss; excess can cause hair loss also. It helps heal wounds, facilitates mental function, and produces red blood cells.

Iodine: Kelp, seaweeds (sushi), eggs, and milk contain iodine. It kills many detrimental bacteria. The mineral concentrates in the thyroid to form T3 and T4 (thyroid hormones), thus deficiency relates to fatigue, obesity, and impaired intelligence. Iodine alleviates dry nails, skin, and hair. It's an essential micro-mineral, which regulates blood sugar, blood pressure, and it reduces total and LDL cholesterol as well as arteriosclerosis. Iodine alleviates diabetes and insulin resistance, and reduces glycation cross-linking. Iodine deficiency increases lipofuscin deposits.

Iron: Seventy-five percent of iron in the body exists in the form of hemoglobin. Meat contains the heme form of iron (well absorbed), while vegetable sources contain a non-heme form (not as well absorbed). The best sources of iron are all dark red meat, kelp, spirulina, cumin seeds, rice bran, brewer's yeast, molasses, beef liver, wheat bran, kidneys, turnip greens, green beans (twice that of spinach), pumpkin seeds, sesame seeds, cocoa, wheat germ, mussels, sunflower seeds, millet, clams, parsley, almonds, prunes, beef, cashews, brazil nuts, tomatoes, dates, walnuts, hazelnuts, black olives, and tofu. Take care with iron supplements because excess iron can cause cardiovascular disease and elevate LDL levels. What's more, there is a strong association between excess iron and various carcinomas. Ask your health professional before taking iron supplements.

Magnesium: Good sources of magnesium are kelp, wheat bran, wheat germ, sunflower seeds, soy beans, brazil nuts, hazelnuts, almonds, cashews, chard, spinach, cauliflower, raspberries, brewer's yeast, tea, peanuts, walnuts, pistachios, pecans, whole wheat flour, macadamia nuts, oatmeal, shrimp, prawns, dried peas, brown rice, dried figs, rye flour, spinach, and dried apricots. Recommendations for supplementation vary from 100 to 400 milligrams per day. Magnesium improves health of the adrenal glands. It is an integral element in the formation of healthy bones, and it modulates the electrical potential of the cell membranes. Also, it can alleviate lethargy and chronic fatigue syndrome. Magnesium deficiency can cause hypertension and various heart problems such as angina and cardiac insufficiency.

Manganese: Tea, pecans, brazil nuts, barley, rye, split peas, buckwheat, whole wheat, spinach, walnuts, cauliflower, garlic, green beans, spinach, pineapple, raspberries, strawberries, peanuts, liver, oats, and brewer's yeast all contain this essential micro-mineral. It is an essential micro-mineral. It aids in bone repair and formation of cartilage. It also helps reduce arteriosclerosis and some heart disease, deafness, tinnitus, vertigo, fatigue, obesity, and gallstones. It may alleviate depression and irritability and may improve memory.

Molybdenum: All dried beans, celery, and tomatoes contain molybdenum. This mineral alleviates symptoms of various arthritis diseases and prevents against various cancers, such as breast and esophagus, by protecting against certain dietary carcinogens.

Potassium: All fruits and vegetables have potassium, but some exceptional sources are cantaloupe, bananas, crimini mushrooms, winter squash, chard, tomatoes, turnip greens, beets, and parsley.

Selenium: This powerful antioxidant comes in brazil nuts (one brazil nut contains 50 to 100 micrograms of selenium depending on the soil in which it is grown), garlic, onions, mushrooms, liver, kidneys, chicken, peanuts, cabbage, radishes, and tuna. Selenium protects against heart disease, arteriosclerosis, hypertension, and stroke. Deficiencies of this mineral can cause hypothyroidism and thyroiditis. It is anti-carcinogenic and may relieve certain autoimmune diseases.

Silica: Get this nutrient from cucumbers, oats, brown rice, bananas, soy beans, sesame seeds, kelp, avocado, cauliflower, garlic, onion, spinach, asparagus, figs, and strawberries. Considered to retard the aging process, silica alleviates arteriosclerosis, strengthens blood vessels, and stimulates production of fibroblasts which produce collagen, which in turn is healthy for hair and skin and reduces premature wrinkling. Silica also alleviates gastritis, excessive perspiration, incontinence, tendonitis, and osteoarthritis.

Zinc: Oysters contain zinc, as do ginger, liver, lamb, beef, sunflower seeds, pumpkin seeds, pecans, brazil nuts, pine nuts, egg yolk, oats, whole wheat, peanuts, butter beans, almonds, chicken, cashew nuts, buckwheat, macadamia nuts, shrimp, green peas, and maple syrup. Zinc is anticarcinogenic and is necessary for numerous enzyme functions throughout the body. Deficiencies are related to reduced function of most organs, which may manifest into learning disorders, depression, periodontal diseases, adrenal insufficiency, male infertility, prostate enlargement, acne, hair loss, Crohn's disease, gastritis, optic nerve function, night blindness, and much more.

APPENDIX 3
HOW TO GROCERY SHOP FOR OPTIMUM HEALTH

By Peter Brodhead, Certified Nutritionist

A good start toward our quest for optimum health is to know how to shop for groceries containing the best quality nutrients, while limiting our exposure to harmful ingredients and unhealthful foods. As with Appendix 1, this section is information-dense, so you may want to use it for reference only.

As a first step toward your goal of healthful eating, explore your local natural foods market to find the cleanest, most healthful foods available. Check out certified organic produce departments, as supermarkets usually carry only prepackaged, expensive organic produce that may not be fresh. Natural foods markets have prescreened ingredient quality for you and can answer your questions about foods and supplements. Also, they may have good specials each month on many products.

The safest way to shop at a regular supermarket is to start at the produce department and stay along the perimeter of the store for all your essential needs. Once you venture into the middle section of the store you enter "no man's land," a world of processed and refined carbohydrates, partially hydrogenated fats (trans-fats), and unknown food additives. That's not to say shopping the perimeter isn't without its pitfalls, though. Be careful, for instance, of the nitrate-ridden wasteland of processed meats like bacon and salami. On entering the produce department, look for brightly colored fruits and vegetables and find out what's in season. South-of-the-equator countries make many products, such as apples from New Zealand, available year round.

Fruits

Look for fresh berries. If berries aren't in season, go to the freezer and get unsweetened frozen berries. Strawberries are the exception here—because of their thin skins and the way they are grown, they tend to have a much higher pesticide and fungicide residue content than any other berry. So buy organic strawberries if you can, and always wash them.

Berries—Blueberries, raspberries, blackberries, and organic strawberries are high in flavonoids for connective tissue enhancement.

Apples—Check for wax on the skin, as this is applied to preserve them and is not natural. Always wash apples with a cloth or paper towel. The skin of the apple is rich in lycopene and quercetin, and pectin in the apple promotes regularity. Also, eating apples before meals helps us lose weight by reducing appetite, so apples really do help keep the doctor away.

Tangerines and navel oranges help the liver detoxify our bloodstreams.

Lemons, limes—Lemon or lime juice makes a great, healthy, flavor enhancer for foods.

Kiwi, mango, pineapple, and pomegranates for ellagic acid.

Pears—Bartlett (yellow), Anjou (green) Bosc (brown), Red Bartlett or Anjou (red).

Grapes of all colors are good for you, but grapes with seeds are richer sources of anthocyanidins.

Cantaloupes, watermelon, and honeydew.

Persimmons—Fuji persimmons can be eaten like an apple even when firm to the touch. Hachiya persimmons have to be really soft or they are astringent.

Bananas are rich in potassium.

Avocados are high in Omega-3 fatty acids.

Vegetables

The produce section includes a number of healthful vegetables.

Spring Mix is a great way to get a large variety of lettuces. Add arugula, radicchio, and other bitter greens in the diet as well as romaine, green leaf, red leaf lettuces, and fresh spinach.

Mustard greens, beet greens, kale, red kale, lacinato kale, and dandelion greens. Bitter greens and lettuces are excellent for the liver and for digestion in general.

Mushrooms—White, crimini (baby portabella), portabella, and shitake (a most nourishing mushroom) are all good choices.

Parsley—both curly and Italian flat, should go in your buggy, along with cilantro.

Radishes—regular and daikon root.

Carrots, parsnips.

Tomatoes—cherry, yellow, and roma.

Bok choy is also rich in nutrients.

Roots and bulbs should go in your buggy as well: beets, rutabagas, turnips, ginger root, red onions, yellow onions, white onions, garlic, elephant garlic, and shallots.

Sweet potatoes and purple potatoes are nutrient rich, as are green, red, yellow, and purple bell peppers.

Other vegetables for your buggy are cabbage, red and green, brussels sprouts, artichokes, asparagus, winter squash (all varieties including spaghetti squash), yellow and zucchini squash, broccoli, cauliflower, romanesco, celery, and celery root, which is excellent grated raw or cooked and mashed like potatoes.

You can save a lot of money by using the storage bags that keep fresh fruits and vegetables fresh for weeks instead of days. Remember to eat a rainbow of colors to get the variety of nutrients (many of which are pigments) necessary for health and longevity.

Beef and Chicken

Look for Maverick beef (grass fed, extra lean) and Laura's beef, which contains 8% fat versus the 20% fat found in regular commercial beef.

Free-range chicken—look for those raised without hormones or antibiotics. Cook it with the skin off to reduce fat (and remember, you should eat less saturated fat, not simply less fat).

Fish

Talapia, catfish

Wild salmon, especially Pacific. Avoid farmed salmon, as it has been found to have a higher toxic equivalency score than any other food. Most Atlantic salmon is farmed. Farmed salmon has more saturated fat and less Omega-3 also.

Cod

Shrimp

Canned sardines, wild sockeye salmon (high in astazanthin)

Mackerel is high in Omega-3 fatty acids

Shellfish is nutritionally dense, high-protein food. It is also high in Omega-3 fatty acids, vitamins, and minerals.

Crustaceans (lobsters, crabs, and shrimp) are also rich in protein and nutrients and low in saturated fats.

Eggs

Buy free-range or organic eggs whenever possible.

Dairy

Butter—buy organic if affordable. Fat is where undesirable hormones and antibiotics accumulate and butter is 100% fat, so organic butter is worry-free.

Earth Balance is a non-hydrogenated soft margarine made with palm, soy, and canola oils. It's a more healthful alternative to Smart Balance, which contains additives, artificial flavor, and preservatives.

Low fat (1%) or skimmed milk, preferably organic.

Cottage cheese is incredibly high in protein and a great convenience food. Stock up!

Buy low-fat plain yogurt, organic with the cream layer on top. You can take cream off the top to lower the fat content.

Frozen Foods

Stock up on frozen berries. Freezing the berries makes the flavonoids in them more bio-available to the body.

When convenience matters or when cooking for one, frozen vegetables can be more economical and less wasteful. Cascadian Farms offers certified organic frozen vegetables.

Tabatchnick Frozen Soups use very clean, simple ingredients and offer six or more varieties to choose from.

Ethnic Gourmet makes tasty Indian dinners. Check the ingredients and carbohydrate count. Try also Amy's frozen meals and Health is Wealth frozen foods.

Edamame (frozen fresh green soybeans) have great flavor and taste. They're fun to eat as a snack food. In the South, they are an alternative to boiled peanuts when watching a baseball or football game.

You've made your journey around the outside perimeter of the store by following the walls. Now it's time to journey in the center aisles. But beware of the many prepared foods like Stouffer's, which are loaded with hydrogenated fats, chemicals, additives, and sodium.

Instead of jelly, look for fruit-only products such as Polaner, Smucker's, Simply Fruit, St. Dalfours (my favorite), or Sorrell Ridge.

Or try apple butter. Look for fruit-only. Chavanprash is an apple-butter-flavored spread from India made with about thirty different herbs from the Aruvedic tradition of healing. It is considered a superior tonic in India. It is available at Indian grocery stores for around six dollars. I use it as an alternative to apple butter to get the tonic benefits of all the herbs.

Teas

For antioxidants try green tea, regular and decaf. I recommend several Celestial Seasonings, Tazo varieties, or Lipton.

Rooibos (Red Tea from South Africa) contains no caffeine, has a good flavor, and is loaded with antioxidants. Of course there are also Chinese oolong, white tea, spice tea blends, and black tea. Theophyllins in black tea are good for lowering cholesterol. I recommend Tazo Awake and Earl Grey. The bergamot oil used in these teas has a mood-uplifting effect.

Try herbal teas with hibiscus. Celestial Seasonings Tension Tamer, Sleepy Time, or Traditional Medicinals Nighty Night are great relaxing teas.

Honest Tea is extremely low in sugar, and it's a great flavored pre-brewed tea.

If you've just gotta have coffee, buy certified organic free-trade coffees. They have better flavor and are better for the environment in coffee-growing areas. What's more, the coffee workers are paid a decent salary, which has made a significant difference in people's lives as well as the environment in coffee-growing areas.

Juices and Seltzer Waters

Tomato, V-8, or Knudsen juices have low-sodium varieties. These juices are loaded with the carotene lycopene and have no added sugar. Take-along small sizes are great when you're on the go.

Look for 100% juice with no added sweeteners. Fructose and corn syrup contribute to obesity and high triglyceride levels.

After the Fall and Lakewood brands are clean. Lakewood has a 100% pure unsweetened cranberry juice that's great and can be diluted with water. The brand also makes a pure black cherry juice that's good for gout and high uric acid levels.

Other good brands are Walnut Acres, RW Knudsen, Libby's Juicy Juice.

Unsweetened seltzer water comes in a variety of flavors. Selzer has no calories and is great with a squeeze of orange, grapefruit, lemon, or lime juice. Get off the cola habit with seltzer.

Breads and Crackers

Try Eziekiel Sprouted Grain Breads or Alvarado Sprouted Grains. Eziekiel breads are delicious.

For crackers try Bran O Crisp, WASA, Ryvita Rye Crackers, or Ak-Mak Armenian whole grain crackers.

Chips

When you just have to cheat, you can do it with clean chips. Try Smart Food Popcorn, Cape Cod Chips, Garden of Eating Blue Corn Chips, or Red Hot Blues (Blue corn contains anthocyanidins), or Kettle Chips.

I definitely recommend salsa. It's high in tomato lycopene, and the hot pepper is good for the metabolism. Try Newman's Own, Green Mountain Gringo (one of my favorites), or any picante sauce. Check for healthful ingredients.

When buying canned beans, look at Bush's Beans or Goya, Eden, or Westbrae brands. The ingredient label should read only "beans and water" or "beans, salt and water."

We should include much more tomato paste, sauce, and whole tomatoes in our diet because lycopene prevents cancer and protects skin. Look for any unsweetened varieties. Check catsup labels carefully for added sugars. Muir Glen is the organic line of tomato products.

Canned Fish

Sardines are high in docosahexanoic acid (DHA) and other Omega-3 fatty acids.

Also look for wild Alaskan salmon. Sockeye is the red salmon. It has the highest amounts of the antioxidant carotene astazanthin, a potent antioxidant, as well as the beneficial Omega-3 fatty acids. Check carefully on the label. Unless the salmon is wild-caught or stated otherwise, Atlantic salmon is farmed.

Grains

Basmati brown rice, a variety of rice originally from India with a wonderful aroma, smells buttery when it's being cooked.

Jasmine brown rice, originally from Thailand, is another wonderful aromatic rice.

Lundberg rice blends, Japonica and Whehani, are great whole grain varieties and very flavorful.

Wild rice is another whole grain option.

Whole barley is low on the glycemic index. Barley grits from Arrowhead Mills make a great alternative to corn grits and have a great flavor.

Stock up on old-fashioned rolled oats, and try quinoa. This comes from the Andes Mountains in Peru and is possibly the best grain you can eat. It's hypoallergenic, high in minerals, easy to cook and digest, and is highest in protein of any grain. You can use it like rice or like oatmeal for breakfast.

Buckwheat can be used as a rice alternative. Properly classified, it should be called a fruit kernel, and the roasted kernel from buckwheat is called kasha. It is an excellent source of amino acids and the bioflavonoid, rutin. It's mainly used for making flour for pancakes.

Dried Fruits

Prunes and raisins are very high on the ORAC list of antioxidant foods. Buy organic if you can. For a discussion about ORAC see the section titled "Free Radicals and Antioxidants" in Chapter 2. Read labels and avoid sulphur dioxide and added sugars or potassium sorbate.

Cooking Oils

Most people in the United States don't know that light, heat, and oxygen can affect the stability of oil, causing oxidation and liberation of free radicals. Refrigerate any oil that doesn't solidify in the refrigerator. If you use peanut oil, keep it in the refrigerator and let it sit on the counter until it turns liquid. In Europe all oils are sold in tin containers to keep them fresher.

If you use olive oil, look for darker-colored, extra-virgin olive oil. Coconut oil is the most stable oil you can use for frying. It is highly saturated but does not raise blood cholesterol levels, and it is good for thyroid function. It also has antifungal properties. It is good for intestinal health and is a good oil to use internally if you get lots of sun exposure. Walnut oil is high in Omega-3 fatty acids and great on salads when you don't want the flavor of olive oil. Stock up on spray canola oil. You use a lot less of this when grilling foods. Also keep on hand high oleic sunflower, safflower, or canola oil. Look for Spectrum brand. Commercial oils are processed with solvents, bleaches, and high temperatures that destroy or alter essential fatty acids. I recommend only high oleic brands of sunflower and safflower oils, as they contain high levels of monosaturated fatty acids, which keep the oil much fresher on the shelf. Eating raw nuts and seeds is the best way to get high-quality Omega-6 fatty acids in the diet.

Breakfast Foods

Cheerios contains only one gram of sugar, no trans-fats or saturated fats, and three grams of fiber.

Kashi (GoLean) is another healthy brand of cereal, or you can try Muesli, made of traditional Swiss raw oats, barley flakes, and dried fruit. Uncle Sam's is high in fiber. Check the health foods section for organic cereals. Go 100% whole grain and as low as possible on the sugar content. Try Irish oatmeal or steel-cut oats or seven-grain hot cereal. Bob's Red Mill and Arrowhead Mills are good brands. Quinoa is good cooked as a hot cereal.

I will put a serving of whey protein into my oatmeal to boost the protein content of my breakfast. I learned about this from Barry Sears, Ph.D., the author of *The Zone*. It blends right in and tastes good. Whey protein is easy to mix (no chalky flavor) and has the highest protein efficiency ratio of any protein source. It's as good as or better than egg white. Add berries to it for extra taste and nutrients. Another interesting and tasteful breakfast choice is low-fat cottage cheese topped with berries and whole bran or low fat granola. You could even add low-fat plain yogurt.

Spices and Hot Sauce

Make sure you have lots of spices from the spice rack. Spices are where your local health foods store or market can really beat the supermarkets on quality price. The spices cost one-third to one-quarter of the price of bottled spices and are much fresher.

Use Cinnamon generously. It has been found to help keep blood sugar levels more stable by assisting the efficiency of insulin. It is also helpful alleviating heartburn.

Ginger helps reduce arteriosclerosis by improving circulation and lowering cholesterol. Ginger also reduces indigestion and colitis, and it is an antioxidant and anti-inflammatory.

Rosemary and turmeric are two of the highest antioxidant and liver-protecting spices.

For sauces, try Sanji Reduced Sodium Tamari sauce, Kikkoman Lite Less Sodium soy sauce, and Tobasco sauce. Look for Yucatan Sunshine or any clean brand of hot sauce. Hot sauce is good for you. It helps stimulate the metabolism, and it has been shown to kill bacteria that might cause food poisoning. Also, it can help people with asthma. Beware, however, if you have gastric ulcers or gastritis.

REFERENCES AND SUGGESTED READING MATERIAL

Book I: Causes of Aging

Chapter 1. Our Universal Wish   pages 3–6

1. V. E. Frankl. *Man's Search for Meaning: An Introduction to Logotherapy.* New York: Simon & Schuster Adult Publishing Group, 1984.

Chapter 2. Why We Grow Old   pages 7–28

1. H. Achat, I. Kawachi, C. Byrne, S. Hankinson, and G. Colditz. "A Prospective Study of Job Strain and Risk of Breast Cancer." *International Journal of Epidemiology* 29 (2000), 22–28.

2. B. N. Ames. "Dietary Carcinogens and Anticarcinogens. Oxygen Radicals and Degenerative Diseases." *Science* 221 (1983), 1256–64.

3. S. Attvall, J. Fowelin, I. Lager, H. Von Schenck, and U. Smith. "Smoking Induces Insulin Resistance—A Potential Link with the Insulin Resistance Syndrome." *Journal of Internal Medicine* 233 (1993), 327–32.

4. N. L. Benowitz. "Drug Therapy: Pharmacologic Aspects of Cigarette Smoking and Nicotine Addiction." *New England Journal of Medicine* 319 (1988), 1318–30.

5. V. W. Bunker. "Free Radicals, Antioxidants and Aging." *Medical Laboratory Science* 49 (1992), 299–312.

6. V. J. Burley. "Sugar Consumption and Human Cancer in Sites Other Than the Digestive Tract." *European Journal of Cancer Prevention* 7 (1998), 253–77.

7. R. A. Carels, A. Sherwood, R. Szczepanski, and J. A. Blumenthal. "Ambulatory Blood Pressure and Marital Distress in Employed Women." *Behavioral Medicine* 26 (2000), 80–85.

8. Jean Carper. *Your Miracle Brain: Maximize Your Brainpower, Boost Your Memory, Lift Your Mood, Improve Your IQ and Creativity, Prevent and Reverse Mental Aging.* New York: Harper Collins, 2000.

9. http://www.cdc.gov/tobacca/factsheets/HealthEffectsofCigarettesmoking factsheet.htm

10. A. Cerami, H. Vlassara, and M. Brownlee. "Glucose and Aging." *Scientific American* 256 (1987), 90–96.

11. Stephen Cherniske. *The Metabolic Plan*. New York: Ballantine Publishing Group, 2003, 58–59.

12. B. Eliasson, S. Attvall, M. R. Taskinen, and U. Smith. "Smoking Cessation Improves Insulin Sensitivity in Healthy Middle-aged Men." *European Journal of Clinical Investigation* 27 (1997), 450–456.

13. F. S. Facchini, C. B. Hollenbeck, J. Jeppesen, Y. D. Chen, and G. M. Reaven. "Insulin Resistance and Cigarette Smoking." *Lancet* 339 (May 9, 1992), 1128–30.

14. Rob Faigin. *Natural Hormonal Enhancement*. [Cedar Mountain, N.C.]: Extique Press, 2000.

15. K. Gey, G. Brubacher, and J. Shahelin. "Plasma Levels of Antioxidant Vitamins in Relation to Ishemic Heart Disease and Cancer." *American Journal of Clinical Nutrition* 45 (1987), 1368–77.

16. V. C. Giampapa, A. Fuente del Campo, and O. M. Ramirez. "Anti-aging Medicine and the Aesthetic Surgeon: A New Perspective for Our Specialty." *Aesthetic Plastic Surgery* 27 (2003), 493–501.

17. T. M. Hagen, R. Moreau, J. H. Suh, and F. Visiol. "Mitochondrial Decay in the Aging Rat Heart; Evidence for Improvement by Dietary Supplementation with Acetyl-L-Carnitine and /or Lipoic Acid." *Annals of the New York Academy of Sciences* 959 (2002), 491–507.

18. P. R. Heaton, C. F. Reed, S. J. Mann, R. Ransley, J. Stevenson, C. J. Charleton, B. N. Smith, E. J. Harper, and J. M. Rawlings. "Role of Dietary Antioxidants to Protect Against DNA Damage in Adult Dogs." *Journal of Nutrition* 132 (2002) (6 Supp. 2), 1720–24.

19. C. B. Hollenbeck. "Dietary Fructose Effects on Lipoprotein Metabolism and Risk for Coronary Artery Disease." *American Journal of Clinical Nutrition* 37 (1983), 740–748.

20. Tobacco toxic effects: http://www.Hyperhealth.com

21. J. W. Kenney and A. Bhattacharjee. "Interactive Model of Women's Stressors, Personality Traits and Health Problems." *Journal of Advanced Nursing* 32 (2000), 249–258.

22. W. S. Marras, K. G. Davis, C. A. Heaney, A. B. Maronitis, and W. G. Allread. "The Influence of Psychosocial Stress, Gender, and Personality on Mechanical Loading of the Lumbar Spine." *Spine* 25 (2000), 3045–54.

23. http://www.mascotcoalition.org/education/facts/mortality.html

24. W. G. Mayham. "Acute Infusion of Nicotine Potentiates Norepinephrine-Induced Vasoconstriction in the Hamster Cheek Pouch." *Journal of Laboratory Clinical Medicine* 133 (1999), 48–54.

25. P. McDonough and V. Walters. "Gender and Health: Reassessing Patterns and Explanations." *Social Science and Medicine* 52 (2001), 547–559.

26. *Natural Foods Merchandiser Magazine.* Sept. 2004.

27. P. H. Proctor and E. S. Reynolds. "Free Radicals and Disease in Man." *Physiology Chemistry Physics and Medicine* 16 (1984), 175–195.

28. J. H. Saurat. "Skin, Sun and Vitamin A: From Aging to Cancer." *Journal of Dermatology* 11 (Nov. 2001), 595–598.

29. Barry Sears. *The Omega Rx Zone: The Miracle of the New High-Dose Fish Oil.* New York: Harper Collins Publishers, 2003.

30. W. Stahl, U. Heinrich, S. Wiseman, O. Eichler, H. Sies, and H. Tronnier. "Dietary Tomato Paste Protects Against Ultraviolet Light-Induced Erythema in Humans." *Journal of Nutrition* 5 (2001), 1449–51.

31. G. Vendemiale, I. Grattagliano, and E. Altomare. "An Update on the Role of Free Radicals and Antioxidant Defense in Human Disease." *International Journal of Clinical Laboratory Research* 29 (1999), 49–55.

32. Maureen Williams. "Science Beat." *The Natural Foods Merchandiser* 25(9) (Sept. 2004), 58–59.

Book II: Nutrition and Supplements

Chapter 3. Nutrition for a Long, Youthful Life pages 31–52

1. Robert C. Adkin. *Dr. Atkins' Age-Defying Diet Revolution: A Powerful New Dietary Defense Against Aging.* New York: St. Martin's Press, 1999.

2. F. J. Ayala and A. A. Escalante. "The Evolution of Human Populations: A Molecular Perspective." *Molecular Phylogenetics and Evolution* 5 (Feb. 1996), 188–201.

3. R. M. Azira-Azira, Mestanza-Peralta, and H. Cardiem. "Omega-3 Fatty Acids in Rheumatoid Arthritis: An Overview." *Seminars in Arthritis and Rheumatology* 27(6) (June 1998), 336–370.

4. M. J. Benton. "Early Origins of Modern Birds and Mammals: Molecules vs. Morphology." *Bioessays* 21 (1999), 1043–51.

5. V. J. Burley. "Sugar Consumption and Human Cancer in Sites Other Than the Digestive Tract." *European Journal of Cancer Prevention* 7 (1998), 253–277.

6. A. Cerami, H. Vlassara, and M. Brownlee. "Glucose and Aging." *Scientific American* 256 (1987), 90–96.

7. Stephen Cherniske. *The Metabolic Plan: Stay Younger Longer.* New York: Random House Publishing Group, March 2004.

8. Michael R. Eades and Mary Dan Eades. *Protein Power.* New York: Bantam Books, May 2001.

9. S. B. Eaton, S. B. Eaton 3rd, and M. J. Konner. "Paleolithic Nutrition Revisited: A Twelve-Year Retrospective on its Nature and Implications." *European Journal of Clinical Nutrition* 51(4) (April 1997), 207–216.

10. E. S. Epel, J. Lin, F. H. Wilhelm, O. M. Wolkowitz, R. Cawthon, N. E. Adler, et al. "Cell Aging in Relation to Stress Arousal and Cardiovascular Disease Risk Factors." *Psychoneuroendocrinology* (Nov 16, 2005). PubMed ID 16298085. (Indexed—for MEDLINE)

11. David Mendosa. *Glycemic index and load.* www.mendosa.com

12. I. Greenwell. "DHEA and Anti-Aging Medicine." *Life Extension Magazine, Collector's Edition* (2003), 42–48. www.LEF.org

13. L. S. Hobbs. "Fat News: Dietary Protein Increases Weight Loss." *All Natural Muscular Development* 34 (1997), 170.

14. C. B. Hollenbeck. "Dietary Fructose Effects on Lipoprotein Metabolism and Risk for Coronary Artery Disease." *American Journal of Clinical Nutrition* 37 (1983), 740–748.

15. F. B. Hu, L. Bronner, W. C. Willett, et al. "Fish and Omega-3 Fatty Acid Intake and the Risk of Coronary Heart Disease in Women." *JAMA* 287 (2002), 1815–21.

16. Y. S. Huang and D. E. Mills. "Gamma-Linolenic Acid: Metabolism and its Roles in Nutrition." (Champaign, Il.): American Oil Chemists Society Press, 1996.

17. A. Jablecka, P. Checinski, H. Krauss, M. Micker, and J. Ast. "The Influence of Two Different Doses of L-Arginine Oral Supplementation on Nitrous Oxide (NO) Concentration and Total Anti-oxidant Status in Atherosclerotic Patients." *Med Science Moniter* 10 (2004), CR29-32. PubMed ID 14704639 (Indexed—for MEDLINE]

18. John C. Jackson. *Man, God and Civilization.* Citadel Press, 1983.

19. D. J. Jenkins, M. S. Thomas, T. M. Wolever, and L. J. Alexander. "Starchy Foods and Glycemic Index." *Diabetes Care* 11 (1988), 149–159.

20. D. G. Jordan. "Carnosine: Nature's Pluripotent Life Extension Agent." *nsion* 7 (Jan. 2001), 24–34. www.LEF.org

. Jordan. "Carnosine and Cellular Senescence." *Life Extension* 7 (Jan. www.LEF.org

22. P. M. Kris-Etherton, W.S. Harris, and L.J. Appel. "American Heart Association, Nutrition Committee. Fish consumption, Fish Oil, Omega-3, and Cardiovascular Disease." *Circulation* 106 (2002), 2747–57.

23. E. Moore and D. Farrell. "Egyptian Food and Cooking . . . Food in the Egyptian Diet. Ancient Methods of Nile Farming. . . . The Egyptian's Basic Food and Drink, Bread and Beer." www.inmamaskitchen.com/FOOD_IS_ART/mid-east/Egypt_food.html

24. Michael Murray. *How to Prevent and Treat Cancer with Natural Medicine.* [New York, N.Y.]: Riverhead Trade Press, Nov. 2003.

25. G. Reaven, T. Strom, and B. Fox. *Syndrome Z: The Silent Killer.* New York: Fireside Press, 2001

26. G. M. Reaven and J. M. Olefsky. "Increased Plasma Glucose and Insulin Responses to High Carbohydrate Feedings in Normal Subjects." *Journal of Clinical Endocrinology and Metabolism* 38 (1974), 151–154.

27. G. M. Reaven. "Role of Insulin Resistance in Human Disease." *Diabetes* 37 (1988), 1595–1607.

28. D. Schwarzbein and N. Deville. *The Schwarzbein Principle.* [Deerfield Beach, Fla.]: Health Communications Inc., 1999.

29. Barry Sears. *The Omega Rx Zone: The Miracle of the New High-Dose Fish Oil.* New York: HarperCollins Publishers, 2003.

30. Barry Sears and Deborah Kotz. *A Week in the Zone.* New York: HarperCollins Publishers, 2000.

31. Eugene Shippen and William Fryer. *The Testosterone Syndrome: The Critical Factor for Energy, Health and Sexuality—Reversing the Male Menopause.* [New York, N.Y.]: M. Evans Press, 1998.

32. A. L. Stoll, W. E. Severus, M. P. Freeman, S. Rueter, H. Zboyan, E. Diamond, K. Cress, and Marangell. "Omega-3 Fatty Acids in Bipolar Disorder; a Preliminary Double-Blind Study-Placebo Controlled Trial." *Archives of General Psychiatry* 56 (1999), 407–412.

33. A. L. Stoll. *The Omega-3 Connection: The Groundbreaking Antidepression Diet and Brain Program.* New York: Fireside/Simon & Schuster, 2002.

34. Gary Taubes. "The Soft Science of Dietary Fat." *Science*, 2001. http://nasw.org/mem-maint/awards/01Taubesarticle1.html

35. O. T. Wolf, I. Dziobak, P. McHugh, V. Sweat, M. de Leon, E. Javier, and A. Convit. "Subjective Memory Complaints in Aging Are Associated with Elevated Cortisol Levels." *Neurobiology of Aging* 26(10) (2005), 1357–63. PubMed ID 16243606 (Indexed—for MEDLINE)

36. Sources benefits, side effects and doses of herbs, vitamins, and minerals can be found on www.hyperhealth.com; www.pdrhealth.com/drug_info/nmdrugprofiles/herbaldrugs; www.pdrhealth.com/drug_info/nmdrugprofiles

Chapter 4. Dietary Supplements and Health Foods pages 53–61

1. A. R. Boldyrev, R. Song, D. Lawrence, and D. Carpenter. "Carnosine Protects Against Excitotoxic Cell Death Independently of Effects on Reactive Oxygen Species." *Neuroscience* 94 (1999), 571–577.

2. A. A. Boldyrev, S. L. Stvolinsky, O. V. Tyulina, V. B. Koshelev, N. Hori, and D. O. Carpenter. "Biochemical and Physiological Evidence that Carnosine is an Endogenous Neuroprotector Against Free Radicals." *Cellularabd Molecular Neurobiology* 17 (1997), 259–271.

3. C. Borek. "Co Q10 Energizes the Heart and Brain." *Nutrition Science News* (July 1999).

4. J. Campisi. "The Role of Cellular Senescence in Skin Aging." *Journal of Investigative Dermatology Symposium Proceedings* 3 (1998), 1–5.

5. P. Chowienczyk and J. Ritter. "Arginine: No More Than a Simple Amino Acid?" *Lancet* 35 (1997), 901–902.

6. H. L. Ford and A. B. Pardee. "Cancer and the Cell Cycle." *Journal of Cellular Biochemistry* 32–33 (1999), 166–172.

7. A. R. Hipkiss, J. E. Preston, D. T. Himsworth, V. C. Worthington, M. Keown, et al. "Pluripotent Protective Effect of Carnosine, a Natural Occurring Dipeptide." *Annals of the New York Academy Sciences* 854 (1998), 37–53.

8. M. S. Horning, L. J. Blakemore, and P. Q. Trombley. "Endogenous Mechanisms of Neuroprotection: Role of Zinc, Copper and Carnosine." *Brain Research* 852 (2000), 56–61.

9. Y. S. Huang and D. E. Mills. *Gammashinolenis Acid: Metabolism and Its Roles in Nutrition.* Champaign, Il.: American Oil Chemist Society Press, 1996.

10. M. Jang, L. Cai, G. Udeani, K. Slowing, C. Thomas, et al. "Cancer Chemopreventive Activity of Resveratrol, a Natural Product Derived From Grapes." *Science* 275 (1997), 218–220.

11. M. Jang, L. Cai, G. O. Udeani, K. V. Slowing, et al. "Cancer Chemopreventive Activity of Resveratrol, a Natural Product Derived From Grapes." *Science* 275 (1997), 218–220.

12. G. A. McFarland and R. Holliday. "Further Evidence for the Rejuvenating Effects of the Dipeptide L-Carnosine on Cultured Human Diploid Fibroblasts." *Experimental Gerontology* 34 (1999), 35–45.

13. G. A. McFarland and R. Holliday. "Retardation of Senescence of Cultured Human Diploid Fibrosis by Carnosine." *Experimental Cellular Research* 212 (1994), 167–175.

14 . T. L. Merimee, D. Rabinowitz, and S. E. Fineberg. "Arginine-initiated Release of HGH." *New England Journal of Medicine* 280 (June 26, 1969), 1434–38.

15. G. Munch, S. Maye, J. Michaelis, A. R. Hipkiss, et al. "Influence of Advanced Glycation End-products and AGE-inhibitors on Nucleation-dependent

Polymerization of Beta-amyloid Peptide." *Biochemica et Biophysica Acta* 1360(1) (Feb. 27, 1997), 17–29.

16. H. B. Murphree, C. C. Pfeiffer, and I. A. Backerman. "The Stimulant Effect of Dimethylaminoethanol in Volunteer Subjects." *Clinical Pharmacology and Therapeutics* 1 (1969), 303–310. PubMed ID 14425373 (Indexed—for MEDLINE]

17. F. Stenback, J. H. Weisburger, and G. M. Williams. "Effect of Lifetime Administration of Dimethylaminoenthanol (DMAE) on Longevity Aging Changes in C3H Mice." *Mechanisms of Aging Development* 42(2) (1988), 129–138, Found on Hyperhealth Pro Version 2.0

18. P. J. Quinn, A. A. Boldyrev, and V. E. Formazuyk. "Carnosine: Its Properties, Functions and Potential Therapeutic Applications." *Molecular Aspects of Medicine* 13 (1992), 379–444.

19. "Bioenergetic Therapy for Aging, the Metabolic Syndrome." *Life Extension* (Feb. 2001). Available online at www.LEF.org

20. "How CoQ10 Protects the Brain." *Life Extension*" (Oct. 2001). Available online at www.LEF.org

21. "How CoQ10 Protects Your Cardiovascular System: Cellular Nutrition for Vitality and Longevity." *Life Extension* (April 2000). Available online at www.LEF.org

22. Other excellent sources are: The Physician's Desk Reference Database for Herbal Remedies: http://www.pdrhealth.com/drug_info/nmdrugprofiles/herbaldrugs.

23. www.hyperhealth.com

Book III: Hormones and Aging

Chapter 5. Hormones and Aging pages 65–83

1. E. Banks, V. Beral, G. Reeves, A. Balkwill, I. Barnes. "Fracture Incidence in Relation to the Pattern of Use of Hormone Therapy in Postmenopausal Women." *JAMA* 291 (2004), 2212–20.

2. J. A. Cauley, J. Robbins, Z. Chen, S. R. Cummings, R. D. Jackson, A. Z. LaCroix, et al. "Effects of Estrogen Plus Progestin on Risk of Fracture and Bone Mineral Density." *JAMA* 290 (2003), 1729–38.

3. C. G. Chute, J. A. Baron, S. R. Plymate, D. P. Kiel, A. T. Pavia, E. C. Lozner, T. O'Keefe, and G. J. MacDonald. "Sex Hormones and Coronary Artery Disease." *American Journal of Medicine* 83 (Nov. 1987), 853–859. PubMed ID 3674092 (Indexed—for MEDLINE)

4. N. F. Col, M. H. Eckman, R. H. Karas, S. G. Pauker, R. J. Goldberg, E. M. Ross, R. K. Orr, and J. B. Wong. "Patient-specific Decisions about Hormone Replacement Therapy in Postmenopausal Women." *JAMA* 277:14 (Apr. 9, 1997), 1140–47.

5. K. M. English, R. Steeds, T. H. Jones, and K. S. Channer. "Testosterone and Coronary Heart Disease: Is There a Link?" *Quarterly Journal of Medicine* 90 (Dec. 1997), 787–791.

6. Y. J. Janssen, F. Helmerhorst, M. Frolich, and F. Roelfsema. "A Switch from Oral (2mg/day) to Transdermal (50 microgm/day) 17 Beta-estradiol Therapy Increases Serum Insulin-like Growth Factor 1 (IGF-1) Levels in Recombinant Human Growth Hormone Substituted Women with Growth Hormone Deficiency." *Journal of Clinical Endocrinlogy and Metabolism* 85(1) (Jan. 2000), 146–147.

7. J. O. O'Sullivan, L. J. Crampton, J. Freund, and K. Ho. "The Route of Estrogen Replacement Therapy Confers Divergent Effects on Substrate Oxidation and Body Composition in Postmenopausal Women." *Journal of Clinical Investigation* 102(5) (Sept. 1998), 1035–40.

8. A. Paganini-Hill and V. W. Henderson. "Estrogen Replacement Therapy and Risk of Alzheimer Disease." *JAMA* 288 (2002), 872–881.

9. The writing group for the PEPI study. "Effects of Hormone Therapy on Bone Mineral Density: Results From the Postmenopausal Estrogen/Progestin Interventions (PEPI) Trial." *JAMA* 6276(17) (Nov. 6, 1996), 1389–96. PubMed ID 8892713. (Indexed—for MEDLINE)

10. R. Schmidt, F. Fazekas, B. Reinhart, P. Kapeller, G. Fazekas, et al. "Estrogen Replacement Therapy in Older Women: a Neuropsychological and Brain MRI Study." *Journal of the American Geriatric Society* 44(11) (Nov. 1996), 1307–13. PubMed ID 8909345. (Indexed—for MEDSCAPE)

11. T. A. Sellers, T. J. Mink, J. R. Cerhan, W. Zheng, K. E. Anderson, et al. "The Role of Hormonal Replacement Therapy in the Risk of Breast Cancer and Total Mortality in Women with a Family History of Breast Cancer." *Annals of Internal Medicine* 127(11) (Dec. 1997), 973–980.

12. R. K. Stellato, H. A. Feldman, O. Hamdy, E. S. Horton, and J. B. McKinlay. "Testosterone, Sex Hormone-binding Globulin, and the Development of Type 2 Diabetes in Middle-aged Men." *Diabetes Care* 23 (2000), 490–494.

13. M. X. Tang, D. Jacobs, Y. Stern, K. Marder, P. Schofield, B. Gurland, H. Andrews, and R. Mayeur. "Effects of Estrogen During Menopause on Risk and Age at Onset of Alzheimer's Disease." *Lancet* 348(9025) (Aug. 17, 1996), 429–432. PubMed ID 8709781. (Indexed—for MEDLINE)

14. S. C. Waring, W. A. Rocca, R. C. Petersen, E. G. O'Brien, E. G. Tangalos, and E. Kokmen. "Postmenopausal Estrogen Replacement Therapy and Risk of Alzheimer's Disease: A Population-based Study." *Neurology* 52(5) (Mar. 23, 1999), 965–70. PubMed ID 10202413. (Indexed—for MEDSCAPE)

15. D. B. Willis, E. E. Calle, H. L. Miracle-McMahill, and C. W. Heat, Jr. "Estrogen Replacement Therapy and Risk of Fatal Breast Cancer in a Prospective Cohort of Postmenopausal Women in the United States." *Cancer Causes Control* 7(4) (1996), 449–457. PubMed ID 8813433 (Indexed—for MEDLINE)

Book IV: Aging and Your Skin

Chapter 7. Aging and Your Skin pages 89–95

1. V. L. Ernster, D. Grady, R. Miike, D. Black, J. Selby, and K. Kerlikowske. "Facial Wrinkling in Men and Women, by Smoking Status." *American Journal of Public Health* 85(1) (1995), 78–82.

2. G. J. Fisher, S. Kang, J. Varani, Z. Bata-Csorgo, et al. "Mechanisms of Photoaging and Chronological Skin Aging." *Archives of Dermatology* 138(11) (Nov. 2002), 1462–70.

3. J. Krutman. "The Role of UVA Rays in Skin Aging." *European Journal of Dermatology* 11(2) (2001), 170–171.

4. C. Lahmann, J. Bergemann, G. Harrison, and A. R. Young. "Matrix Metalloproteinase and Skin Aging in Smokers." *Lancet* 357(9260) (2001), 935–936. PubMed ID 11289356 (Indexed—for MEDLINE)

5. W. G. Mayham. "Acute Infusion of Nicotine Potentiates Norepinephrine-Induced Vasoconstriction in the Hamster Cheek Pouch." *Journal of Laboratory Clinical Medicine* 133(48) (1999), 133–148.

6. Y. Miyachi. "Photoaging From an Oxidative Viewpoint." *Journal of Dermatological Science* (1995), 79–86.

7. M. Wlaschek, K. Briviba, G. P. Stricklin, H. Sias, K. Scharffetter-Kochanek. "Singlet Oxygen May Mediate the Ultraviolet A-induced Synthesis of Interstitial Collagenase." *Journal Investigative Dermatology* 104 (1995), 194–198.

Chapter 8. Skin Care and Treatment pages 96–109

1. C. L. Broadhurst. "Antiaging Products for Skin, Hair, and Nails." *Nutrition Science News* 4 (1999), 524–528.

2. V. Goffin, F. Henry, C. Pierard-Franchimont, and G. E. Pierard. "Topical Retinol and the Stratum Corneum Response to an Environmental Threat." *Skin Pharmacology*. 10(2) (1997), 85–89.

3. G. S. Kelly. "Squalene and Its Potential Clinical Uses." *Alternative Medicine Review* 4(1) (1999), 29–36.

4. S. Miners. "Green Supetrods: Plant Chemicals that Heal." *Well Being Journal* 8(2) (1999), 5. Reference from Hyperhealth Pro Version 2.0

5. M. A. Mitchnick, D. Fairhurst, and S. R. Pinnell. "Microfine Zinc Oxide (Z-cote) as a Photostable UVA/UVB Sunblock Agent." *Journal of the American Academy of Dermatology* 40 (1999), 85–90.

6. K. Repinski. "Moisterizers That Do More Than They Say: Keeping the Surface Young." *Longevity* 3(3) (1991), 28–32.

7. Y. Sheng, L. Li, K. Holmgren, and R. W. Pero. "DNA Repair Enhancement of Aqueous Extracts of Uncaria Tomentosa in a Human Volunteer Study." *Phytomedicine* 8(4) (2001), 275–282. PubMed ID 11515717 (Indexed—for MEDLINE)

8. P. K. Thibault, K. J. Wlodaczyk, and A. Wenck. "A Double Blind Randomized Clinical Trial on the Effectiveness of a Daily Glycolic Acid 5% Formulation in the Treatment of Photoaging." *Dermatological Surgery* 24(5) (1998), 573–577.

9. J. Varani, R. L. Warner, M. Gharmani, S. H. Phan, et al. "Vitamin A Antagonizes Decreased Cell Growth and Elevated Collagen-degrading Matrix Metalloproteinases and Stimulates Accumulation in Naturally Aged Human Skin." *Journal of Investigative Dermatology* 114(3) (2000), 480–486.

Book V: Exercise, Why and How

Chapter 9. Exercise Programs for Age Reversal pages 113–126

1. American Diabetes Association. National Diabetes Fact Sheet. Available online at http://www.diabetes.org/diabetes-statistics/national-diabetes-fact-sheet.jsp

2. R. Biswas-Diener, E. Diener, and M. Tamir. "The Psychology of Subjective Well-being." *Daedalus* 133 (2004), 18–25.

3. W. M. Bortz, IV, and W. M. Bortz, II. "How Fast Do We Age? Exercise Performance Over Time as a Biomarker." *The Journals of Gerontology: Series A: Biological Sciences and Medical Sciences* 51A (1996), 223–227.

4. F. Dimeo, M. Bauer, I. Varahram, G. Proest, and U. Halter. "Benefits From Aerobic Exercise in Patients With Major Depression: A Pilot Study." *British Journal of Sports Medicine* 35 (2001), 114–117.

5. D. Feskanich, W. Willett, and G. Colditz. "Walking and Leisure-time Activity and Risk of Hip Fracture in Postmenopausal Women." *JAMA* 288 (2002), 2300–06.

6. D. M. Gilcrest and K. Mayo. "Type 2 Diabetes, Health Disparities, and Exercise: A Review of the Literature." *Journal of Multicultural Nursing and Health* 10 (2004), 62–67.

7. S. A. Hawkins, R. A. Wiswell, and T. J. Marcell. "Exercise and the Master Athlete: A Model of Successful Aging?" *The Journals of Gerontology: Series A: Biological Sciences and Medical Sciences* 58A (2003), 1009–11.

8. R. Kagan. "Exercise and Bone Health." *Female Patient* 27 (2002), 49–50.

9. M. L. Kohut, M. M. Cooper, M. S. Nickolaus, D. R. Russell, and J. E. Cunnick. "Exercise and Psychosocial Factors Modulate Immunity to Influenza Vaccine in Elderly Individuals." *The Journals of Gerontology: Series A: Biological Sciences and Medical Sciences* 57A (2002), M557–M562.

10. P. Manninen, H. Riihimaki, M. Heliovaara, and O. Suomalainen. "Physical Exercise and Risk of Severe Knee Osteoarthritis Requiring Arthroplasty." *Rheumatology* 40 (2001), 432–437.

11. R. S. Mazzeo and H. Tanaka. "Exercise Prescription for the Elderly: Current Recommendations." *Sports Medicine* 31(11) (2001), 809–818.

12. H. C. McGill and C. A. McMahan. "Starting Early to Prevent Heart Disease." *JAMA* 290 (2003), 2320–22.

13. S. Mora, R. F. Redberg, R. Cui, M. K. Whiteman, et al. "Ability of Exercise Testing to Predict Cardiovascular and All-cause Death in Asymptomatic Women: A 20-year Follow-up of the Lipid Research Clinics Prevalence Study." *JAMA* 290 (2003), 1600–07.

14. K. Mummery, G. Schofield, and C. Caperchione. "Physical Activity Dose-response Effects on Mental Status in Older Patients." *Australian and New Zealand Journal of Public Health* 28 (2004), 188–192.

15. R. Oida, R. Kitabatake, Y. Nishijima, T. Nagamatsu, et al. "Effects of a 5-year Exercise-centered Health-promoting Program on Mortality and ADL (Activities of Daily Living) Impairment in the Elderly." *Age and Ageing* 32 (2003), 585–592.

16. B. W. Penninx, W. J. Rejeski, J. Pandya, M. E. Miller, et al. "Exercise and Depressive Symptoms: A Comparison of Aerobic and Resistance Exercise Effects on Emotional and Physical Function in Older Persons with High and Low Depressive Symptoms." *The Journals of Gerontology: Series B: Psychological Sciences and Social Sciences* 57B (2003), 124–132.

17. W. J. Rejeski and S. L. Mihalko. "Physical Activity and Quality of Life in Older Adults." *The Journals of Gerontology: Series A: Biological Sciences and Medical Sciences* 56A (2001), 23–35.

18. J. Roomi, A. M. Yohannes, and M. J. Connolly. "The Effect of Walking Aids on Exercise Capacity and Oxygenation in Elderly Patients with Chronic Obstructive Pulmonary Disease." *Age and Ageing* 27 (1998), 703–707.

19. "Tai Chi Improves Balance in Older Adults." *Journal of Physical Education, Recreation, and Dance* 75 (2002), 5–8.

20. U.S. Centers for Disease Control and Prevention. National Center for Health Statistics. Available online at http://www.cdc.gov/nchs/default.htm

21. K. E. Yarasheski. "Exercise, Aging and Muscle Protein Metabolism." *The Journals of Gerontology: Series A: Biological Sciences and Medical Sciences* 58A (2003), 918–922.

INDEX

(In this index, *f* denotes figure or photo and *t* denotes table.)